W9-ADH-240

A Campaign of
Quiet Persuasion

Making the Modern South

David Goldfield, Series Editor

A Campaign of Quiet Persuasion

HOW THE COLLEGE BOARD DESEGREGATED
SAT® TEST CENTERS
IN THE DEEP SOUTH, 1960–1965

JAN BATES WHEELER

FOREWORD BY DAVID COLEMAN
President, College Board

Louisiana State University Press)((Baton Rouge

Published by Louisiana State University Press
Copyright © 2013 by Louisiana State University Press
All rights reserved
Manufactured in the United States of America
First printing

Designer: Barbara Neely Bourgoyne
Typefaces: Verb, display; Whitman, text
Printer and binder: Maple Press

Library of Congress Control Number: 2013944432
ISBN 978-0-8071-5271-3 (cloth) — ISBN 978-0-8071-5272-0 (pdf) — ISBN 978-0-8071-5273-7 (epub) — ISBN 978-0-8071-5274-4 (mobi)

SAT and the College Board are registered trademarks of the College Board, which was not involved in the production of, and does not endorse, this product. In the material, the author refers to the SAT as the Scholastic Aptitude Test. This description is accurate for the time presented and is how the test was referred to in the 1960s. Currently, however, the proper name for the test is SAT.

Created and designed by educators, the SAT is a valuable and reliable measure of college readiness for students seeking admission to undergraduate colleges and universities in the United States. The SAT tests the academic skills and knowledge that students acquire in high school. It also shows how well students can apply their knowledge, a factor that educators and researchers agree is critical to success in college course work.

The SAT is consistently shown to be a fair and valid predictor of first-year college success for all students. A study including data from more than 100 colleges and universities demonstrates that the best predictor of college success is a combination of SAT scores and high school grades. In addition to admission, many colleges use the SAT for course placement. The SAT is administered annually to more than 2 million students at approximately 6,000 test centers located in more than 170 countries.

Jacket photo used by permission of the Educational Testing Service. ETS disclaims all warranties, representation and liabilities to true ownership of the image and ETS may or may not be the owner of the image.

The paper in this book meets the guidelines for permanence and durability of the Committee on Production Guidelines for Book Longevity of the Council on Library Resources. ♾

For my family, especially Mark and Millicent

Contents

Acknowledgments

This study began in 2002 as a research paper for Professor Thomas G. Dyer's course, The History of Higher Education, at the University of Georgia's Institute of Higher Education. Later, it grew into my dissertation. Tom's sustained enthusiasm for the project—and especially his patience in advising a nontraditional student with no formal education in history—are remarkable. The very same can be said for John C. Inscoe, who helped me find my way to the Louisiana State University Press and volunteered his valuable counsel throughout the dissertation-to-final-manuscript period. I can't thank them enough.

I am grateful to the Educational Testing Service and College Board archivists, who welcomed me to their facilities, helped me find obscure materials, and, in the case of the College Board, entrusted me with many hundreds of original documents. I appreciate the contribution of College Board president David Coleman in writing the foreword and also thank Jenny Krugman, director of the College Board's Southern Regional Office, for her guidance. I am also grateful to Marcia G. Synnott, who saw potential in the project in its early stages. Jean Gibson and Doug Cameron provided insights into the characters of their fathers, Ben Gibson and Ben Cameron, who are the story's protagonists. I thank them for sharing their memories.

I also thank my colleagues at the University of Georgia for their support, in particular, John Albright, Allan Aycock, Robert Boehmer, and Jerry Legge, from the Office of Academic Planning, my campus home, and Michael F. Adams, who read my dissertation and provided encouragement. I am indebted to my dissertation committee—Tom Dyer, Melvin Hill, Libby Morris, and Scott Thomas; to Edward Simpson, who prodded me to enter the Institute's doctoral program; and to fellow IHE graduates Lloyd Winstead and Haixia Xu. I am also indebted to E. M. Beck for his apt suggestions and to Robert Pratt, who directed my readings on the civil rights movement. Jöelle Walls and Anne Sidner helped me assemble the pieces, and I appreciate their attention to every detail.

It has been a pleasure to work with LSU Press, and I would like to acknowledge especially David Greenfield, who saw potential in my original manuscript, and Rand Dotson, who patiently guided me through the entire publishing process. I also value the expertise and good judgment of Lee Sioles, Maria denBoer, and Lauren Tussing-White in the production of the book.

Many friends, especially those from our church and my venerable book club, have generously given their moral support. I thank them most sincerely.

The encouragement and understanding of my wonderful family have been essential. Each member has inspired and encouraged me, especially my mother, Millicent Bates, who has consistently cheered me on in all my pursuits; my husband, Mark—a fine editor and critic; our children, Anna and Samuel; and children by marriage, Niels and Michela.

I wish I could thank Ben Cameron and Ben Gibson, the two men whose story I have recorded. Their dedication, persistence, writing excellence, and senses of humor persuaded me to do what they could not—publish the story of their good work. It is my hope that they would be pleased.

Foreword

By David Coleman, President of the College Board

Founded in 1900 by leaders from colleges and universities across the country, the College Board was born from the shared belief that equal access to education was a right, not a privilege. More than a century later, we recognize that there is still much work to be done to ensure that all students—regardless of their circumstances—have access to an excellent education. And as we continue to pursue this goal, we can find inspiration in one of the proudest episodes in the history of the College Board, which has remained largely untold until now: the campaign to desegregate test centers in the Deep South.

Jan Bates Wheeler details the courageous work of the two men who led this campaign: Southern Regional Office director Ben Cameron and his aide, Ben Gibson. Wheeler offers a superb, accessible narrative of this five-year campaign, filled with fine-grained details that portray the key players with depth and humanity. Her analysis reveals the maneuvering—strategic and tactical—that went into this historic campaign, and celebrates the men and women who led its charge.

As Wheeler notes, the successful desegregation of test centers was not preordained and did not come without great risk—both personal and professional. At a time when Jim Crow still ruled the South, Cameron and Gibson's overtures placed them in direct conflict with many school officials. "Both men were aware of the potential for the ostracism of and violence against those who supported school desegregation to any degree. They had no reason to believe they would be exempt," writes Wheeler.

The College Board also risked alienating many new customers who were uncomfortable with desegregation at a critical time when demand for standardized testing was growing. Local superintendents were incensed at what they perceived to be the College Board's interference in local matters, and some threatened to arouse anger against the Board by making the integrated testing policy public. According to Wheeler, one disgruntled superintendent from Jackson, Mississippi, Kirby Walker, told Gibson that parents "'need to know what you all are up to, and that the public schools are not having anything to do with it.'" To make clear the threat, Walker pointed to the virulently segregationist Jackson press, telling Gibson, "the College Board will have it rough in Mississippi, maybe before December. The papers are just biding their time." Similar threats came from Toombs County, Georgia, where the superintendent told Gibson that "publicity on the closing of the [segregated] centers would have 'far-reaching effects.'"

But Cameron, Gibson, and their colleagues persevered. Working closely with the Education Testing Service (ETS) and community, religious, political, and military leaders, they slowly and stubbornly brought change to the nation's most heavily segregated states. At a time when few schools in the Deep South were integrated, they negotiated district by district, and occasionally school by school, to end segregation in test centers. And by the conclusion of this "campaign of quiet persuasion," black and white students sat together for College Board exams throughout much of the region.

Inspired by the example of Cameron, Gibson, and the many partners who fought alongside them, the College Board today is committed to upending a new status quo that has emerged over the past fifty years. It is a status quo that tolerates far too little diversity at the highest levels of academic achievement. Fifty years after the great battles of the Civil Rights Movement, we find that high-achieving black and Latino students with the same readiness to take challenging Advanced Placement Program® (AP®) courses as their white and Asian peers are less likely to do so. Most low-income, high-achieving students in our country do not even apply to, much less attend, the selective colleges for which they are qualified.

At the same time, academic gains at the highest levels by minority students on the SAT® have stagnated. In 2012, 1 out of every 189 African American students and 1 in every 87 Latino students scored in the top 5 percent on the SAT. These results are substantially worse than they were 20 years ago. By contrast, today 1 in every 18 white students and nearly 1 in every 7 Asian students scored in the top 5 percent.

These statistics have endured too long and are unacceptable. As a country, we cannot tolerate such inequity at the highest levels of academic performance, leaving vast reserves of humanity, creativity, and ingenuity untapped. Following in the footsteps of Cameron and Gibson, the College Board today must be willing to make the investments and take the risks required to address these inequities. As the battle to desegregate test centers shows, such audacious work will require remarkable partners. We must draw on great individuals and organizations in technology, the arts, the military, and others—the widest range of talent possible and leaders from all sectors—to make a sustained effort to create lasting change.

The campaign to desegregate test centers was driven by the belief that discriminating against black students taking College Board exams was "morally wrong, unlawful, and counter to [the Board's] core precept of providing appropriate and standardized test conditions," as Wheeler writes. Just as Cameron and Gibson were motivated by that belief, the College Board today must be driven by the belief that all students, regardless of their background, have a right to practice the kind of rigorous, challenging work necessary for success in college and beyond.

Research shows that access to rigorous work that emphasizes the concepts and skills most essential for later success is what makes students truly ready: ready for work, ready for college, ready for citizenship, ready to live more fully. And such work makes students ready for a world that is challenging and always changing. In our schools today, this challenging work is too often available to only a portion of students.

One promising sign for equity and excellence in our time can be found in the most recent results from our AP program. The body of students taking AP is now more diverse than ever, and scores are the highest they've been since 2004. AP shows promise to deliver the kind of work that advances both equity and excellence.

Yet we must continue to do better, and to this end we have launched an initiative to dramatically increase the number of low-income and minority students participating and succeeding in college-level AP courses. Similarly, we are also investing in innovative technologies and partnerships that will fuel a campaign to ensure that academically ready students from low-income and minority backgrounds apply to, attend, and graduate from college.

The desegregation campaign reminds us of the power of the College Board as a force for change. As Wheeler writes in the epilogue of her narrative, "Perhaps taking the SAT together on a Saturday morning was the first integrated event in the lives of both black and white students, and they gained something important from that experience."

Today, our work remains rooted in the same commitment to equity and excellence that Ben Cameron and Ben Gibson fought for so tenaciously. And by insisting that *all students* deserve access to a high-quality education, we honor the legacy of their work and the founding principles of the College Board.

A Campaign of
Quiet Persuasion

Introduction

Separate educational facilities are inherently unequal.
—U.S. Supreme Court, May 17, 1954

The movement to desegregate southern schools, colleges, and universities was a critical step in a broadening of access to higher education in the United States. Post–World War II America demanded training beyond high school for a much higher percentage of its citizens, including those who had been left behind in the "separate but equal" racially segregated schools allowed by law. The *Brown v. Board of Education* Supreme Court decision of 1954 marked the beginning of the end of segregated public education, and in 1955 *Brown II* famously established the timeline "with all deliberate speed." The 1964 Civil Rights Act further supported the desegregation of schools by imposing financial penalties on those that refused to desegregate.

This book chronicles a five-year period, 1960–65, during which the College Entrance Examination Board through its activities in southern schools and colleges unexpectedly became a participant in the school desegregation movement. Working with its partner organization, Educational Testing Services (ETS), the College Board quietly desegregated its Scholastic Aptitude Test (SAT) centers in the five states of the Deep South—Alabama, Georgia, Louisiana, Mississippi, and South Carolina. Traveling from state to state, taking one school district and even one school at a time, two men waged "a quiet campaign of persuasion" and

succeeded, establishing a roster of desegregated test centers within segregated school districts while the historic battle for civil rights unfolded
around them. Significantly, they accomplished most of their work prior
to the passage of the 1964 Civil Rights Act that would substantially accel-
erate the pace of school desegregation. At its outset, their job seemed so
daunting that on first hearing about it, College Board staff members were
stunned. Even ETS president Henry Chauncey, who supported the idea
wholeheartedly, had second thoughts just a few months into the project.

Involving judges, attorneys, activists, school officials, politicians, police officers, religious leaders, members of the military, and private citizens, the desegregation of schools and colleges became an unavoidable
concern for all individuals and organizations interested in the future of
education, especially in the South. Among those keenly interested were
the College Board and ETS, whose tests and other programs aided high
school students, school officials, and college admissions officers in their
admissions and academic placement processes and generally promoted
college attendance. By the mid-1950s, the College Board was already
developing and supporting programs designed to improve educational
opportunities for minority students. These included its demonstration
guidance projects (long-term, remedial math and reading programs for
underprivileged children), scholarship service, and efforts to address the
use and misuse of the SAT in college admissions and placement processes.
But the College Board, launched by the Ivy League in 1900, was active
primarily in the Northeast. In the late 1950s, the gains of the civil rights
movement, efforts by southerners to improve public education, and competition from a new, rival organization drew the attention of the College
Board toward opportunities in the South.[1]

Beginning in the 1930s, civil rights attorneys won opportunities for
black students to attend white colleges and universities in many states of
the South. At the end of the 1950s, only five states—Alabama, Georgia,
Louisiana, Mississippi, and South Carolina—still maintained total segregation in their state colleges and universities as well as in their public schools.[2] Feeding on the grass-roots, "massive resistance" movement
against integration spawned by the *Brown* decisions and supported by
state law, state officials denied black applicants access to white colleges

and universities in a variety of ways, including the creation of new admissions criteria. Personal interviews and alumni recommendations became standard components of a college application and were effective in both identifying black candidates and barring them from enrollment. Another new requirement was the SAT, initially imposed by some white colleges and universities to keep black applicants out of their institutions. The cost of the test, the travel to the test site, the racist treatment of some black test candidates, and the lack of test preparation arising from poor public schools for black children were all factors contributing to black students' below-average test performance; hence, the SAT was often an effective barrier to their admission. Some black students, barred from the test sites altogether, were unable even to sit for the test. At the same time, black colleges and universities that had previously not required the SAT for admission began to consider doing so. It became clear to the College Board and ETS that for the first time significant numbers of black high school students in the South would be taking College Board examinations. Unfortunately, with few exceptions, test centers, the places where candidates sat for the tests, were located in white schools and colleges, locations forbidden by law and custom to black students. Clearly, this was a dilemma for the College Board and ETS leadership. The solution, reached after considerable research and discussion, was to desegregate the test centers.

The College Board assigned that responsibility to Ben Cameron, a Mississippi native and director of the newly formed Southern Regional Office of the College Board. Over a five-year period, Cameron worked with a small staff and an ad hoc College Board committee to accomplish his assignment. One of those staff members, fellow southerner Ben Gibson, collaborated with Cameron to perfect a strategy the two men employed as they quietly traveled the South, patiently "negotiating" with school and college officials for desegregated test centers.[3]

Their story, told primarily through their candid records of conversations and confrontations with individual school officials, offers a unique perspective on school desegregation. The responsibility of the two men, especially that of Gibson, placed them in the unusual position of advocating for school desegregation on a day-to-day basis as part of their jobs.

Their abundant, thoughtfully written correspondence, reports, and other writings supplied most of the information on which this book is based.

Clearly, without those documents, this book would not exist; without them, the significant accomplishment of providing desegregated testing within segregated school districts would remain only a footnote in the histories of the College Board and ETS. The substantial collection of documents, apparently untouched for nearly fifty years, reveals the day-to-day persistence required to reach a goal many thought unachievable and possibly foolhardy. The charge to the College Board's new Southern Regional Office was to expand College Board programs throughout the South. Requiring desegregated SAT test centers placed the College Board and ETS squarely in opposition to prevailing laws, customs, and attitudes—an unenviable and ill-advised position for any nascent business venture, particularly one experiencing competition from a new, rival organization purported to accommodate openly those same laws, customs, and attitudes.

In addition to the known financial risk accepted by the College Board, Cameron and Gibson assumed the personal risk of involving themselves directly in confrontations with school officials. At the least, these confrontations might prove uncomfortable or embarrassing; at worst, dangerous. Both men were aware of the potential for the ostracism of and violence against those who supported school desegregation to any degree. They had no reason to believe they would be exempt.

Assuming even greater risk were the school, college, and military base officials who cooperated with Cameron and Gibson. They clearly risked criticism and worse from the segregationists in their schools and communities. In order to minimize the risk to all concerned, the College Board, ETS, and especially Cameron and Gibson pledged not to publicize their efforts. Even years after their work had ended, the two men refused to write about their campaign for fear of compromising the people who had helped them. Their legitimate concern has kept this story largely untold until now.

In order to appreciate the difficulty of the work Cameron and Gibson undertook, it is necessary to recall the scope and nature of segregation as it existed in the United States in the middle of the twentieth century.

Sustained by a philosophy of white supremacy, the practice of segregation permeated everyday life. The massive resistance to desegregation that arose in opposition to the first *Brown* decision was enabled by state and local laws that ignored individual rights and undermined the dignity of both races. These laws reached beyond public education into other areas. For example, during this period in Montgomery, Alabama, racially mixed participation in every organized sport—and even in games of cards, dominoes, and checkers—was expressly prohibited by law. In 1957, two years following the second *Brown* decision, Eugene Cook, attorney general of Georgia, reminded his fellow citizens that in order to preserve segregation as "an integral part" of state "traditions," they must practice segregation "twenty-four hours a day, seven days a week, and three hundred and sixty-five days a year." In complying with that directive, the Georgia board of education resolved to prohibit public school organizations "from planning or participating in any integrated activity." Testing black students at white schools, or vice versa, would have been forbidden under this ruling.[4]

The five "hard core" states that Cameron and Gibson dealt with all had similar laws that kept black and white young people from taking College Board examinations together. In an effort to explain test center segregation to his New England colleagues, Ben Gibson wrote, "Some communities just don't want Negroes sitting in a white student's desk"—even for a few hours on a Saturday morning when school was not in session.[5]

From the perspective of the College Board and ETS, the idea that black students were being turned away from white schools or otherwise being discriminated against when they arrived to take College Board examinations was morally wrong, unlawful, and counter to their core precept of providing appropriate and standardized test conditions. They believed that all students should be tested impartially, which meant under the same conditions. In fact, the very integrity of the examinations depended on standardized test conditions. From the perspective of black students, the idea that they were treated differently from white students, by either being turned away from a center altogether or taken to a separate room or building for testing, was morally wrong, unlawful, frightening, and humiliating. Many teachers and counselors at black high schools were aware of the growing importance of College Board exams in the admission of their brightest students to more selective institutions in the South and elsewhere. But convincing students and their parents of the need to register for testing and to travel to the test site (possibly up to seventy-five miles away) was often difficult, especially in cases where the test registration fee and transportation meant sacrifice for the family. By the day of the exam, many students were already nervous, convinced that their future success depended on their test scores. Those scheduled for testing at white schools were especially apprehensive. Fannie Phelps Adams, assistant principal and guidance counselor at black Booker T. Washington High School in Columbia, South Carolina, described to a colleague what a group of her students experienced at a test administration in the early 1960s:

> On the day of the exams the children go to a white school (their first experience in an all white environment). This is rather unsettling. . . . When they enter the school they are told to stand in a corner of the hall. . . . They see the white children ushered into a nice bright study hall while they stand and wait. After a while they get a little panicky and begin to feel they should never [have] dared to come there.[6]

Eventually, the children were "led to the basement," where they took the SAT in a room with dim lighting. The test proctor distracted the students by talking to an assistant throughout the test period. Students who also had registered for the afternoon College Board Achievement Tests watched while white children took their lunch break in the school cafeteria. But, Fannie Adams explained, "Since this is a white neighborhood there is no place where the Negro children can be served." Adams believed her students were filled with tension, fear, and humiliation as a result of their treatment and predicted that their test scores would reflect their emotions rather than their abilities.[7]

In addition to recalling the scope and nature of segregation, one does well to remember that the desegregation of schools was a long process, not a single event. The *Brown* decisions of 1954 and 1955 made segregated public schools unlawful and provided an imprecise timetable—"with all deliberate speed." But there was certainly no rush toward compliance with the law. On the contrary, desegregation progressed at a painfully slow pace over a period of many years. It did not occur regionally or even state by state; instead, desegregation unfolded largely one school district at a time. Some schools desegregated voluntarily, while others waited for the courts to force the issue. The five states of the Deep South were the last to desegregate their schools. By May 1964, 10 years after the first *Brown* decision, of the 636 school districts in those 5 states, only 11 school districts, fewer than 2 percent, were desegregated. While the passage of the Civil Rights Act in July 1964 did spur the overall rate of desegregation, it also hardened the resolve of die-hard segregationists in many areas of the Deep South, including those with whom Cameron and Gibson negotiated.[8]

Finally, it is important to remember that desegregation was an exercise in tokenism. A white school was classified officially as desegregated if it enrolled a single black child. Those who waged war against desegregation gave as little ground as possible, as slowly as possible.

In general, the South of the 1960s did not welcome liberal ideas, liberals (including southern liberals such as Ben Cameron and Ben Gibson), or liberal organizations. The College Board and ETS, headquartered in New York and New Jersey, respectively, represented the northern, "Yankee" establishment and were looked upon with skepticism or worse by segregationists whose words and actions are part of this story. To accomplish what they had determined to be morally right, both organizations risked the prospect of diminished influence on education in the South. Throughout both organizations there were also concerns about the related financial risk, expressed most strongly by ETS president Henry Chauncey who worried that desegregating the test centers would harm seriously the prospects of the College Board and ETS in the South.

Cameron and Gibson soon discovered that the massive resistance to school desegregation was not impenetrable. In many communities, they found school and college officials who were willing to accommodate black test candidates even though their schools and communities remained strictly segregated. Some officials struggled with their decisions, while others acted with little apparent thought for any professional or personal risk. A few were unwavering in their faith in segregation, and Cameron and Gibson listened to their opinions also, nearly always with patience and understanding. Describing a particularly difficult conversation with a segregationist school superintendent "[whose] normally ruddy complexion became white" when Gibson asked him to accommodate black SAT candidates, Gibson wrote, "It actually hurt me to make this man so miserable."[9]

In order to accommodate the predicted growth in SAT testing, Ben Cameron needed to prepare for a lack of cooperation from some school districts. Fortunately, the College Board and ETS had earned considerable respect in national education circles. As a result, requesting help from a variety of highly influential sources came easily, so it seemed natural to seek assistance from the military in providing alternative testing facilities in areas where the desegregation of traditional test centers proved impossible. Individual military base commanders from locations in the Deep South also enter the story.

And Cameron formed a special committee of men with varied backgrounds and different perspectives on desegregation to discuss strategy and advise him on specific situations. Among them was Cameron's associate Stephen J. Wright, president of Fisk University, a leading private black university in Tennessee, which under Wright's leadership became a center for student activism in the civil rights movement. Wright, the only black member of Cameron's committee, fully supported school and test center desegregation and provided valuable insight throughout the endeavor.

ETS brought to the project of desegregating SAT test centers in public schools its recent experience of desegregating its Law School Admissions Test (LSAT) centers in southern colleges and universities. The desegregation of educational institutions in the United States began in earnest in the 1930s with the desegregation of graduate and professional education, particularly law schools. The desegregation of the LSAT centers, as a general precedent and especially as it relates to the desegregation of law schools themselves, offers important context for this book. The ETS organization, formed in 1947 through a merger of the testing functions of the American Council on Education, the Carnegie Foundation for the Advancement of Teaching, and the College Board, maintained a close relationship with the College Board, its largest client, and provided Ben

Cameron a starting point for his work. Representatives from the College Board and ETS attended each other's meetings and kept in close communication. Officials of each organization shared a culture of integrity, and the related, institutionalized precision of their record-keeping made this book feasible.

Readers should know that the long and complex history of the SAT is not a significant part of this book. However, it is helpful to understand that at the time this story takes place the test was in its ascendancy. Standardized testing, an important placement tool for schools and colleges, was also used to identify talented young people who might otherwise be overlooked due to various socioeconomic factors. As such, some tests, particularly the SAT, became factors in a larger effort to broaden the public's access to higher education. The SAT, the most prevalent of standardized tests used for college admission, and its guardians, the College Board and ETS, commanded the attention and regard of educators at the highest levels: educators had faith in the test and in the organizations that provided it. The College Board and ETS felt the weight of that faith and took their responsibilities seriously, including their responsibility to test equitably all students who registered for the SAT.

Largely missing from the ETS and College Board records are the voices of individual black students and school officials speaking about their experiences with test centers. Apparently, the organizations did not retain for any considerable period of time most records of complaints from individual black students and teachers. After investigating each individual complaint and taking appropriate action, at a certain point staff members destroyed the records. It is fortunate that a few records, such as the letter from teacher Fannie Phelps Adams, cited above, were saved. References to and descriptions of similar complaints are part of the record and strongly indicate that such discriminatory treatment was not unusual.

The project to desegregate test centers displays the willingness of two organizations and two committed men to make a singular contribution to the desegregation of education in the South. Their success in this task demonstrates that Cameron and Gibson were uniquely positioned to negotiate with both secondary and postsecondary school officials. Armed with the right strategy, they met a difficult challenge.

A Precedent

DESEGREGATING THE LAW SCHOOL ADMISSIONS

TEST CENTERS, 1960–1962

All tests so given are grossly unfair to Negro applicants. We urge
prompt revamping of [segregated] testing practice.
—Roy Wilkins, executive secretary, NAACP, telegram to
Educational Testing Service, August 1960

Almost from its formation in 1948, Educational Testing Services (ETS)
had been concerned about segregated conditions at centers for its several
test programs. Complaints from black candidates in the South arrived
regularly at the ETS campus in Princeton, and the organization addressed
them on a case-by-case basis, offering apologies and making special accommodations when appropriate. Meanwhile, demand for all tests administered by ETS was growing steadily, with more candidates each year
for Graduate Record Examinations, Secondary School Admissions Tests,
College Board tests (including the Scholastic Aptitude Test [SAT]), Law
School Admissions Tests (LSAT), Secondary School Admissions Tests,
National Teachers Examinations, and others. ETS was enjoying this growth
and knew that it risked losing test centers and white candidates in the
South if it insisted on integrated centers. The LSAT centers became the
first that ETS studied with the idea of desegregation in mind. Its success
in that arena led to a much more ambitious plan to desegregate College
Board test centers. These two efforts parallel the movement to desegregate

public law schools that eventually led to the desegregation of public higher education generally and then, finally, to the desegregation of public schools. Background on the LSAT and the desegregation of law schools, outlined in this chapter, provides a context for what follows.[1]

The College Entrance Examination Board developed the LSAT in the late 1940s in response to a request from Frank Bowles, director of admissions at Columbia University and later president of the College Board. Columbia and Yale University had the longest histories of administering legal aptitude tests, both having begun that practice in the 1930s. Bowles was dissatisfied with the entrance test Columbia was using at that time. He and other Columbia representatives met in July 1947 with Henry Chauncey, then treasurer of the College Board, and other College Board officers to discuss alternatives.[2]

Those attending the July meeting issued an invitation to representatives of Harvard University and Yale to join Columbia in a project wherein the College Board would develop and administer an aptitude examination for the three universities to use as part of their law school admissions process. Harvard and Yale agreed to the proposal. When the university and College Board representatives met in August, they decided to include several other law schools, inviting all institutions holding membership in the College Board and having law schools to form a group that would finance the development of the test.[3]

In November 1947 the Conference on the Legal Aptitude Test took place. Those present agreed to offer the opportunity to participate in the project to any law school that belonged to the Association of American Law Schools, an organization encompassing the country's most prestigious law schools. In the end, 22 law schools participated. Pretesting was conducted at 9 law schools in the fall of 1947, and 2,753 candidates took the first form of the test the following spring. Having assumed responsibility for all College Board test administrations on January 1 of that year, ETS administered the test. During the 1948–49 academic year, ETS tested approximately 7,500 LSAT candidates. By the end of 1948 the LSAT had become a self-supporting division of ETS, and all of the original donors to the program were reimbursed from the collection of test fees.[4]

The year 1948 was a banner one for law schools, which enrolled more first-year students during that academic year than in any prior year due largely to the influx of World War II veterans; moreover, the 1948–49 academic year would continue to hold that record for nearly two decades. Because postwar candidates were so diverse in their academic backgrounds and because they were applying from all over the United States, law school admissions officers needed a standard measure of aptitude to aid them in their selection processes.[5]

By 1953, the fifth anniversary of the LSAT, the number of those taking the test, after an initial dip from its starting point of 7,500, had reached 8,283. In addition to the usual logistical challenges of test administration—finding facilities; hiring, training, and evaluating test center supervisors; processing registrations; and shipping test materials—ETS faced an additional challenge in some of its southern locations. That challenge was racial segregation in the colleges and universities where ETS administered the LSAT in the South. ETS found itself in the difficult position of attempting to accommodate black test candidates in colleges and universities where they were not at all welcome.[6]

In the South of the early 1950s, education at every level was a strictly segregated enterprise. Southern states consistently supported the "separate but equal" system established in 1896 by the Supreme Court in the *Plessy v. Ferguson* case. In upholding a Louisiana law pertaining to segregated railway accommodations, the Court ruling allowed states to create and perpetuate separate facilities of all types, including schools, for whites and blacks, effectively legalizing the South's Jim Crow laws. Historian Robert Pratt observes that the *Plessy* decision was "the most devastating judicial decision ever rendered against African Americans in the United States."[7]

These segregated facilities were purported to be equal, but rarely if ever were. Over time, the southern states created a dual public education system that included separate black and white schools at the elementary, secondary, and college levels. But this system did not extend to graduate or professional education for blacks. Studying for a doctorate in the South was simply impossible for black people. The situation for professional education was nearly as dire: the historically black Howard University School of Medicine (District of Columbia) and Meherry Medical

College (Nashville, Tennessee), also historically black, were the only two accredited medical colleges available to blacks in the South. For aspiring black lawyers wishing to attend an accredited law school in the South, Howard's law school was their single option.[8] Howard Law School was responsible for training nearly all black lawyers in the United States, having graduated 80 percent of their number by the early 1930s. More than thirty years later, Howard could still claim as alumni most of the black lawyers in the United States. For many reasons—lack of good preparation, lack of money, and increasingly more rigorous requirements for enrollment and graduation, among others—the total number of black lawyers remained a very small percentage of total U.S. lawyers, increasing from 0.80 percent (1,450 of 180,461) in 1950 to only 1.16 percent (2,440 of 209,684) in 1960. While some gains were made in the enrollment of black law students in the 1960s, the number enrolled would not reach even 5 percent until the 1970s.[9] In the South, the numbers were particularly low. Mississippi, with a black population of approximately one million, claimed only nine black lawyers in 1967.[10]

Access for blacks to white law schools in the South finally began to improve in the late 1930s due to efforts on the part of the NAACP Legal Defense Fund under the leadership of Thurgood Marshall. Marshall, who in 1967 would become the first black Supreme Court justice, had himself been denied admission to the University of Maryland Law School. Instead, Marshall attended Howard Law School, graduating in 1933 and taking a position with the NAACP shortly afterward. It was therefore fitting that Marshall would play a role in the case that led the University of Maryland Law School to admit its first black student in 1936.[11]

In the 1940s, Marshall and other NAACP Legal Defense and Educational Fund attorneys established the goal of desegregating public law schools within their broader cause of improving the education of blacks generally. They concentrated on law schools for several reasons. First, the U.S. Constitution clearly supported their position. The Fourteenth Amendment, ratified in 1868, established that states could not "make or enforce any law which shall abridge the privileges or immunities of citizens of the United States; nor shall any State deprive any person of life, liberty, or property, without due process of law; nor deny to any person within its jurisdiction the equal protection of the laws." Denying black students access to state-supported law schools was an undeniable affront to constitutional law.

Second, by choosing public law schools as their focus, Marshall and his colleagues could operate within the prevailing "separate but equal" environment handed down in the 1896 *Plessy* decision. The NAACP lawyers based their law school desegregation case arguments on the fact that the states in question provided absolutely no opportunities for black citizens to study law within their borders, a privilege that white citizens unquestionably held. By focusing on only the "equal" portion of *Plessy*, the NAACP could postpone confronting the very essence of segregation—the "separate" portion—until a later time, one they hoped might be more conducive to their success.

A third reason for choosing law schools, as opposed to other professional or graduate education, stemmed from the fact that the white judges who would hear the Fund's cases were themselves very familiar with the resources necessary for a sound legal education. They were not likely to accept the makeshift, substandard remedies offered by states resisting desegregation. Fourth, states under court order to provide "equal" legal education to their black citizens might well find that desegregating their existing, white law schools would be a cheaper alternative than funding new law schools solely for black students. This in fact is precisely what happened in several instances.[12]

Finally, the NAACP attorneys must have considered that resistance to desegregation and any corresponding mistreatment of black students on the part of white law faculty members would be minimal when compared to that in other higher education settings. As reported in a 1957 *American Bar Association Journal* article on the position of law faculty regarding the desegregation of law schools, law faculty "do not enjoy being put in the position of defying the law which they teach. . . . They recognize the inconsistency which their institutions enforce upon them." The author, writing on behalf of the Association of American Law Schools, added that most law faculties would be willing to admit black students if it were not for the opposition of their administrators and trustees. If the NAACP attorneys succeeded in forcing law schools to admit black students, those students were likely to be treated relatively well by faculty, a factor that could not be taken lightly.[13]

Throughout the 1940s and early 1950s, Thurgood Marshall and his colleagues won opportunities for black students to enter state-sponsored, white professional and graduate programs. However, these hard-won accomplishments were only a beginning. In June 1950, with the conviction that desegregating white educational institutions at all levels was the only way black people would ever have access to an education equal to that of whites and with the corresponding realization that their new strategy was replete with risk, they decided to address the "separate" side of *Plessy* and challenge segregation head-on.[14] In December 1952, the Supreme Court heard five cases involving elementary school desegregation; collectively, the cases would become known as *Brown v. Board of Education.* By mid-1953, the Court requested more evidence from the attorneys and then in December reheard the cases. Finally, on May 17, 1954, the Supreme Court ruled unanimously in favor of the plaintiffs in *Brown,* marking the beginning of the end of segregated schools as well as the beginning of the protracted and massive resistance to school desegregation in the Deep South.[15]

By 1954, public law schools in Arkansas, Kentucky, Louisiana, Maryland, Missouri, North Carolina, Oklahoma, Tennessee, Texas, and Virginia had been desegregated by court order. William and Mary in Virginia, and eight, white, non-state, southern university law schools (in Kentucky, Missouri, Texas, and the District of Columbia) voluntarily admitted black students. In 1950, under federal court order, only one of the Deep South or hard core southern states, Louisiana, had quietly desegregated its law school at Louisiana State University (LSU) in Baton Rouge. The states of Alabama, Florida, Georgia, Mississippi, and South Carolina maintained a rigid segregated status in their schools of law, as they did in virtually all other aspects of life.[16]

In 1953, while the law, medical, and graduate schools at LSU together enrolled one hundred black students, the total undergraduate enrollment consisted, though only briefly, of one student. LSU soon reversed its admissions decision and cancelled that student's registration pending further litigation, effectively expelling the recently admitted student. This extremely limited degree of desegregation at LSU reflected the magnitude of Louisiana's resistance to school and college desegregation generally and contributed to the difficulties of some of the LSAT candidates reporting to LSU facilities for testing.[17]

In the early 1950s, LSU's law school was one of the very few desegregated enterprises in Baton Rouge. Jim Crow practices of all kinds were pervasive, no more so than in public schools that would remain segregated for another dozen years. Black laborers had not benefited in any significant way from the prosperity that Baton Rouge's booming oil refineries brought to the area. There, blacks working in the refineries filled only low-paying jobs that required little in the way of skill or education; skilled and white-collar jobs were strictly for white people. The same was true in the shipbuilding industry, another thriving sector of the Baton Rouge economy. Labor unions and government jobs also were for whites only. In June 1953, responding to another daily injustice, black bus riders staged a brief boycott of the city's bus system in protest of segregated seating. The seats in the back of the bus were reserved for blacks, who were forbidden the more comfortable and convenient front seats, even when no white passengers were present. More significant than the physical discomfort and inconvenience was the clear message of inequality. Historian Adam Fairclough writes: "The symbolism of being assigned the back of the bus rather than the front was unmistakable, and it sank in at a tender age . . . the system clearly put blacks at a psychological disadvantage." The white drivers (there were no black drivers) were openly disrespectful to their black passengers while treating whites with deference. The Baton Rouge bus boycott, which spawned an improvised, efficient, and free alternative transportation system for blacks, did not succeed in bringing equality to the seating of passengers on that city's buses. But in predating the iconic Montgomery bus boycott of 1955–56, it made its own mark on the civil rights movement as a model of direct-action, church-based protest.[18]

An incident that occurred in Baton Rouge at the LSU LSAT test center in August 1953 was typical of the kind of racial discrimination black LSAT candidates were experiencing at test centers throughout the South. On August 8, three black candidates arrived at the center along with approximately twenty white candidates. In a formal complaint made following the incident, W. O. Powell, one of the three blacks, explained that all candidates, black and white, waited together pleasantly enough for a few minutes prior to the arrival of the test supervisor. When the supervisor, Tandy McElwee, arrived, however, he told the three black candidates that they would have to move to another room. McElwee's stated reason was his fear that one or more of the white candidates might resent the presence of blacks, and he wanted each candidate to do his best on the exam. Powell asked McElwee if he was acting in compliance with a law requiring the segregation of candidates. McElwee answered that he simply did not wish the black candidates to be offended by any comments the white men might make. Powell then asked if the policy of segregation during testing was approved by ETS, and McElwee said, incorrectly, that it was.

The supervisor then moved the three men to a third room; allegedly, it was more comfortable because it was equipped with fans operating against the August heat. In his letter of complaint to ETS, Powell described the room as a small office being used as a stationery stockroom. Located next to that small room was an administrative office occupied by several LSU employees who, according to Powell, talked loudly throughout the test. The three candidates complained to the supervisor about the noise, but it continued. Powell also wrote that one of the fans in the test room was so noisy that it had to be turned off.

Powell concluded that the supervisor intentionally made the testing conditions difficult for the three black candidates. "No one could do his best under the conditions in which we took it." In an aside, Powell mentioned that at the end of the exam one of the "white boys" offered him a ride back to town and during the drive "emphatically expressed" his disagreement with the way Powell and the other two black candidates had been treated. This attitude among white test candidates was not unusual. While a small number of whites did complain to test supervisors about being tested with black students, ETS and the College Board discovered that most were too absorbed in taking the tests to care, and few reported such incidents to their parents or others who might object. More than one school official rightly observed that a "new breed" of young person was emerging, one less adamant about segregation than its predecessors. Powell closed his letter of complaint expressing his hope that in the future ETS would be able to put all candidates "on an equal footing."[19]

Josephine Hammond, head of the ETS centers and supervisors section, responded to Powell's complaint and stated "emphatically" that ETS "does not 'authorize' segregation at all and accepts it only in cases where local laws would otherwise prevent the testing of Negro candidates [with whites]."[20] Hammond then wrote to McElwee, the LSU test center supervisor, stating that ETS found the incident "disturbing." Especially disturbing was McElwee's claim that ETS policy actually authorized racial segregation. ETS's strong preference, she explained, was for all candidates to be seated for exams in the same room; exceptions were tolerated only when local law dictated segregation. In those cases, ETS policy was that candidates be treated impartially. Like Powell, Hammond closed her letter expressing the hope that the LSU center would not separate candidates in the future.[21]

McElwee responded defensively, arguing that all candidates had been moved once, due to the room's size being inadequate, and that Powell's other complaints, including those involving the distractions from conversations and the noisy fan, were unjustified. In fact, according to McElwee, the fan, which had a "slight squeak," had been turned off when one of the candidates complained. McElwee reminded Hammond that, in a letter dated October 17, 1950, she had written to McElwee that all candidates should be tested under "competent supervision and comparable conditions." In a subsequent letter, dated January 22, 1952, she had agreed that McElwee had proceeded appropriately in preparing for an earlier exam by "engaging Miss Hatcher . . . to administer the test to Mr. Turner," a black candidate who had been tested away from white candidates. If since that event ETS had changed its testing policies, McElwee stated, he had not been notified. McElwee, unable or unwilling to comprehend that he had offended the black candidates by segregating them from the larger group, stubbornly added that it was his opinion that the black candidates indeed had been tested under the same conditions as the white candidates; moreover, he thought the room where the black candidates had been placed was superior because it was cooler. McElwee closed his letter with the statement that segregated conditions would be continued "until the policies of the University are changed."[22]

Hammond answered McElwee's letter immediately. In her succinct, two-sentence response she ignored McElwee's several arguments, thanked him for his "explicit account" of the incident, and expressed ETS's confidence that he would do everything he could to avoid "future embarrassment to LSAT candidates and ETS." The individual hopes of W. O. Powell and Josephine Hammond that blacks and whites would be tested together at LSU in the near future were not realized, as an incident that occurred in 1960, fully seven years later, illustrated.[23]

By 1960, the number of candidates taking the LSAT each year had reached more than 23,000; the test had become a standard requirement for admission to law schools across the United States.[24] During the 1960–61 academic year, in Alabama, Florida, Georgia, Louisiana, Mississippi, and South Carolina—those states most solidly resistant to desegregation—ETS administered the LSAT at thirteen locations. Of course, based on the very low numbers of black students attending law school, the number of black LSAT candidates was correspondingly very small.[25]

In 1960, 6 years following the first *Brown* decision, little progress had been made toward desegregating the South's schools, colleges, or universities, with only 6 percent of black elementary and secondary school children in the entire southern region (17 states plus the District of Columbia) attending school with whites. Out of a total of more than 6,000 school districts in the region, only 765, about 13 percent, had desegregated. In fact, instead of moving toward school desegregation, much of the South was resolutely engaged in its massive resistance movement against it. Of the hundreds of public school districts located in the 6 hard core states, only a lone district in Miami, Florida, was considered desegregated as fall term classes began. In addition, no public colleges or universities in Alabama, Georgia, Florida, Mississippi, or South Carolina were desegregated.[26]

In 1960 ETS had no formal policy requiring that its test centers be desegregated, with the exception of its Navy College Aptitude Test centers. The Navy, like other branches of the armed forces, had been integrated for more than a decade and naturally required desegregated testing.

However, since the 1954 *Brown* decision and the resistance that followed, there had been mounting concern among ETS's leadership about segregated testing conditions throughout the South, as a small but growing number of southern black candidates sought entry to law schools there and elsewhere.

As a result of segregation in general and the segregation practiced by the colleges and universities that served as LSAT test centers in particular, black candidates, like W. O. Powell, often experienced racial discrimination when they appeared at a testing center. Typically, black candidates were taken to a room apart from the white candidates, and it appears that the facilities provided for them were not always equal to those provided for whites, an intolerable situation for an organization that insisted on optimal testing conditions for all. ETS records reveal that complaints from black candidates in the South were regular occurrences. In some cases, a candidate who had faced racial discrimination would report his or her experience to a local chapter of the NAACP instead of or in addition to ETS. When ETS received a complaint from the NAACP, it investigated the incident and determined whether the testing conditions had indeed been inferior. If their investigation confirmed inferior conditions, ETS offered the candidate an immediate special administration of the test.[27]

In August 1960, seven years after W. O. Powell's experience, ETS learned of a complaint from another black LSAT candidate, again involving its center at LSU in Baton Rouge. It was this incident that finally compelled ETS leaders to institute formal policies and procedures for desegregating LSAT centers. Their work toward desegregating the LSAT centers soon led to the joint ETS and College Board campaign to desegregate the SAT centers.

By 1960 ETS had established three LSAT centers in Louisiana: McNeese State College at Lake Charles, Louisiana State University at Baton Rouge, and Tulane University of New Orleans. McNeese State, a public college, had been ordered to admit black students in 1954. LSU, still resisting desegregation in its undergraduate programs despite having enrolled black graduate and professional students, was, by 1960, under two federal injunctions ordering the university to discontinue its racially discriminatory practices, including "internal segregation," the Jim Crow practice of separating its own enrolled students from each other on the basis of race within the university itself. As a private institution, Tulane was free to operate with segregated or integrated facilities and would not admit black students until the 1964–65 academic year.[28]

If they had been aware of the imposed federal injunctions, some at ETS might have expected LSU to conduct its administrations of the LSAT under integrated conditions. However, that was not the case, as LSAT program director John Winterbottom learned in a memo from his assistant Ethel Kaveney. The memo, dated August 12, 1960, and written during Winterbottom's absence from the office, begins "I am sorry to have to greet you with a small bombshell in the form of a letter from the Baton Rouge Supervisor."[29]

The letter, signed by George Deer, dean of the junior division at LSU, and Amelia Hatcher, proctor for the August 9 test administration at LSU, referred to the "racial problem faced by institutions in this area" and explained that "Donald Moss, a Negro applicant for the Law School Admissions Test, declined to take the test as a protest against the separation of Negro and white students." Furthermore, Deer and Hatcher wrote, Moss requested that his name be struck from the test roster and stated his intention to file a complaint with ETS.[30]

Kaveney consulted Moss's test registration form and learned that he lived in Baton Rouge, had attended Southern University's School of Law, and had requested that his scores be sent to Howard University. "Apparently segregation is no novelty to him," Kaveney quipped in reference to the two black universities. Kaveny's memo to Winterbottom ended with her hope that Moss's letter of complaint would not arrive at ETS prior to Winterbottom's return.[31]

If Kaveney had done additional research she would have learned that Donald T. Moss, in addition to being a former law student at Southern University, an historically black university located in Baton Rouge, was applying for a transfer to Howard University because he, along with fifteen other Southern University students, had been expelled for attempting to desegregate the lunch counters of two Baton Rouge establishments. The students had also been barred by Louisiana's governor and state legislature from ever again attending any public college or university in

Louisiana. In the meantime, Moss was working for the NAACP on a project in Louisiana to revive chapters that had become dormant due in part
to internal strife, but primarily because of pressure from segregationists.

During March 1960, inspired by the North Carolina Agricultural and
Technical College students' sit-in at the Woolworth lunch counter in
Greensboro, North Carolina, and many other student sit-ins that followed,
sixteen Southern University students, who became known as the Southern Sixteen, had participated in a series of sit-ins in Baton Rouge. Donald
Moss and six other students were involved in the S. H. Kress Department
Store sit-in. Upon entering the store they made several purchases and
then seated themselves at the lunch counter. Predictably, the waitress
ignored them. The manager eventually instructed the waitress to tell one
of the women in Moss's group that they would not serve "colored" at the
lunch counter. The students could order food and beverages at the counter
but would have to take them to a table behind a curtain. Hoston Harris,
Moss's fellow student, replied that she preferred to drink her beverage
at the counter.[32]

Summoned by the management, police arrived and told the students
to leave or face arrest. The six quietly refused and were jailed for several
hours. Within a few days, Southern University president Felton G. Clark
called the students to a meeting and expelled them, following up on his
own threat made prior to the sit-ins and obeying the order of segregationist governor Earl K. Long.[33] Claiming that "some radical outfit" had
encouraged them, Governor Long urged the expelled students to go back
to Africa "where colored men don't have any more privileges as a good
mule does in Louisiana."[34]

In ordering their expulsion, Long acted in concert with the Louisiana
legislature which, as a result of the sit-ins, amended the state's constitution to allow the "owner, lessee, or custodian" of a structure to forbid
entry to any "unauthorized" person. Members of the legislature also for-
bade the presidents of all public colleges and universities in Louisiana
to enroll any of the sixteen expelled students.[35] The experience of the
Southern Sixteen was not unique. During the spring of 1960, more than
one hundred students from historically black colleges throughout the

South were expelled by their institutions for participating in sit-ins and other peaceful demonstrations.[36]

Meanwhile, ETS's Ethel Kaveney acknowledged Deer and Hatcher's letter about the Moss incident in a brief note. Writing on August 15, she stated that no letter had yet been received from Moss and closed with her regret that Deer and Hatcher had been confronted "with this embarrassing problem."[37] Within the next few days, Winterbottom returned to his office at ETS and telephoned the LSAT supervisor at LSU, an individual referred to as "Mr. Firnberg." Firnberg explained that Moss was the only black candidate that day and that he had asked Moss to take the test in an office. Firnberg stated that the office was air-conditioned and was located on the same floor as a larger room where the white candidates were tested. According to Firnberg, Moss stated that he had received such a shock from being asked to be tested separately that he simply could not take the test. Moss had then left the center.[38]

Clearly, the incident upset Moss at the time and remained a vivid and troubling memory. In a 2005 interview he exclaimed, "They were trying to put me in a broom closet!" Moss added that Firnberg blamed the necessity of his separation from other test-takers on the Louisiana legislature and state law. But Moss recalled not showing his anger: "I was cool."[39]

ETS's Winterbottom was surprised to learn from Firnberg that LSU actually admitted black students to its law school, where they routinely took exams related to their coursework with white students. The law school's policy, which must have seemed bizarre to Winterbottom, sitting in his office in Princeton, stated that only *enrolled* LSU students were allowed to take examinations in an integrated setting. This practice of "integrating" schools and colleges in such a restrictive way became pervasive, with many white colleges remaining off-limits to any black people who were not enrolled students. In his record summarizing their telephone conversation, Winterbottom concluded that he believed Firnberg had not acted with any "personal" discourtesy toward Moss.[40]

If Moss wrote a letter of complaint to ETS officials, it is not to be found in the ETS Archives. Based on his experience with LSU's Firnberg, likely the only ETS representative Moss had ever encountered, the disgusted

Moss may have decided that he would receive little understanding from the organization Firnberg represented. Drawing on his direct, professional link with the NAACP, Moss complained to that institution instead. Within days, the NAACP responded.

While ETS records do not yield a copy of Moss's complaint, they do contain many references to a telegram regarding the Moss incident from NAACP executive secretary Roy Wilkins. Wilkins's telegram, quoted in full in at least one newspaper, stated that segregating a Negro candidate from the main testing room "made it virtually impossible for him to give a good accounting of himself." Wilkins added, "In addition to depriving a particular applicant of a fair chance, such tests pile up group statistics which flagrantly misrepresent Negro capabilities." The telegram ended, "We urge prompt revamping of testing practice." Wilkins's prominence put ETS on alert. It was conceivable that the NAACP would file an official complaint with ETS, something the organization clearly wanted to avoid.[41]

In 1960 Roy Wilkins was fully engaged in his work. Energized and encouraged about the momentum that student sit-ins were generating in the civil rights movement, he nevertheless was concerned about how to keep that momentum going over the long term. He was keenly interested in the upcoming presidential election between John Kennedy and Richard Nixon and how its outcome would affect the movement. He was very much aware that the NAACP was not the only group vying for the loyalty of black citizens—the Congress on Racial Equality (CORE), the Southern Christian Leadership Conference (SCLC), the Student Non-Violent Coordinating Committee (SNCC), and the National Urban League (NUL) were all seeking followers and financial support. As a result, Wilkins was working to revitalize his organization in the South, particularly in Alabama and Louisiana, where those states' attorneys general had issued court orders that had effectively forced local NAACP units underground. It was this revitalization that engaged Donald Moss in Baton Rouge.[42]

A few days after ETS received Wilkins's telegram, Winterbottom met with Malcolm Talbott, a law professor at nearby Rutgers University and chair of the ETS policy committee for the LSAT, to discuss how ETS should respond to the situation at LSU and the dilemma of segregated test sites in general. Talbott had learned about the LSU incident prior to his September 13 meeting with Winterbottom and then had sought out his colleague Clyde Ferguson, a fellow law professor at Rutgers and black. Talbott and Ferguson had agreed that because the test in question was an aptitude test for the study of law and because members of the LSAT policy committee would probably be particularly "sensitive" to potential civil rights cases, the NAACP "might be especially inclined to bring suit in this instance."[43]

Talbott also had communicated with Paul Herbert, dean of LSU's law school. Herbert suggested that LSAT centers in the South might be located only at law school facilities where integrated conditions were more likely to be possible than at other on-campus sites and further suggested that LSU should make that change. Herbert warned against a "dramatic move" in this direction, however, fearing that any publicity about the change in location could hurt the ability of people such as himself to be effective in promoting integration on their campuses. This concern about publicity from someone supporting desegregation was the first of dozens of similar messages expressed to ETS and the College Board. Avoiding publicity would become one of the hallmarks of efforts to desegregate test centers.[44]

Talbott and Winterbottom agreed that before they tackled the problem of segregation at test centers they needed much more information. ETS staff, located in New Jersey, had no realistic idea as to how extensive the segregation problem was; they also had limited information on the most current legal status of segregation in southern schools and colleges. In addition, although ETS kept meticulous records on the numbers of its test candidates, no records existed on the race of candidates. However, based on the low number of black lawyers and black law students, plus anecdotal evidence from test centers, the leadership at ETS would have known that the number of black LSAT candidates was small. Before their meeting ended, the two men drafted a four-step plan.

First, Talbott would engage Clyde Ferguson, the black Rutgers law professor, to report on the status of segregation in each of the communities in the southern states where LSAT centers operated. Second, Ferguson, Talbott, and other ETS representatives would meet to review the report and determine a course of action. Third, Winterbottom would talk to LSU

Law School dean Herbert and request that the November LSU LSAT be administered at the law school. Finally, because Talbott had friends at many law schools on southern campuses hosting LSAT centers, he agreed to telephone his contacts to learn what they knew about testing conditions with regard to segregation. In situations where conditions were unknown, Talbott planned to ask his friends to visit those centers personally and find out whether segregation was being practiced and, if so, what the facilities were like—were they "really equal even though separate"?

In Talbott's opinion, Roy Wilkins was "a reasonable though determined man" who would respect good faith efforts toward desegregating the centers. Talbott doubted, however, that Wilkins would be able to stop local chapters of the NAACP from taking legal action against ETS. Winterbottom ended his memo about the meeting with a statement describing Talbott's belief that it might not be possible to desegregate centers in states such as Louisiana. If so, the result could be closing centers, to the detriment of all candidates, who then would have to travel out of state for testing.[45]

On September 16, 1960, Talbott wrote Winterbottom to say that he had engaged Ferguson to do the legal research necessary to their plan.[46] Ferguson went to work immediately and submitted a twenty-page opinion on whether, from a legal perspective, desegregated testing centers could be established for administration of the LSAT in each of eleven southern states—Alabama, Arkansas, Delaware, Florida, Georgia, Louisiana, Mississippi, North Carolina, South Carolina, Texas, and Virginia—plus the District of Columbia. In each instance he presented information on existing test centers and whether it was known if they were desegregated; a summary of current state laws with regard to segregation; a summary of relevant cases in federal courts as well as information on any relevant federal injunctions; and his own conclusions about the legal position of institutions that continued to operate on a segregated basis.[47]

In addition to preparing the legal opinion on the "validity" of ETS establishing desegregated LSAT centers, Ferguson also had conferred directly with NAACP officials. Ferguson noted that the NAACP was particularly interested in testing conditions for the LSAT in the southeastern states where segregation was the most firmly entrenched. He had assured

Roy Wilkins that ETS was actively reviewing testing conditions there and that ETS would take whatever measures it could to correct the situation. Wilkins had responded that the NAACP would not consider legal action until ETS had a chance to end racial discrimination at the centers.[48]

Talbott, Ferguson, and Winterbottom met on September 23 with William Turnbull, ETS executive vice president and ETS president Henry Chauncey's right-hand man. Although the men found Ferguson's legal summary informative, they agreed that it could not take the place of an ETS representative being on the spot, observing what actually transpired at centers during a test administration. As Winterbottom correctly observed, "Integration may take place on an informal basis where it is officially forbidden and segregation may exist as a matter of custom even though not required by law." The four men determined that for the upcoming November 1960 test date, they would send "observers" to selected centers where they suspected supervisors were segregating candidates. Observers were to note what took place during test administration, question the supervisor about conditions in order to determine any underlying policy, avoid publicity through "discretion," and avoid offending the supervisors. These four goals later became the basis of the strategy developed by the College Board in their much more challenging task of desegregating the SAT centers. The ETS plan called for sending observers to approximately fourteen LSAT centers in seven southern states. Observers also traveled to western test sites where ETS suspected discrimination against Mexican and Mexican American candidates. All indications were that racial discrimination in testing was limited to those two regions.[49]

Not everyone at ETS agreed with Ferguson's legal opinion or approved of his taking it upon himself to represent ETS in his conversation with Roy Wilkins. ETS staff member A. L. Benson, in a memo to Winterbottom, said that he was "shocked" to learn that Ferguson had been allowed to speak "so broadly" on behalf of ETS and "in language tantamount to admission of the existence of 'objectionable circumstances'" at the centers. Benson was also concerned about the validity of Ferguson's assumption that court decisions that applied to public institutions would apply to all ETS test centers, some of which were located at private institutions. Furthermore, because Ferguson was black, Benson questioned his impartiality in the matter. Finally, he expressed his reluctance for ETS's development of a policy for its LSAT centers without additional and more objective study, reminding Winterbottom that differences in opinions "are what make horse races and courts." There is no evidence that Winterbottom and Talbott considered taking Benson's advice. Realizing the legitimacy and urgency of Roy Wilkins's complaint, they took immediate action.[50]

Meanwhile, a plan was under way at LSU to move the test center to the law school facilities. Dean Herbert had asked LSU's legal counsel to determine the conditions under which the LSAT could be administered at the law school and hoped to have an answer by the end of September. ETS officials needed as much notice as possible in order to mail entry tickets to candidates well in advance of the November 12 test date because those tickets included test center locations.[51]

During October and November 1960, reports began arriving at ETS from Talbott and Winterbottom's southern law school associates and ETS observers. Some had actually attended the November examinations, while others had made phone calls to people upon whom they could depend to provide accurate and candid information. Not surprisingly, reports varied, including those included here, all from white, segregated universities. Emory University's center, the sole LSAT center in Georgia, was reported to be "integrated," but black candidates were seated in a separate block of seats and were forced to find an off-campus restaurant that would serve them at lunchtime. Washington and Lee's center was also reported to be integrated, but, to the knowledge of the test supervisor, an eight-year veteran, the center had never had a black candidate. Duke University's center, which was investigated by a Duke law professor whom Winterbottom thanked for his "great tact" in collecting his facts, was integrated. A second report about Duke supported that claim, but informed ETS officials that black candidates at the Duke center tended "to segregate themselves in a group at the back of the room."[52]

The center at Florida State University had been integrated since the recent arrival of a new supervisor. Integration there had been "hastened" due to the fact that the administrators of a national testing program for nursing students had threatened to remove their center from Florida State and offer the test only at a nearby black institution, compelling white students to take the test there. The University of Miami center truly was desegregated, by both room and seating arrangement. Ray Forrester, dean of the Tulane University School of Law, wrote that its center did not practice segregation and that they had had "no difficulty in this connection." The observer who reported on South Texas College's center stated: "Mr. Walker [the center supervisor] indicated he would certainly expect to admit Negro students to the center and to test them in the same room with other students. He seemed somewhat surprised that the question had been raised." Mr. Walker's accommodation went only so far. The observer, describing the restrooms for black test candidates, noted that those facilities were "separately labeled" (by race), which she supposed was "standard" for the college.[53]

A lively report from ETS staff member Carol McDonough, dispatched to observe the center at the Stetson University College of Law in Florida ("supported by the hat man," McDonough wrote), included a statement that, despite the fact that Stetson University itself was a conservative, "hard shell Baptist institution" that practiced segregation, the law school, which many years prior had moved from the main campus in Deland to St. Petersburg, practiced integration as "a law of the land." McDonough offhandedly attributed this achievement to law school dean Harold Sebring, who had participated in the Nuremberg trials prosecuting Nazi war criminals.[54]

Elmer Day, an ETS department head and the observer who traveled to the University of South Carolina test center for the November exam, submitted a report that must have disappointed, but probably not surprised, his ETS colleagues. The university's center supervisor, Rollin Godfrey, who was "Southern by birth and inclination," had graduated from Teachers College of Columbia University and was well acquainted with ETS and some of its staff members. Godfrey favored testing all candidates together; however, if there were complaints from whites he would test black candidates in his office.

Day felt Godfrey was doing his best to accommodate black candidates. He had moved the test center from the Navy ROTC Armory, located at the very hub of the all-white campus, to a building that was on university property but situated off-campus several blocks away. In fact, it stood, well camouflaged, next to "a Negro business college." ETS's Day assumed that Godfrey had chosen that particular location because a casual observer would probably not notice that blacks were entering a university facility. Day noted that segregated restrooms and water fountains had not been installed during the building's recent renovation and feared that ETS should expect "violent community reaction" if it became widely known that the center was being operated on a fully integrated basis. After all, the building stood "within the shadows of the State Capitol," a facility that hardly symbolized racial tolerance. Day recommended two alternative locations should the LSAT policy committee insist on fully integrated centers: the Naval Reserve Training Center, a federal facility used for ETS Navy ROTC examinations, or Columbia College, a private institution thought to be sympathetic to integration. The College Board staff later would adopt the idea of using federal facilities in their campaign to desegregate the SAT centers.

Day concluded that because Godfrey was taking steps toward operating an integrated center, ETS should take a wait-and-see position before changing locations. Godfrey was not optimistic about the future of integration in his state: "The climate of the community is in direct opposition, and there are few educated people who feel that there will not be bloodshed in rural areas before integration is ever accomplished in the State of South Carolina."[55]

On November 3, Henry Chauncey presented a report entitled "Integration at Testing Centers" to the ETS executive committee. First, referring to the long history of complaints from black test candidates, he reminded the members that test center segregation had been a "delicate problem" and a "potentially sensitive area" for many years. He then recited the details of the Donald Moss incident at LSU in August and explained that initial efforts were under way to discover the facts regarding center segregation at several locations.[56]

Next, Chauncey listed the principles governing the current initiative. They were: (1) to abide by the law, following the rulings of the federal courts in line with the Supreme Court decisions (Chauncey was referring to the 1954 and 1955 *Brown* rulings); (2) to take steps so that all candidates were tested under equitable conditions; (3) to "encourage and speed integration" at the centers to the extent possible.[57]

Chauncey stressed that the organization's first responsibility was to administer tests to candidates, meaning that in some cases that responsibility would override the objective of desegregating the centers. Because state and local laws and customs still dictated segregation, Chauncey polled the committee as to how far ETS should go in insisting that its centers operate on an integrated basis. Committee members responded that they supported the principles of integrated education along with ETS efforts to ensure the most fair and positive test conditions possible. They also backed the plan to move toward integrated centers, acting in "the spirit of the Supreme Court rulings." During the discussion that followed, one member suggested that ETS should maintain the expectation that centers be desegregated within the timeframes prescribed by federal court orders for school desegregation. Where time limits had not been established and integrated education was not practiced, ETS should investigate, but not require, the option of moving the centers. It was also suggested that ETS officers write a statement of the "principles and policies" the organization would use as it moved toward desegregating the centers and present the statement to the ETS trustees for possible adoption.[58]

By mid-October 1960, LSU law school dean Herbert had telephoned Winterbottom to report that the LSU legal counsel had determined that integrated testing could take place at the established test center; there would be no need to move the examination to the law school. LSU's president specifically had asked test supervisors not to change locations "in order to avoid undue publicity." This news spread through the ranks at ETS so that examination tickets, which indicated the center's address, could be sent to candidates assigned to Baton Rouge. Diana Lucas, assistant department head for operational services, circulated a memo about the newly desegregated Baton Rouge location, advising staff members to begin processing test admission tickets and to "Cross your fingers!" for a trouble-free test administration.[59]

While ETS officials, like the LSU leadership, wished to avoid publicity, the involvement of the NAACP made that unlikely. Articles about the

LSU incident appeared in several newspapers. Yale University law professor Jack Tate sent a copy of one such article to his friend John Winterbottom in October. He blamed LSU policies for the incident rather than ETS. In responding to Tate's letter, Winterbottom referred to other "less virulent" newspaper articles and assured Tate that ETS was working to eliminate the possibility of more incidents occurring in the future.[60]

At their November 29, 1960, meeting, ETS trustees discussed the executive committee's report and decided not to issue a policy statement regarding integrated testing at that time. In what might seem an unusual action, the trustees also decided that ETS officers should accommodate any black candidates requesting permission to be examined separately from whites. The committee wished to minimize any embarrassment on the part of black candidates who might be placed in an uncomfortable, desegregated environment for testing. In addition, ETS officials were to question their other clients about test conditions in order to avoid similar problems at those centers. At the close of their discussion, the trustees recommended that at subsequent meetings their officers would report on the progress made toward integrating the centers.[61]

On December 2, Winterbottom dictated a memo to Talbott summarizing all reports from observers at the November 12 test administration. He recommended that ETS review all the centers they planned to use for the rest of the academic year and to "check by phone or visitation additional ones which are likely to be trouble spots." In Winterbottom's opinion, the generally positive nature of most of the reports indicated that further incidents such as the one at LSU were unlikely; however, he admitted that there was no guarantee that another incident might not occur. He suggested to Talbott that ETS let the NAACP know what action ETS had taken so far and of the testing organization's intention to deal with any "isolated incidents" by either receiving assurance from the center involved that it would be operated on an integrated basis or closing it and moving to another location.[62]

The executive committee next met on December 27, 1960. Discussion centered around a means of obtaining detailed information regarding segregation at all LSAT centers so that ETS would be able to write an informed policy. The committee asked Winterbottom to draft a survey and a cover letter, which would be addressed to "a high administrative official, probably the president or dean," of each center to be surveyed, to be presented for approval at the January 1961 policy committee meeting. With the committee's approval, ETS would mail the survey immediately and share the results with the executive committee as soon as possible. The executive committee also decided to explore the possibility of using federal facilities as centers, an idea that would surface again during SAT center desegregation efforts. The committee ruled out approaching parochial schools since "many of them are in a ticklish enough situation as it is with respect to integration" but agreed to consider cancelling centers where desegregation would be impossible.[63]

The draft of the cover letter explained the need for the survey information and cited the LSU incident as being one that "had implications of a very basic nature for the conduct of the LSAT program." Winterbottom emphasized ETS's responsibility to ensure that each candidate be tested under fair circumstances and not "handicapped in taking the test because of race, religion, or national origin." He acknowledged that the survey might offend some recipients, but that giving offense was not the policy committee's intent.[64]

The LSAT policy committee met next on January 20, 1961, and, for reasons that are not clear, but probably included the fear of publicity, decided to defer mailing the questionnaire. It appears that it was never sent. Acting in part on the information gathered from November test observers, the committee passed the following motion:

> That "upon discovery that a center is segregated with respect to room, seating, rest-room facilities, or meal facilities, ETS will be empowered to negotiate in an attempt to achieve desegregation. In the event that the negotiations are unsuccessful, the center will be discontinued and an attempt will be made to establish a substitute center."[65]

Meanwhile, as resistance to desegregation persisted throughout the South, including determined resistance to the integration of colleges and universities, ETS's attention was drawn once again to an LSAT test center in Louisiana, this time its desegregated center at white Tulane University in New Orleans. Following the February 1961 test administration,

Murray S. Work, center supervisor, wrote to Harold L. Crane, director of
test administration at ETS, to report an incident that he believed might
"forebode of things to come." Work had supervised LSAT tests at Tulane
for several years and, as Tulane's Law School dean Ray Forrester had reported a few months earlier, had never experienced any trouble or even
a "hint of trouble" with regard to his fair, nondiscriminatory administration of tests. He estimated that the Tulane center had, on average, about
10 percent black candidates at each LSAT administration and repeated to
Crane that no one, meaning no white person, had "ever complained . . .
or indicated concern in any way about the presence of Negroes."[66]

Nonetheless, on the previous Saturday morning when the examination was well under way, two young white men appeared at the center
"stalking about . . . and brandishing a flash camera." They told Work that
they were there to take a photo of the testing for the school "scrapbook."
Work was understandably suspicious, having recognized the pair as members of a "small, but highly motivated group of racists" at Tulane. When
pressed, they could not name the publication for which they were allegedly taking the photograph and became "flustered," asking Work what he
had to hide and by what authority he could tell them that they couldn't
take a picture. Work assured the students that they would have to have
permission "from Princeton," the location of ETS, before they could photograph test candidates, and he returned to the testing room. The two
"fussed about" in the hall for a few more minutes and then left.[67]

Work explained that a similar occurrence had taken place just the night
before. A campus organization had invited a black visiting professor to
speak to its membership, and an uninvited photographer had appeared.
Work thought that the photographer was from the same group as his two
interlopers and believed that racist students were collecting pictures of
integrated campus activities in order to "stir up" interest among people
outside the university. While Work had heard of complaints from "out-
siders" about desegregated testing at Tulane, this was the first instance
of internal dissent of which he was aware. Work warned Crane that tensions in the South, and particularly in New Orleans, were escalating and
that ETS might receive some "crank letters" about desegregated testing.

He doubted that the white candidates themselves had any objections to being tested along with blacks.[68]

Murray Work was correct about current tensions in New Orleans. Three months earlier, in November 1960, New Orleans public schools had begun court-ordered school desegregation by enrolling four first-graders in two schools. Under the city's desegregation plan, integration would occur one grade at a time. Within a few days of the black children's enrollment, riots broke out, and black people were attacked and beaten in the streets. The Greater New Orleans Citizens' Council, a powerful segregationist group, led a highly successful boycott of the schools, harassing any white parents who dared send their children to school. The boycott lasted to the end of the 1960–61 school year, when resistance subsided to some degree. School desegregation in New Orleans would continue, but at a painfully slow pace. Some white parents sent their children to private schools in New Orleans, paying for tuition through a system of state-sponsored grants devised specifically for that purpose. Others simply left the city. Thousands of black students remained in crowded, substandard schools.[69]

Tulane University seemed to be in no more hurry to integrate than the New Orleans public schools had been. Benefactor Paul Tulane, who left a fortune to the university in the late nineteenth century, stipulated that Tulane was intended only for young white people from New Orleans. Over the years, Tulane University had reinterpreted Paul Tulane's wishes to include students from around the world and students of other races; however, black applicants were still barred from attending. In 1961, advised that it would be denied a large Ford Foundation grant if it continued to refuse admission to black applicants, Tulane, rather than simply agreeing to admit blacks in the future, invited a "friendly" lawsuit on behalf of two black applicants to force integration through the courts. The attorney for the applicants argued that, although it represented itself as a private institution, Tulane had received enough state support over the years to fall under the Fourteenth Amendment and was therefore guilty of racial discrimination in its admissions practices. This strategy, in effect an effort to negate Tulane's elite, "private" status, infuriated its governing

board. Historian Adam Fairclough writes, "The suit turned out to be anything but 'friendly.'" Rather, the lengthy process of desegregating Tulane
would expose the degree to which the white elite of New Orleans persevered to maintain "the marriage of wealth, class, and racial privilege that
they personified." Tulane did not admit its first black student until 1963,
two years after the incident Murray Work reported to ETS.[70]

At the April 1961 ETS executive committee meeting, Henry Chauncey
reported that the LSAT policy committee had "recently adopted a quite
stringent policy regarding conditions under which the LSAT would be
administered." In addition, ETS had changed the wording of its formal
letter of agreement with all center supervisors to include a paragraph
stating that ETS expected supervisors to operate test centers on an "entirely non-segregated basis." If a supervisor did not believe he or she
could meet that expectation, ETS should be notified.[71]

Maintaining fully integrated conditions at LSAT centers became a
routine part of ETS work, with updates on any changes in a center's status or lack of compliance included in periodic reports. At least two LSAT
centers were closed because they would not comply with the policy to
desegregate—a center in Virginia that is not named in the record and
the center at McNeese State College in Lake Charles, Louisiana. Significantly, ETS also began discussing steps to desegregate the centers for its
other clients' tests, including the College Board's SAT.[72]

In early 1962 ETS staff member Layton Wolfram compiled a follow-up
report for Winterbottom on the subject of the LSAT centers in several
southern states. Of the eighteen LSAT centers in Alabama, Florida, Georgia, Louisiana, Mississippi, South Carolina, and Virginia, sixteen were
considered "unconditionally desegregated." Only the centers at Florence
State College, Florence, South Carolina, and the University of Alabama,
Tuscaloosa, were listed as "conditionally desegregated," able to accommodate a "small number of Negroes" in an integrated setting but having
to test "large numbers" in a separate room.[73] Unfortunately, black test
candidates still faced segregated lunch facilities at some locations, including Emory University in Atlanta. It is not known how news of this
problem at Emory reached Winterbottom, but once he learned that black

LSAT candidates were having difficulty finding a place to have lunch near the campus, he wrote to both the test center supervisor and the dean of the law school reminding them that in order to keep their center they must make available "satisfactory luncheon facilities of equally convenient accessibility and equally satisfactory service for candidates of all races, at or adjacent to test centers." Winterbottom acknowledged that Emory was in compliance with all other requirements, and said that he would be "most reluctant to take any such drastic action [closing the center]" should Emory not comply by providing adequate lunch facilities for black candidates by July 1962. Emory complied.[74] The test center at the University of Richmond, which had reported earlier that it was desegregated, became a problem due to its lunch and restroom facilities for black candidates. An ETS report read in part: "No rest rooms or lunch facilities available at this location" for black candidates. The outcome of this situation is not known.[75]

ETS periodically received requests for new LSAT centers to be opened, and their new policy on requiring all centers to be unconditionally desegregated became another standard against which a possible center was measured. In April 1962, Layton Wolfram telephoned two potential center supervisors at Howard College, a private, four-year, white, Baptist institution in Birmingham, Alabama, and Centenary College, a private, four-year, white, Methodist college in Shreveport, Louisiana.

Howard College's representative reported that he had accommodated black students for other kinds of tests and had seated them in the same room as whites, but in assigned seats. Lunch facilities on the campus were segregated, so black candidates would have to patronize restaurants located approximately one mile from the campus. Restrooms would be desegregated on the day of the examination.

The Centenary College representative responded that all races would be tested under unconditionally desegregated conditions. Restrooms were desegregated, but black students would have to go off campus to find a place to have lunch. Wolfram sent his report on these two institutions to Winterbottom, asking if he, Wolfram, could be of further help. The outcome of these institutions with regard to their status as LSAT centers is unknown, but it is highly unlikely that they were added to the ETS list of test centers until ETS was assured that they had corrected any discrepancies and could conform to the new ETS policy.[76]

Throughout their dealings with center officials and test candidates and in communications with each other, ETS and College Board staff members maintained the highest level of professionalism, exhibiting courtesy to and respect for all. The only known deviation from this pattern involved a black LSAT candidate from Savannah State College, a black institution and part of the University System of Georgia. In this instance, Martha Wilson, professor of mathematics and director of testing at Savannah State and black, intervened on behalf of a student, Bobby Hill, addressing the problem he would have in finding a place to eat lunch at or near the LSAT center at Armstrong College, a public, white institution. On-campus lunch facilities were closed on Saturday, the day the LSAT was administered, and all candidates were expected to find places to have lunch on their own. Wilson, in a telephone conversation with ETS's Wolfram, insisted that no black person would be served in any restaurant in the area near the test center. Wolfram then suggested to Wilson that Hill bring his lunch, as many candidates did, but she rejected this idea, stating that Hill lived in a dormitory and lacked facilities to make his own lunch. Wolfram then asked Wilson if she had any suggestions, but she had none and ended the conversation with the statement that she would try to help Hill work something out. Wolfram told her to call him if he could help. In his report to Winterbottom, Wolfram stated that, should Wilson insist that Hill had been treated unfairly by being assigned to a center that lacked desegregated lunch facilities, his only alternative would be to make special arrangements to administer the test to Hill at a later date on his own, black campus.[77]

In a departure from ETS style and his own usual professional behavior, Wolfram exposed his frustration with Wilson and the situation by including an "editorial" section at the conclusion of his formal, and otherwise civil, report. First, he complained that Wilson "carried a chip on her shoulder which could be seen between the lines of our telephone conversation." "Apparently," he continued, "a big wary eye was open for any cracks in the ETS defense and if she found one she was prepared to split it open with a black wedge." Martha Wilson, in Wolfram's opinion, believed that it was ETS's responsibility "not only to test the candidates but also to feed them between sessions." Wolfram then sarcastically suggested that ETS "air-express" a box lunch to Bobby Hill at the test center, making sure that "None of the sandwiches were made with only white bread." Otherwise, Wolfram facetiously predicted Wilson would file a complaint with ETS about unfair test conditions. Wolfram did concede that test center lunch facilities were in fact a legitimate concern for ETS.[78]

Wolfram's slide into what could be interpreted only as racial slurs was addressed immediately by Winterbottom. In a memo to Crane and Joseph Terral, two of the other recipients of Wolfram's report, Winterbottom came down hard on Wolfram's behavior, writing that he had shown "very bad judgment" in the "editorial" section of his report. Winterbottom wrote:

> The paragraph . . . contains some heavy-handed humor which is in very poor taste and also potentially dangerous. The plight of the people we are dealing with here is too serious to permit bad jokes at their expense, particularly when such jokes are given the permanence afforded by inclusion in a memorandum. It seems to me that our attitude should be one of scrupulous fairness, even sympathy—but certainly not hostility.[79]

Winterbottom also reminded Crane and Terral, and undoubtedly Wolfram, that if anyone outside ETS read such a memorandum that there would be "real danger of serious embarrassment." He was further distressed that Wolfram had sent a copy to Ben Cameron, director of the newly opened Southern Regional Office of the College Board, who had helped ETS assess the racial situation in the South as it pertained to test center locations. The fact that the memo had made its way to Cameron "put it out of our control," even though it had been marked confidential. Winterbottom closed his message with this sentence: "The probability of accidental disclosure is probably not great but the effects might be very damaging."[80] ETS and the College Board would remain scrupulous in all subsequent communications and would continue efforts to limit strictly any kind of publicity about test center conditions.

By mid-1962 ETS considered its task of desegregating LSAT centers essentially complete. The job had taken less than two years from that day in August 1960 when Donald Moss walked away from the LSU Baton Rouge center rather than be tested in a separate room, and had been accomplished quietly. Amid the LSAT efforts, ETS also studied access for black candidates at the test sites of its other clients—those sponsoring Graduate Record Examinations (GREs), Secondary School Admissions Tests (SSATs), National Teacher Examinations (NTEs), and others. Where ETS found segregated centers, the staff looked for alternatives, in the end adopting a standardized policy of requiring desegregation for all testing centers.[81]

The task of desegregating the College Board SAT centers would prove to be a much more arduous one, involving more than ten times the number of test centers and taking more than twice as many years. Fortunately, lessons learned from the LSAT desegregation project instructed the College Board and ETS in desegregating College Board test sites. Establishing policies, procedures, and a general strategy—including defining the process as a series of quiet negotiations; avoiding publicity; considering the option of using federal facilities as alternate sites; and dispatching staff members to each center to assess its particular situation became hallmarks of the College Board SAT test center desegregation campaign. In addition, the research on the status of segregation in the hard core states, provided in part by Ben Cameron, College Board Southern Regional Office director, laid the foundation for further research, subsequent negotiations, and, eventually, success. Most importantly, the satisfaction that ETS experienced in doing what was right and its knowledge that centers for its other tests might soon come under NAACP scrutiny motivated ETS and the College Board to move forward.

① ● ③ ④ ⑤ ⑥

The Way Things Were, 1959–1961

Impossible!

—Response from white Deep South school officials when asked to consider
desegregated testing, ETS telephone survey, spring 1961

In 1959, the College Entrance Examination Board opened its Southern
Regional Office in Sewanee, Tennessee, in response to a growing demand
for its services in the South. College Board president Frank H. Bowles
hired Ben F. Cameron as office director and charged him with establishing "channels of communication" between secondary schools and colleges in the South, with the ultimate goal of "improving the prepared-
ness of high school students for college." The College Board anticipated
that its presence in the southern region would also improve college admissions practices there, which in turn would raise the academic standards of those institutions. It did not anticipate its almost immediate
entanglement with the racial struggles of the region. In addition to his
more obvious duties, Ben Cameron would be charged to assess the level
of resistance to or support for desegregated testing and then to develop
and execute a plan to achieve a roster of test centers accessible to all.[1]

Cameron, a former chemistry professor and director of admissions at
the University of the South, Sewanee, Tennessee, was a likely choice for
the position. Born and raised in Mississippi, he understood the plight of
education in that region and was dedicated to improving it. His teaching
experience, work in the selective admissions process, and service as a

41

College Board trustee qualified him for his new job. During World War II, Cameron had served as a bomb disposal officer, and this experience, too, may have prepared him for some of his more sensitive duties as director of the Southern Regional Office.[2]

Also important to the task that lay ahead was Cameron's liberal stance on civil rights. Cameron believed in and openly supported the movement, a position he attributed in part to having served in a segregated navy. Cameron's liberalism in matters of race increasingly put him directly at odds with his father, Judge Ben F. Cameron. An Eisenhower appointee to the U.S. Court of Appeals for the Fifth Circuit, the elder Cameron opposed his son's views on race and remained an ardent segregationist all his life.[3]

The opening of the Southern Regional Office and of regional offices in the West and the Midwest in 1959 coincided with the establishment in 1957 of the American College Testing (ACT) program, the College Board's first rival in its then fifty-seven-year history. The College Board, along with ETS, a former division of the College Board and now its partner, had long enjoyed a monopoly in the business of testing high school students for admission to college. The leadership of the ACT program operated out of the University of Iowa in relationship with the American Association of Collegiate Registrars and Admissions Officers (AACRAO), an organization made up of officials from public colleges in the Midwest. ACT intended to make inroads in areas where the College Board had not yet established a loyal clientele, including many parts of the South. One of the ways the College Board planned to compete with ACT was to open regional offices that would tailor services to the specific needs of the schools and colleges in their respective areas. Frank Bowles was confident that the College Board and ETS had a superior product in the Scholastic Aptitude Test (SAT), in use primarily in the Northeast since 1926. He believed the College Board could compete with ACT by maintaining that superiority and by offering school and college personnel additional support in their professional development and in their interactions with regional and national colleges. This strategy required the establishment of regional offices.[4]

If choosing Cameron as director of the Southern Regional Office made good sense to those familiar with the goals and challenges of the College Board, locating the office in Sewanee, Tennessee, initially did not. Atlanta seemed the obvious choice, but Cameron had two reasons for wanting to stay on the mountaintop where Sewanee was located. First, his wife, a pediatrician, had a thriving practice in the area, and, second, Cameron believed he could better service the entire South from a somewhat remote location. Had the office been in Atlanta, he later stated, he would have become "the College Board director for Atlanta, and for the state of Georgia. . . . I would have been almost completely cut off from the rest of the region." And eventually, the College Board and ETS would have additional justification for agreeing to Cameron's request to stay in Sewanee—being off the beaten track made it easier for him to be involved in controversial activities.[5]

Cameron spent his first year on the job setting up his office on the Sewanee campus, hiring a few staff members, and traveling extensively throughout the South to become acquainted with its school districts and colleges. That year, Texas and South Carolina claimed most of Cameron's time, and he was successful in his negotiations with both states, which agreed to adopt College Board testing programs. The University of Texas would require both the SAT and the College Board's English Composition Test for all applicants for fall 1962, and other Texas colleges planned to follow suit. Because Texas was one of the few states outside the Midwest that ACT had made a priority, the majority of colleges in Texas remained listed as ACT institutions, but most would accept either SAT or ACT scores. In South Carolina every accredited, four-year college for white students had begun to require the SAT, and in some cases College Board Achievement Tests, for admission. Within the southern region, only Georgia had a similar, but more sweeping, requirement. In 1957, the board of regents of the University System of Georgia had begun requiring the SAT for admission to all of its public, four-year colleges, both white and black, placing it well ahead of all other states in the Deep South in terms of numbers of SAT candidates. Georgia's predominance as a College Board state would make it of special interest to Cameron and his staff.[6]

Cameron also traveled to Louisiana but did not succeed immediately in selling College Board tests to schools there. The governing board of public education was considering a statewide testing program to be used for counseling and placement purposes rather than for admissions, and it seemed that ACT would be filling that role. Institutions in Kentucky and Arkansas had shown interest in College Board programs, while the ACT had established support in Alabama and Oklahoma. Cameron, a native Mississippian and conscious of the low standing of education there, quipped that his home state was "warily standing off. And, wisely so, since there is no need for entrance examinations within the state." On the whole, Cameron ended his first year as director of the regional office with optimism: "Within a year," he predicted, "virtually every college north of Florida along the Atlantic Seaboard will have [College] Board test requirements."[7]

Cameron was not so naïve as to think that all institutions using College Board tests for admissions purposes were doing so simply to enhance their college admissions and class placement processes. Some, he was convinced, used standardized tests as mechanisms for keeping black students out of white institutions. Though he never mentioned specific evidence, Cameron firmly believed this was the case in Georgia. But, he wrote, "this idea has been completely lost in the growing consciousness of the fact that no test will exclude all Negroes from the colleges." With more students, both black and white, wishing to attend college, admissions officials were beginning to grasp completely the fact that a common measure of academic aptitude was a helpful tool in making good admissions decisions—those that placed students in colleges and universities where they could succeed academically.[8]

In addition to his work trying to convince schools and colleges to participate in College Board test programs, Cameron also became involved in the administration of the tests themselves, something that would normally be the sole responsibility of ETS. In January 1960, he convened a meeting in Atlanta to "discuss the problems encountered in testing Negro candidates for College Board examinations in the state of Georgia, and in Atlanta particularly." Those attending the meeting included two prominent black educators, Rufus E. Clement, president of Atlanta University and the first black member elected to the Atlanta board of education, and L. H. Pitts, executive secretary of the Georgia Teachers and Education Association, the black counterpart to the all-white Georgia Education Association. John R. Hills, director of testing and guidance for the University System of Georgia, and Ben W. Gibson, liaison officer for Atlanta's board of education, also attended.[9]

When the Georgia board of regents established its policy that all system colleges and universities, black and white, require the SAT, the resulting increase in the number of test-takers caused ETS, school districts, and participating colleges and universities to scramble for additional testing dates and/or locations. In Georgia in 1960 there was absolutely no racial integration in the schools or colleges, but the information ETS asked a test candidate to provide on the test registration card did not include the candidate's race. ETS assigned candidates to test centers on the basis of geography only, with each candidate typically requesting and being assigned to the test center closest to his or her school, potentially creating problems of access to testing sites for black students. While a small number of school districts in Georgia would quietly allow a few black students to spend a Saturday morning in one of their white schools, in defiance of state law, most would not even consider doing so. The few centers that were located in the state's black high schools and colleges sometimes lacked the seating capacity to test all potential candidates, and often were not open as centers for all test administration dates.[10] After discussing several approaches to the complex problem, the group Cameron assembled in Atlanta unanimously agreed on several recommendations that he relayed to his superiors. One of the most important was that the Georgia Department of Education would provide ETS with a list of high schools in Georgia, including black schools. This information would prove valuable to ETS staff in their unprecedented and time-consuming task of identifying black students and assigning them only to centers willing to accommodate them.[11]

Another outcome of the January meeting was Atlanta University president Rufus Clement's offer to establish a test center at his black campus, on condition that neither every black candidate from the area nor only black candidates be assigned to his center. Accordingly, the committee recommended that ETS establish a center at Atlanta University and also at the historically black, state institutions in Georgia—Albany State, Fort Valley State, and Savannah State—of which only Albany State had a center at that time. Paine College, a private black college, had a center, but did not administer the August test, which was especially popular with black students and black colleges. In general, lack of funding and staff training resulted in inadequate college counseling in many black high schools, so college-bound black students often were unaware of the board of regents' requirement that the SAT be part of the application process. Perhaps in part as a result of this lack of awareness, or perhaps because Ben Cameron was right about the racist motive behind its requirement, the board of regents had not enforced the requirement at the system's black colleges. It was often only upon admission that the black students were informed by their colleges that SAT scores were necessary for enrollment. At that point, usually during the summer just prior to entering college, they registered to take the SAT, creating much greater demand for test center space for black students during the August test administration. Instead of using the test scores as part of their admissions process, the colleges could have used them to place students in classes of appropriate difficulty, but it is not clear from the record if or to what extent this was actually done. The men meeting in Atlanta recommended that ETS ask Paine College to operate a center in August and that the five centers located in black high schools in Georgia—which previously had not operated in August—be sent the same request.[12]

Those attending the Atlanta meeting agreed that these steps would take care of the immediate problem of providing adequate seating capacity. With a growing number of black students wishing to enter college, however, the College Board and ETS would have to further expand center capacity soon. The possibility of school desegregation in Georgia in the near or even more distant future apparently was not discussed at the meeting and was clearly not anticipated as an easy way out of the testing problem.[13]

While it was only one event during the hectic first year of Cameron's work for the College Board, the meeting in Atlanta was nevertheless significant. First, it allowed Cameron to meet and become better acquainted with four men whom he would call upon to help him during his subsequent years as director of the regional office—Rufus Clement, L. H. Pitts, John Hills, and Ben Gibson. Second, the meeting forced Cameron to face the problems that segregation created for the test centers.[14] As a southern liberal, Cameron had long known segregation to be a blight over the entire region. In his new role as director of the Southern Regional Office, Cameron now also identified segregation as a challenge he himself would have to confront directly in his professional life. Early in his tenure, Cameron reflected that his work as director of the Southern Regional Office would be influenced constantly by two factors, each related to the region's poverty—the very low level of funding available to education in the southern states and "the presence of and discrimination against" the large population of black people in the South.[15]

Still, Cameron could be optimistic about the potential of the Southern Regional Office, not only because of his successes in Texas and South Carolina in signing on colleges and universities to use the SAT, but also because in his first months on the job he had found school officials, both black and white, in the South "hungry" for help in improving the quality of education. They needed assistance and believed that College Board programs and staff could provide it.[16]

Cameron knew that the recommendations made by his Atlanta group in January 1960 were only stop-gap measures, but nevertheless he went to work arranging for additional centers to accommodate the anticipated increase in the number of black students taking the SAT in Georgia. In most communities where a center had been established in a white public school (there were approximately 60), Cameron arranged for an additional center at a black public school, resulting in a dual system of around 120 segregated centers—72 in white schools and colleges, about 45 in black high schools (an increase from only 13), and 5 in black colleges. He allowed this dual, segregated system only for the sake of expediency. Cameron expected the number of black candidates to grow considerably in the near term, creating a need for even more spaces for testing. With racial tensions escalating in many of Georgia's cities and rural areas, especially those located in the state's "black belt," Cameron thought this segregated testing to be the only way to operate centers without fear of racial incidents.[17]

ETS put the plan into practice at once, opening a testing center at a black public school in most districts with a center at a white school. This dual system required no explanation to students and parents, black or white. They were thoroughly familiar with segregation, so the assignment of test sites based on race was expected. Names of all the schools where the tests would be given were included in the registration information provided by the College Board and ETS, and students selected a site based on their race. When the Georgia board of regents, under pressure from the black colleges, ruled in 1961 that it would begin enforcing its 1957 requirement that all state colleges require the SAT prior to enrollment (the same requirement for white state institutions had been enforced rigorously since 1957), the dual system succeeded insofar as it accommodated all candidates without incident. Of course, this practice did nothing to move ETS and the College Board closer to having only desegregated test centers.[18]

Cameron regularly encouraged the commitment of the College Board to the regional office and to the South by reminding the trustees of the educational and commercial significance and potential of the region. In his inaugural report to the board of trustees, in December 1959, he pointed out that the southern region made up one-fourth of the land area of the United States and claimed one-fourth of its colleges. Moreover, nearly 20 percent of the College Board's membership was located in the South, and one-third of those institutions recently elected to College Board membership were southern.[19]

The College Board, born and bred in the Northeast, needed Cameron's regular reminders that it was no longer the same organization it had been in the 1930s. It was now a national, not a regional, organization. In a report subsequent to his inaugural report, Cameron again stressed this point, warning the trustees that they should guard against provincialism in their planning and decision-making.

> Although 48 percent of the Board member colleges now lie outside the area defined by the New England and Middle States Associations, and these

Johnny-come-lately states now enroll 72 percent of the students in higher education in the country, the Board, through the Trustees, the standing committees, and the staff, is still primarily engrossed in the problems of its traditional clientele.[20]

Cameron emphasized that the organization needed to think in broader terms, not only regarding the geographic expansion of its membership, but also concerning how institutions outside the East used its tests. Colleges and universities beyond the Board's traditional area, such as the black colleges in Georgia, frequently used the tests for guidance and course-placement purposes rather than for admissions, administering the tests to students after their admission to colleges, many of which used the "open door" (nonselective) admissions process then prevalent throughout the South. As the quality of those institutions improved and they became more selective, Cameron believed they would also use the SAT and other College Board tests for admissions purposes. Significantly, Cameron placed in his files a typed roster of the 1960–61 trustees, with each of the twenty-five members' names marked in ink with an "E," "M," "W," or "S" (East, Midwest, West, or South) to indicate the location of that person's home school or college. Eighteen members, 72 percent, were marked with an "E"; only one, Fred C. Cole, president of Washington and Lee University in Virginia, bore an "S." Clearly, the predominance of trustees from the Northeast vexed Cameron.[21]

Nevertheless, Cameron was pleased with the progress he and his small staff had made during their first year of operation. As he made plans to attend the trustees' meeting on December 8, 1960, in Palo Alto, California, Cameron knew he would present a favorable report, especially pertaining to the progress he had made in Texas and South Carolina, and his confidence concerning the ability of the Southern Regional Office to compete with the ACT. He would also report that demand for College Board-sponsored workshops for guidance counselors was so high that the office could not handle all requests. Plans were under way to expand the number of various workshops, and Cameron would propose adding a fourth person to his staff by 1962, someone "skilled in secondary school counseling, and fairly sophisticated in the interactions of schools and colleges." His written report concluded with the observation that he found the work of the regional office "exciting and rewarding." In his report, however, Cameron made no mention at all of test center problems related to segregation.[22]

The regularly scheduled December 1960 meeting of the College Board trustees began as usual with recently elected chairman Frank D. Ashburn, headmaster of the Brooks School of North Andover, Massachusetts, presiding. All twenty-five College Board trustees were present, and the meeting opened with typical announcements of committee appointments and a report from acting president Edward S. Noyes.[23] The report from ETS, originally a division of the College Board itself and regularly represented at College Board meetings, was the next item on the agenda. Founded in 1947 through a merger of the testing operations of the College Board, the American Council on Education, and the Carnegie Foundation for the Advancement of Teaching, ETS provided testing services to a number of organizations, but the College Board was easily its most important client, not only because of the common origins of the two organizations, but also because of the scale of its programs. In addition to the college admissions-related Scholastic Aptitude Test (SAT), Achievement Tests, and Writing Sample, ETS also supported the College Board Preliminary Scholastic Aptitude Test (PSAT), Advanced Placement (AP) Examinations, and Secondary School Aptitude Test (SSAT). Collectively, the College Board tests had consistently made up a majority of tests administered by ETS. During the 1960–61 academic year, College Board tests, with nearly two million candidates, had a volume of more than four times that of the ETS's next largest client, the National Guidance Testing Program.[24]

ETS president Henry Chauncey reported on behalf of his organization. Chauncey had worked at the College Board for several years prior to his appointment as the first president of ETS in 1947. He developed an interest in mental testing, a relatively new course of study, in 1923, during his first year of college. In his youth Chauncey, whose father was a Harvard graduate, attended the Groton School, as his father had. Unlike most of the families of his Groton classmates, Henry Chauncey's had little money. Consequently, he spent his first year of college at tuition-free Ohio State University in Columbus, where his father was rector of Trinity Episcopal Church. In a psychology class at Ohio State, Chauncey studied and soon fell in love with the idea of mental testing. Meanwhile, his father's friends raised the funds to send him to Harvard for the rest of his schooling. Chauncey graduated in 1928 with a degree in philosophy and psychology, having taken coursework in testing and education. Nicholas Lemann, writing about Chauncey's life in *The Big Test*, speculates that it was Chauncey's poverty relative to that of his Groton and Harvard classmates that allowed him the freedom and motivation to become interested in something so new and different as testing.[25]

After thirteen years at ETS, Chauncey still held the position of president and regularly addressed the College Board trustees at their meetings, held each March, September, and December. Chauncey's reports to the trustees typically reflected his passionate interest in the tests themselves—their design and implementation, the machines that graded them, and the countless studies of test validity and other factors that ETS generated to evaluate tests. That December day, at Stanford University's Bowman Alumni House, Chauncey's report was running true to form, involving a detailed description of the technical difficulties caused by ETS's recent conversion to a new grading machine. During the previous few months ETS had been very much engaged in solving those problems and, simultaneously, in dealing with a positive but complicating factor: because of the increase in the number of students applying to college and the increase in the number of colleges requiring the SAT, the number of students registering for tests scheduled for December had increased by 80 percent instead of the 41 percent that ETS had forecast. Chauncey assured the trustees that delivery of a second grading machine in the next several months would allow ETS to accommodate the increase in demand for the SAT. Chauncey next reported that ETS had completed some new "cramming" studies and that in three out of four trials, control groups had actually performed better than coached groups, again substantiating the College Board and ETS's strong position against SAT coaching.[26]

Ben Cameron may have been only half listening to Chauncey, anticipating his own presentation that was to follow shortly. But Chauncey's next statement grabbed his full attention. Chauncey announced that he and others at ETS had discussed the problem of test center segregation and that they believed that centers for all the tests ETS administered, including College Board centers, should be integrated as soon as possible.[27]

In his own words, Cameron was "aghast." It was a reaction he would remember for years to come. Although Cameron personally supported racial integration, he never would have imagined that ETS and the College Board would take on the job of desegregating SAT test centers. He likely assumed that test center desegregation would follow school desegregation—a process under the purview of government agencies, not organizations such as the College Board. In January, he had been satisfied with the outcome of his Atlanta meeting—all black students in Georgia could be accommodated in segregated centers. None would be turned away or embarrassed, and a potential barrier to their access to higher education had been eliminated. Even though Cameron was aware of ongoing efforts by ETS to desegregate centers for the Law School Admissions Test (LSAT), he would have been forgiven for not concluding that SAT centers would be expected to follow suit. The vast differences in the numbers of candidates; in the numbers and locations of centers (most LSAT centers were located on college campuses that were at least beginning to integrate while most SAT centers were located in high schools); and in the levels of education of those involved in each test made it too great a leap for Cameron to imagine. Cameron, along with the other College Board staff members present, "argued against Henry's urging that there be immediate action by the College Board's trustees to eliminate any of this discrimination because we simply were not ready and didn't know when we might be ready." Cameron especially must have been apprehensive. Of all those in attendance, he, a native southerner living and working in the South and charged with the responsibility of making the Southern Regional Office a success, was in the best position to know what such an attempt would mean. And, because ETS had no southern regional office, he surely must have projected that he and his staff would be heavily involved in any work to desegregate the centers.[28]

After a lengthy discussion, the trustees, echoing the Supreme Court's implementation decree in *Brown II* in the last phrase of their motion, voted to ask the staff to make a study of the facts in regard to segregation at centers for the Board's tests and to report to the Trustees at their March 1961 meeting, looking toward appropriate action. It was the sense of the meeting that the Trustees favored testing at integrated centers and wished to move in that direction *with all deliberate speed* [emphasis added].[29]

It is important to note that while Roy Wilkins's telegram to ETS about LSAT testing may have been part of the discussion, it is not mentioned in the minutes. Pressure from the NAACP, or any other outside agency, does not appear to have motivated the College Board in its decision to pursue SAT test center desegregation. Rather, the trustees were motivated by their desire to do the right thing.

The trustees anticipated that the study would enable them to "take appropriate action." The meeting continued with no further surprises, and the three regional directors made their reports. Not unexpectedly, it was Ben Cameron who was dispatched to gather and "make a study of the facts."[30]

Richard Pearson, executive vice president for the College Board, and Henry S. Dyer, an ETS vice president, organized the fact-finding effort, and within three weeks after the December 1960 meeting, the two decided what to do. Because the College Board normally had very little to do with the test centers themselves (Cameron's involvement with the centers in Georgia was atypical), the first step was for ETS to explain how centers were operated under the current system. In light of this need, Dyer formed a staff committee composed of Joseph E. Terral, executive director of administrative and operational services; Harold L. Crane Jr., director of operational services; and William Bretnall, director of administration for College Board programs, to collect the information. Both Terral and Crane had played roles in the LSAT Center desegregation effort just a few months earlier. In addition to basic information on test center operations, Pearson and Cameron requested that the ETS committee provide a list of all College Board centers in the southern region for the 1959–60 and 1960–61 test years, including their seating capacities and for which of the five possible dates of test administration the centers were used. Pearson and Cameron were particularly interested in the Atlanta metropolitan area and New Orleans, two areas that attracted large numbers of test candidates, requesting the number of candidates being tested at each center and which high school each of those candidates attended. They also wanted an accounting of any complaints regarding center facilities from 1954 to the present, as well as a report on how ETS had addressed those complaints.[31]

Meanwhile, Cameron returned to Sewanee, where he recovered from his initial shock and began to feel a little less apprehensive about Chauncey's proposal. At the December meeting, one of Cameron's main concerns had been the general state of race relations in the South. During the discussion he had "underscore[d] again the fact that the climate in the south right now is in a state of turmoil. It would be easier to do something like this in the future rather than right now." He told the trustees that there had been no trouble with integration in the schools following the *Brown* decision in 1954, only because "there has been no integration." Cameron's statement was certainly true of the hard core states.

Cameron's worry about establishing desegregated centers in the southern region stemmed in part from his knowledge of a situation with another ETS-administered test, the Navy Reserve Officer Training Corps test, which, like the SAT, was given primarily in high schools. The navy, like other branches of the military, was integrated and required that testing be integrated also. Many white high schools had actually closed their test centers rather than allow black students into their segregated facilities. Cameron was concerned that if the College Board did not move very carefully, the attempt to desegregate test centers would result in many students, both white and black, not being able to take the SAT and Achievement Tests at all. Also, some black colleges (Cameron specifically cited those in North Carolina) wanted their candidates for admission to have the choice of being tested in nonintegrated conditions, believing that black students could be at a disadvantage at an integrated center. Agreeing with a point Chauncey had made during the discussion, Cameron had reminded the trustees "it is our principal function to get the students tested." For example, he wondered how a blanket policy disallowing segregated centers would play out in his home state.[32]

In Mississippi most Negroes are tested with the whites. Granted, there are very few Negro candidates; the situation might change if suddenly there got to be larger numbers of Negro candidates. But if this policy were announced, then tomorrow it would be impossible for a Negro to be tested in an integrated center in Mississippi.[33]

Cameron agreed entirely with the "moral stand" behind Chauncey's recommendation, but he knew how difficult it would be to accomplish. One thing the College Board could do to make the task less onerous was to keep absolutely quiet about it. Cameron hoped that the College Board "would not take an action resulting in the announcement of such a policy because it would create a lot of ill will in the area where we want to push ahead." No one argued against this point.[34]

By the end of January 1961, Cameron had developed a preliminary, four-part position paper on the issue of desegregating College Board centers. His primary concern was to get all students tested. Next, the first effort in desegregating centers should be made in metropolitan areas, where the majority of testing took place; if any of those current centers would not desegregate, he would relocate the testing center. Third, the College Board would require that all new testing centers be integrated from their inception, unless there was absolutely no other option available to get students tested. Fourth, should "trouble" develop at a testing center, it should be closed and a new, integrated center opened in its place if at all possible.[35]

In arriving at his position, Cameron had turned for advice and inspiration to two black leaders in education, Fisk University president Stephen J. Wright and Atlanta University president Rufus Clement. Fisk, located in Nashville, Tennessee, was one of the leading black colleges in the United States and, under Wright's leadership, provided both intellectual and practical guidance to the student sit-in movement and other student actions. Since becoming director of the regional office, Cameron had worked with Wright on the change at Fisk from the Cooperative Intercollegiate Examination Program (CIEP), an ETS test developed for the United Negro College Fund (UNCF), to the SAT. Wright would later become president of the UNCF and already had considerable influence with that group, eventually persuading its member colleges to adopt the SAT. Wright was also responsible for Fisk gaining membership in the College Board. Cameron respected Wright's judgment. Discussing his relationship with Wright in a 1989 interview, Cameron recalled that "[Wright's] office door was always open to me and I could pick up the phone and call him wherever he was, which was likely to be anywhere. . . . I checked every idea [about desegregation] with him . . . and he knew the South well enough and the people well enough and the whole movement well enough to have sound advice always." Cameron found Wright to be "consistently pressing ahead" in the area of civil rights, something Cameron deeply respected as he himself pressed ahead of prevailing conditions in his work to desegregate the SAT centers.[36]

Like Fisk, Atlanta University was a center of civil rights activity. Students there also staged sit-ins and in March 1960 published in Atlanta newspapers "An Appeal for Human Rights." The full-page ad was signed by student leaders and outlined in detail their grievances and their intention to "use every legal and non-violent means" to win equality. Historian Kevin Kruse writes, "The city was stunned by the 'Appeal' and the civil rights revolution it heralded." Rufus Clement, elected to the Atlanta board of education in 1953 and thus Atlanta's first elected black official since Reconstruction, was also helpful to Cameron.[37]

The ETS committee and Cameron were to complete their studies prior to the March 15–16, 1961, meeting of the College Board trustees. Richard Pearson, College Board executive vice president, reviewed both reports and mailed them to the trustees on March 6. In his cover memo Pearson explained that ETS was engaged in examining its policies for the test centers of all its clients, not only those of the College Board. ETS trustees planned to meet in April and would discuss the report at that time. Pearson added that College Board senior staff had "wholeheartedly" endorsed "the Cameron plan" and encouraged its adoption by the trustees. Pearson agreed with Cameron about avoiding publicity, noting that a public announcement about the proposed policy on desegregating the centers would not "serve any useful purpose."[38]

ETS had been thorough in compiling the available facts. Their report, written by Joseph Terral, explained that the primary purpose of a test center was "to serve the needs of as many applicants as it can, as efficiently and conveniently as it can." In order to fulfill that purpose, ETS required competent, trained supervisors and proctors; an accessible location; and buildings that offered ample capacity, appropriate seating, satisfactory lighting, adequate restrooms and lunchrooms, quiet surroundings, and "general comfort." Significantly, ETS also charged center supervisors with testing each candidate "under competent supervision and standard testing conditions." The key phrase "standard testing conditions" meant not only that the centers met ETS requirements in terms of the items listed above, but also that all students at a given center were tested under identical conditions. The ETS policy that students be seated equitably for the exam was central to the concern about racial discrimination at testing centers.[39]

In January 1961, an ETS representative traveled to the Southern Education Reporting Service (SERS) in Nashville, Tennessee, to retrieve the most accurate and up-to-date information available on the progress of school desegregation in the seventeen southern and border states and the District of Columbia. SERS, a nonprofit agency organized in anticipation of reaction to the first *Brown* decision, objectively researched, maintained, and shared data about "developments in education arising from the Supreme Court decision of May 1954." SERS correspondents throughout the region were charged with collecting clippings from local newspapers, thoroughly investigating local news stories, and forwarding to SERS each month a report on events related to race and education. SERS staff then compiled the data in a monthly publication with the innocuous title *Southern School News*. They also cultivated state-by-state, comprehensive lists of legislation and litigation bearing on school desegregation. Anyone with a serious concern about the status of the desegregation of schools and colleges was interested in SERS research and reports. As a result of the richness and accuracy of its data and its strict policy of reporting without editorializing, SERS attracted a diverse group of subscribers. These included southern governors and other elected officials, school officials, and many organizations and individuals interested in the status of desegregation in schools and colleges. Members of both the Ku Klux Klan and the NAACP subscribed.[40]

On the basis of information SERS provided and ETS's own experience with test centers, Terral divided the seventeen southern and border states and the District of Columbia into four main categories based on levels of segregation in their public schools and colleges. Those in the first category, the most segregated, were the five states comprising the hard core states, or the Deep South, those states with the largest black populations: Alabama, Georgia, Louisiana, Mississippi, and South Carolina. These states maintained "complete" segregation and would become the focus of Cameron's work to desegregate test centers. Terral did cite two exceptions to this nearly perfect record: four black first-graders were attending public school in New Orleans, and two black students, Hamilton Holmes and Charlayne Hunter, had just been admitted to the University of Georgia. Terral may have been unaware of LSU's desegregated professional and graduate programs. He stated emphatically: "ETS could definitely not successfully require desegregated testing at public institutions in these states." Florida and Virginia stood in second place in Terral's hierarchy, having had only "very limited" desegregation of public schools. Terral thought ETS might succeed in requiring desegregated test sites in a few of the public schools and colleges in these two states.

Arkansas, Delaware, Kentucky, Maryland, Missouri, Oklahoma, Tennessee, and Texas were ranked in third place, and Terral believed that North Carolina, which he had relegated to its own subcategory of "spotty" desegregation, might shift to that group soon. In those states, Terral reported, desegregation of the schools was "essentially achieved" or "making rapid progress," and ETS could probably achieve desegregated testing at nearly all of its public school and college centers. However, Terral believed that to require immediately the total desegregation of all test sites in these states would "retard rather than speed the total process." Instead, since there were very few problems associated with testing black students in these nine states, ETS and the College Board should allow for desegregation of test sites to unfold as a natural outcome of school and college desegregation. A similar position was adopted in connection with testing in Florida and Virginia. West Virginia and the District of Columbia, in Terral's fourth category, were already "completely desegregated for testing purposes."[41]

The significant conclusion from Terral's study of SERS data was that, with the exception of the five hard core states, the desegregation of schools was occurring at a pace that would very shortly accommodate all SAT candidates. In other words, the desegregation of test centers in the majority of the states should be allowed to follow that of the schools themselves. Conceptually, Terral's four categories of states were then reduced to only two: twelve states, plus the District of Columbia, which were not of significant concern to ETS and the College Board with regard to testing black candidates, and five states where resistance to school desegregation was so formidable that it was difficult to even imagine let alone plan for a viable solution.

Other information ETS collected in its own limited telephone survey of selected high school administrators corroborated SERS findings about the degree of segregation in Alabama, Georgia, Louisiana, and Mississippi (the omission of South Carolina from the survey was not explained). Terral's summary statement about those four states reads, "Negro candidates at secondary schools are tested under segregated conditions, and the trend toward desegregation in the schools, and hence toward segregation in the test centers, is, at best, both slow and painful." The telephone survey conversations with school administrators in the four surveyed states yielded a telling and nearly unanimous response to the possibility of testing black candidates in white schools: "impossible!"[42]

The ETS committee report also described four different methods center supervisors in the southern states used when testing candidates of both races at the same test administration. Based to a large extent on the supervisors' own personal assessments of racial tolerance in their communities, some centers operated impartially, with absolutely no distinctions made between students of different races, thereby conforming to ETS's definition of a desegregated center. Some supervisors seated all candidates in the same room but assigned black students to a separate block of seats. Some seated black and white candidates in separate rooms in the same building. And some transferred black candidates to a separate building, frequently a nearby black high school. Because the race of the students was not known in advance, supervisors at white schools had no idea if any black students would appear. To prepare for the possibility of testing black candidates, some supervisors arranged for standby proctors who accompanied black students to a separate room or building.[43]

Center supervisors in some white schools differed substantially from ETS in their definitions of "desegregated." Supervisors who tested black students in the same room or even the same building as the white students considered testing conditions to be desegregated. From their perspective, organizing students by race in blocks of seats in the same room or in separate rooms in the same building, clearly in keeping with pervasive Jim Crow practices, did not constitute segregation. Thus, the ETS committee cautioned that any general survey of southern centers would have to "probe" all respondents for an accurate assessment "and it is the probing necessary to get this explicit information that makes investigation at most centers in the Deep South a delicate matter."[44]

In response to Pearson and Cameron's question about complaints from black test candidates made to ETS between 1954 and 1960, Terral cited nine known "incidents." All nine had occurred in Alabama, Georgia, North Carolina, South Carolina, and Virginia.

> Two Negroes refused to wait until arrangements could be made to transport them to another location; five objected because the tests were administered in a separate room; one was refused admittance to the center because the supervisor had not made the necessary arrangements for testing Negroes; and ETS's investigation of one complaint revealed that a Negro candidate's father had misunderstood our transfer of his son from a center filled to capacity to one nearby where there was room for him and where, incidentally, the boy was tested in a completely desegregated situation.[45]

Terral assured the College Board trustees that ETS had responded promptly to each complaint and that its investigations and subsequent remedies "apparently were completed to the satisfaction of the complainants since no further word has been received from any of them." The ETS staff may have been too sanguine about the outcomes of these nine cases; there was really no way to know how well satisfied the students and their families were, nor the possible effect of these incidents on the students' test scores. While Terral did not say so, it is almost certain that the nine reported incidents represented a much larger number of similar (or worse) incidents that went unreported.[46]

Terral closed the ETS report with an important point about the recent development in Georgia of opening centers at both white and black schools and colleges. While this dual, "separate but equal" practice eliminated the problem of black students being turned away from white centers, it unfortunately seemed "to be taking us in an undesirable direction" in terms of eliminating segregated centers.[47]

Terral's and Cameron's reports to the trustees quantified the scope of the southern SAT center situation for the first time. The College Board's southern region consisted of 13 states, the 5 hard core or "die-hard" states, as Cameron referred to them—Alabama, Georgia, Louisiana, Mississippi, and South Carolina—plus Arkansas, Florida, Kentucky, North Carolina, Oklahoma, Tennessee, Texas, and Virginia. Because Kentucky and Oklahoma no longer classified high schools by race, Cameron did not include those states in his statistics. During the 1959–60 testing year, the total number of candidates taking the SAT in the whole southern region (minus Kentucky and Oklahoma) exceeded 87,000. The total number of centers was 317. The number of students from black high schools taking the test while still in high school (many others, black and white, took the SAT for placement purposes after being admitted to college) was pitifully low with fewer than 1,200 black test-takers (about 1.4 percent) in the entire 13-state southern region. These statistics demonstrate not only the small number of black test candidates relative to their large numbers in the general population, but also the disproportionate amount of effort ETS and the College Board were willing to expend for the sake of so few students.

During the same school year, 1959–60, in the 5 hard core states (the ones with which Cameron would soon become most concerned), the number of black students taking the SAT while still in high school had totaled only 619. There were 122 test centers in those states and a total of 29,000 candidates. Georgia, due to its 1957 mandate requiring the SAT for admission to public colleges, led in both categories with 467 black candidates and 74 centers. Louisiana stood last both in its number of black students taking the SAT, 31, and its number of centers, 11. For the 1960–61 year, the implementation of the dual center system in Georgia raised the state's number of centers to 120, nearly 10 times that of each of the other 4 hard core states. The number of students tested and the number of centers in the southern region represented only a small fraction of the total number of SAT test candidates and centers throughout the United States and abroad. For the same period (1959–60), ETS and the College Board reported that 574,368 candidates had taken the SAT at more than 1,400 centers worldwide, compared with 29,000 candidates and 122 centers in the Deep South states.[48]

In his report to the College Board trustees, Cameron praised ETS for operating its centers in the southern region as equitably as possible under difficult conditions. Its just policies were "primarily responsible for the fact that College Board testing centers in all parts of the South are well ahead of either community attitudes or judicial decrees in fostering the progress of desegregation." Nevertheless, Cameron now urged the trustees to take an even more active approach, pushing ahead of any progress in school desegregation wherever possible. The positive responses of many school officials to whom Cameron had spoken about desegregation were responsible for his change of outlook since the December 1960 meeting, and, despite the negative reaction ("impossible!") from Terral's school survey contacts, Cameron believed that progress in center desegregation was possible. He agreed with Terral's assessment as to which states were the most segregated in terms of test centers. In writing about these, he focused on four—Alabama, Georgia, Mississippi, and South Carolina. Louisiana, included in this category by ETS, was omitted by Cameron in this instance because nearly all students in that state took the test in New Orleans, where all five centers, located in white private schools largely outside of state control, were "completely desegregated."[49]

In his report, Cameron reflected state by state on the task ahead. In Cameron's opinion, it would be difficult to discover exactly how the centers in Alabama and Mississippi were operated—an opinion likely based on his personal knowledge of several school districts—but he suspected that practices varied widely. South Carolina had three centers (out of thirteen) which Cameron had learned were desegregated, at least to some degree. Georgia, which with the exception of Kentucky and Oklahoma was the only southern state with a significant number of black candidates, tested under segregated conditions in most centers. The Atlanta area centers were exceptions, due to the changes Cameron and his colleagues had initiated in January 1960. Cameron reserved his harshest criticism for his home state of Mississippi. With regard to the desegregation of any institutions, public or private, the state of Mississippi was "the worst" in all the South. He wrote with disgust: "a Roman Catholic seminary is the only desegregated institution of any type in the state."[50]

Cameron noted that conditions in the South were changing rapidly and in "complex" ways. Following the 1954 Supreme Court *Brown* decision, he explained, "there has been a marked decrease in tolerance in some areas, and an equally marked increase in others." For example, a Montgomery, Alabama, high school that had tested black and white candidates in the same room in 1953 could no longer do so in 1957 and had requested a separate center for black students. On the other hand, the desegregation of all levels of education in Kentucky had taken place with little difficulty. Cameron attributed these differences in reactions to the 1954–55 *Brown* decisions largely to differences in local leadership.[51]

Underscoring his point, Cameron added: "It is a fact . . . that there is more racial tension now in the more difficult areas than there was before 1954. Those difficult areas are the only ones in which the College Board is faced generally with segregated testing now; it will be harder to change these conditions immediately than it would have been eight years ago."[52]

Cameron's astute observations about increased racial tensions in "difficult areas" encapsulate the phenomenon of massive resistance to desegregation following the *Brown* decision in 1954 and, with regard to his remarks about testing in Alabama, evoke the Montgomery bus boycott of 1955–56 and the riots following the failed attempt to desegregate the University of Alabama in 1956. Coined by Senator Harry Byrd of Virginia, the term "massive resistance" referred to the collective efforts of segregationists to maintain a segregated society. In anticipation of, and later in reaction to, the Supreme Court's rulings on school desegregation, the southern states adopted nearly three hundred new resolutions or laws all related to preventing, restricting, or controlling school desegregation.[53] Eight states passed resolutions approving "interposition," a means of placing the barrier of state sovereignty between local school officials and the federal courts and allegedly giving those states permission to ignore *Brown*. Historian Numan Bartley explains, "Interposition was the theory and the battle cry of massive resistance." It provided, its sponsors believed, a legal basis for states to stand against the social changes that threatened white southerners' sense of superiority and "the southern way of life." Interposition proponents, Bartley writes, "sought not so much to avoid or evade the Court order as they did to defeat it— to achieve total victory." With school governance transferred from local school districts to the states, legislatures could close schools in defiance of *Brown*, and the South would in effect nullify the Supreme Court decision.[54] In 1960, according to SERS data, Louisiana led the five hard core southern states with more than forty acts designed to defy school desegregation. These ranged from interposition to lifting compulsory school attendance in desegregated schools, the dismissal of teachers and other school officials found to be in favor of school desegregation, a ban on interracial sports and other social activities, tuition grants for private education, the withdrawal of funding for integrated schools, and the revoking of teaching licenses of teachers in integrated schools, all enacted to throw up effective legal barriers to desegregation.[55]

Examples of massive resistance legislation in other states included the provision for the secession of schools from local and state systems into independent districts (Alabama), the forfeiture of retirement benefits of state law officers who did not enforce segregation (Georgia), an outright ban on white and black attendance at the same school (Mississippi), and the removal of funding of any school to which a student was transferred by court order (South Carolina).[56]

Massive resistance legislation was not limited to school desegregation and was at times absurd. In the two-year period following the *Brown* decision, the Georgia House brazenly voted to re-segregate the armed forces, while the legislature as a whole voted to impeach the U.S. Supreme Court justices and nullify the Thirteenth and Fourteenth Amendments to the Constitution. Another law called for the state flag to be altered to include the battle flag of the Confederacy.[57]

In 1956 the southern states joined forces against *Brown* when a large majority of U.S. senators and representatives from 11 states (101 out of a possible 128 national legislators) hammered out the "Southern Manifesto." Led by Senators Strom Thurmond of South Carolina and Harry Byrd of Virginia, the document attacked the *Brown* decision, stating that the Supreme Court had "no legal basis" for its ruling, and instead had "substituted their personal political and social ideas for the established law of the land." Praising the merits of *Plessy*, the signers of the manifesto pledged "to use all lawful means to bring about a reversal of this decision which is contrary to the Constitution and to prevent the use of force in its implementation." It was, to say the least, an arrogant document.[58]

Massive resistance was not limited to legal obstructions. Inspired by the actions of their state and national representatives in opposing *Brown*, southern whites, in groups or as individuals, felt empowered to resist desegregation. The fact that black parents, encouraged by the NAACP in the wake of the Supreme Court decision, had begun to file petitions for the desegregation of their local school systems was a further motivation. By the summer of 1955, sixty petitions had been submitted. Many of those petitioners faced not only disappointment but also harsh reprisals. Numan Bartley writes that they found themselves "without jobs, credit, or even the meager benefits of white paternalism," a heavy price for seeking a better education for their children.[59]

This escalation of racist emotions contributed to a resurgence of the Ku Klux Klan and the formation of many new segregationist groups, the most prominent being the Citizens' Councils, or White Citizens' Councils. Originating in 1954 in Indianola, Mississippi, the Citizens' Councils soon festered into a coordinated organization of more than 250,000 members across several southern states. Influencing many thousands beyond its official membership rolls, its tactics were varied, but its primary tool was economic discrimination. Council members, most often members of the middle class occupying leadership positions in their communities and in business, deprived blacks attempting to vote or support school desegregation of not only their jobs and credit, but also of access to insurance coverage and even medical care. Reaching its peak membership in 1957, the organization maintained significant influence for several years, especially in Mississippi and Alabama.[60]

The Citizens' Councils' success was fed largely by white southerners' fear of losing their supremacy over black people. It is not a coincidence that the five hard core states—those most adamantly fighting desegregation—had the highest black populations. The U.S. Census of 1950 shows that in those five states the black percentage of the population ranged from 30.9 in Georgia to 45.3 in Mississippi, considerably higher than that of neighboring southern states.[61] Also at the root of southern racism was the fear of loss of racial "purity" through intermarriage. The belief that the black race was inferior was pervasive, and most whites could not fathom allowing their children to "mix" with black children. Historian James Patterson writes, "Mixing in the classroom . . . could also lead to mixing out of class, and even (a horror scarcely to be imagined) to interracial dating or marriage." This way of thinking was largely responsible for making school desegregation such a protracted and difficult struggle.[62]

Clearly, Ben Cameron was well aware of the formidable resistance to school desegregation. But, as director of the Southern Regional Office, he regularly came in contact with people throughout the South who were more moderate in their views. Cameron held a sufficient degree of confidence that, as a starting point, he and his staff could appeal successfully to this more circumspect group. Cameron believed that the trustees had two fundamental duties related to testing and desegregation. The first was to ensure that all candidates be tested under satisfactory conditions; the second, that the College Board "conduct itself in a socially, morally, and educationally responsible manner in all of its activities."[63]

Cameron reminded the trustees that southern colleges differed from the traditional clientele of the College Board in terms of mission, student bodies, and use of the SAT. He assured the trustees that the presence of the College Board in the region was already improving the educational climate there. For example, the University System of Georgia, which he noted had initially required the SAT mainly for the purpose of keeping black students out of its white colleges, was now beginning to make "valid and valuable use of the examination data," thereby improving college guidance procedures. In addition, as shown by the recent case of the court order to admit two black students, Hamilton Holmes and Charlayne Hunter, to the University of Georgia, SAT scores were actually being used to strengthen rather than weaken the argument for the admission of some black students to white colleges. Cameron also underlined the significant increase he expected in the numbers of black students in the southern region who would take the SAT and possibly the College Board Achievement Tests. While one result of this situation could be a worsening of the problems associated with segregated testing, some school administrators, Cameron believed, might actually react strategically to the threat of an increase in the numbers of black test candidates. If test centers were desegregated while the number of black candidates was still small, perhaps only one or two per test administration, the event itself and the administrators who allowed it might escape notice.[64]

Cameron recommended in his report that even though total center desegregation would remain the College Board's ultimate goal, the College Board should take a practical position that would continue to allow centers in black institutions, giving black students a choice of testing centers during a difficult and probably prolonged period of transition. He remained adamant about avoiding publicity having to do with efforts to desegregate the centers. Cameron feared that white test supervisors, usually high school teachers and administrators, who had been operating desegregated centers quietly might come under fire from local school boards if it became known that they allowed black and white students to sit together for the tests. For example, if a public announcement were made in Georgia, Cameron warned, the board of regents would drop its SAT requirement and switch to "another testing program" (meaning the ACT), which would agree to test in segregated centers only, causing the College Board to "lose its opportunity for leadership in education as well as in desegregation."[65]

Cameron had cause for concern about "another testing program." He was well aware of ongoing aggressive efforts by ACT to promote its tests throughout the South and may have heard of an unusual tactic ACT was alleged to employ in enlisting the participation of some southern schools and colleges. The rumor that circulated during this time was that ACT, tailoring its services for a segregated South, was promising potential southern clients not only segregated test centers but also segregated machines for grading the tests. The test answer sheets submitted by white students would not touch those submitted by blacks. Whether the rumor was true or false, the fact that College Board staff members found it a plausible ACT marketing strategy is striking.[66]

Finally, anticipating that progress toward desegregation would not be steady, Cameron asked the trustees to expect "temporary local regressions in some of the more difficult areas . . . in the long-term pursuit of the stated goal." Cameron condensed his findings and opinions in a policy he recommended for the trustees' consideration at their March 1961 meeting.[67]

> The first responsibility of the College Entrance Examination Board is to provide for the testing of all candidates under standard, equitable conditions. The Board will, however, make a definite and specific effort in all areas to assure that all testing centers will be equally accessible to all candidates without regard to race when this can be accomplished without definitely jeopardizing the Board's ability to test all candidates.[68]

Modifying and expanding his earlier four-part plan, Cameron outlined a new and more detailed, seven-part plan for implementing the policy should the trustees adopt it. First, the College Board staff would determine to the extent possible the testing conditions under which all black candidates had been tested in 1959–60 and what changes, if any, had been implemented for 1960–61. Next, all new centers would be open to candidates of all races, except when "local conditions will definitely prevent" establishment. Third, ETS and the College Board would close those centers where candidates had been unfairly treated because of race. Fourth, supervisors would be instructed to accommodate all candidates in the same building except for reasons of space and, when separating candidates, not to divide them by race in any way. Fifth, in metropolitan areas, ETS and the College Board would provide only desegregated centers whenever possible. Sixth, they would open new, desegregated centers where both black and white centers currently existed, gradually phasing out the dual system of black and white segregated centers. Finally, the staff would evaluate progress closely, keeping the trustees informed. Like Terral, Cameron found it necessary to define a "desegregated" center, explaining that at such a center candidates "will be admitted, seated, and tested with no regard to race."[69]

College Board chairman Frank Ashburn opened the March 15–16, 1961, meeting of the College Board trustees at the Board offices on Riverside Drive in New York City. After addressing all routine business matters during the afternoon, the trustees reconvened that evening for a special session, and the only two items on the agenda were Cameron's and Terral's reports.[70]

Unlike Cameron, Henry Chauncey had found no reason for optimism or resolve during the three months since the December 1960 meeting. On the contrary, according to Cameron, Chauncey had become "scared to death" that desegregating test centers would "kill" the College Board. In Chauncey's new frame of mind, it was something they simply couldn't afford to do. He had become convinced that their efforts would end in having to close all testing centers in the South. Cameron was annoyed with Chauncey's change of mind. He himself had "been frightened at first but . . . was a lot more relaxed by this time."[71]

The reasons for Chauncey's reaction are not entirely clear. He may have found Terral's and Cameron's reports disheartening, or he may have been deterred by news of the lack of progress regarding school desegregation generally in so many southern states. Chauncey had spent most of his life in the northeastern United States; it would have been impossible for him to have acquired Cameron's knowledge of and commitment to the South. Also, as president of ETS, Chauncey was ultimately responsible for the organization's financial position, and he legitimately feared losing testing volume and regional influence to ACT. Whatever his reasons for wishing to reverse the movement he had begun three months earlier, Chauncey failed to convince the trustees that they should pull back. Although they tabled their decision until the next morning, the trustees voted to implement both Cameron's test center desegregation policy and his seven-part plan of action. Word for word, the "Cameron plan" had prevailed. And, logically, Cameron was made responsible for its execution, armed with his plan, his belief in the College Board's moral stand, and the early stages of an idea for a support system.[72]

Ben Cameron in the late 1950s

Ben Gibson in the early 1960s

The Cameron Plan Is Implemented and the Special Committee Is Established, 1961–1962

Three states—Alabama, Mississippi, and South Carolina—
continue to have complete segregation at all grade levels in the ninth
school year after the U.S. Supreme Court ruled in 1954 that
compulsory school segregation was unconstitutional.
—*Southern School News* (September 1962)

Cameron didn't have to wait long for the implementation of his seven-part plan. Within days of its adoption at the March 1961 board of trustees meeting, Justine Taylor, executive secretary to Harold Crane, director of test administration at ETS, exercised the new plan's second principle when she refused to establish new testing centers at two white Georgia high schools located at opposite ends of the state. Both schools, when making their requests, had explicitly stated that they would test only white students. In a letter to Taylor, J. H. Wells, principal of Brooks County High School in Quitman—a small, rural community in the south-central part of the state and considered part of Georgia's "black belt"—explained that Georgia law allowed only white students to enter his school. In his letter to Taylor, D. W. Bramlett, principal of Hart County High School in Hartwell—a small, rural community in northeast Georgia—did not refer to Georgia law, but instead stipulated that "Under no condition are colored pupils to be assigned to this testing center." Doing so "at this time would create an atmosphere in which no pupil could do his best work." Presumably acting under the direction of Crane and ETS assistant director of test administration Layton Wolfram, Taylor promptly denied both requests for centers "in view of the fact that you will not accept colored students." Both Quitman and Hartwell students would have to continue traveling some distance to be tested, and their schools would forgo the prestige associated with becoming test centers for the College Board.[1]

While Cameron agreed with the outcome of the two requests, he asked to be involved from the outset in future inquiries about opening centers. The second part of his center desegregation plan made room for flexibility in at least considering the opening of a segregated center if "careful investigation indicates that a center is needed, and that local conditions will definitely prevent the establishment of a desegregated center sufficiently close to provide the testing of all candidates." Cameron's flexibility would extend to permitting segregated testing at both white and black schools in a given community if absolutely necessary. Cameron then asked Crane to alter ETS procedures for responding to requests from schools in Alabama, Florida, Georgia, Louisiana, Mississippi, and South Carolina, the states Cameron felt confident would "normally" operate only under segregated conditions, directing all such inquiries to the Southern Regional Office. Cameron also suggested that telephone requests from schools in those states could be managed by ETS staff who would inquire "about the accessibility of the center to Negroes, and, if a negative reply is received, state simply that the request will be considered." ETS staff would then relay the request to Cameron. Requests for centers from schools located in the other states served by the Southern Regional Office would continue to be handled by ETS for the most part since school desegregation was occurring in at least some of the school districts in those states.[2]

The College Board and ETS agreed that their most important goal was to test every student who registered for the SAT: no student should be turned away. Another goal was to offer the test at as many school districts as possible, so that students would not have to travel far from their communities. This was an important consideration especially for rural black students who frequently lacked transportation. Clearly, Cameron needed some flexibility in his test desegregation plan in order to balance the desegregation of test centers with his other responsibilities. Some centers would simply have to operate temporarily on a segregated basis. College Board executive vice president Richard Pearson agreed with Cameron. In a note to two staff members, Pearson, referring to the bureaucracy at ETS, confessed that "ETS's need for routine often means inflexibility—and we can't have that here."[3]

Conversations and correspondence about procedures and policies for the implementation of the test desegregation plan flourished throughout the spring of 1961 and involved upper-level staff members at both the College Board and ETS, including College Board acting president Edward S. Noyes and ETS president Henry Chauncey, each of whom took an active interest in the process of desegregating all of ETS's test sites.[4] Among the points of discussion was how the new policy should be communicated to the College Board membership and to test center supervisors. At an April meeting of the American Association of College Registrars and Admissions Officers (AACRAO) in Miami, a meeting that Cameron was unable to attend, John Hills, director of testing and guidance for the public higher education system in Georgia, was surprised to learn from College Board staff members that the College Board and ETS were working to desegregate SAT centers. Hills, who had attended Cameron's meeting in Atlanta in January 1960 about the difficulties of testing black candidates in Georgia, had two primary concerns that he confided to Cameron as soon as he returned to Atlanta. First, Hills, who supported desegregation, believed the College Board trustees should have brought the new policy to the entire College Board membership for discussion. In response, Cameron argued that the trustees' action, in addition to being the moral thing to do, had been legal. Establishing policy was the role of the trustees. Hills accepted that point, albeit reluctantly. Cameron also stressed that, as a practical matter, taking the policy to the entire membership for deliberation "would lead inevitably to some sort of open warfare which could result only in a net loss for all." Keeping their work quiet was critical.[5]

Hills's second concern was the question of his responsibility to inform his employer, the board of regents of the University System of Georgia, about the test center desegregation plan. As a result of his conversations with College Board staff members during the Miami meeting, Hills was under the impression that all test centers, both current and new, would be sent a letter at once stating that they would have to "accept all candidates under standard conditions." Hills, according to Cameron, "was ready to go to his board of regents with a report" about the policy. Cameron, worried that such a public disclosure of the plan would only impede its progress, argued that Hills's report would be premature and persuaded Hills not to inform the board of regents about the plan.[6]

This incident brought home to Cameron that there was still a great deal to accomplish in getting all the involved parties "on the same road" and asked Harold Crane of ETS to include him in any future decisions about information being mailed to test center supervisors. In keeping with the intent of the College Board trustees, Cameron did not want ETS to distribute information about the desegregation policy to supervisors of existing test centers. Instead, in order to proceed as quietly as possible, he and his staff would deal with each center in the hard core states on a case-by-case basis, certainly an ambitious undertaking given the geographic area and the undoubted range in attitudes they would encounter.[7]

Throughout the summer of 1961, ETS staff spent considerable time and energy debating questions surrounding center desegregation for all of its clients, not only the College Board, giving particular attention to the wording of a policy and how it would be communicated to center supervisors. In a confidential memo for the record, Crane reiterated the general desegregation policy for all ETS test administrations, including the SAT:

> The first responsibility of ETS is to provide for the testing of all candidates under standard, equitable conditions. ETS will, however, make a definite and specific effort in all areas to assure that testing centers will be equally accessible to all candidates without regard to race when this can be accomplished without definitely jeopardizing the ability to test all candidates.[8]

Fortunately for Cameron, the policy reflected the realistic and flexible approach that his job would require.

In his memo, Crane officially defined "desegregation" at a test center as "the admission and seating of all candidates without regard to race," establishing a standard definition that would prove contrary to others developed by many southern principals and superintendents. Except for the LSAT program, ETS would postpone requiring desegregated center lunchroom and restroom facilities.[9]

ETS staff agreed that a paragraph requesting desegregated testing conditions be sent to all test center supervisors, with the exception of those administering the College Board SAT and Achievement Tests. Slightly different wording was to be used for the various ETS tests, and the most explicit version, sent to LSAT supervisors, read as follows:

> The test application does not in any way indicate the race of the candidate, who himself chooses a center from the list in the bulletin of information. We expect that, unless you notify us to the contrary, you will operate the center on an entirely non-segregated basis.[10]

The first sentence was used in all the letters. For unknown reasons, ETS used somewhat different wording in letters to the supervisors for its other tests. It may be that because each test operated under the direction of its own governing body, ETS allowed flexibility in the exact wording of letters to center supervisors. For example, the LSAT policy committee had been responsible for establishing its own specific desegregation policy and its own wording.[11]

At any rate, ETS was characteristically very particular about how the desegregation of test centers should proceed, cautioning its staff to take "great care" in their correspondence and telephone conversations with supervisors. All "doubtful issues" were to be referred to Crane himself. If supervisors did not agree to desegregate their centers, ETS was prepared to deal with those situations in one of three ways: closing the uncooperative center, while establishing a new center at a nearby site; transferring candidates to a more distant, desegregated center; or, in what they hoped would be rare cases, being forced to continue to operate the center on a segregated basis.[12]

ETS worked with Cameron to make special arrangements to inform the SAT center supervisors about the new policy on desegregation. In the past, letters to SAT center supervisors in the southern states had included the following paragraph:

> The test application which is filed with Educational Testing Service does not in any way indicate the race of the candidate, who himself chooses a center from the list published in the bulletin of information. Since it is most important that no candidate be prevented from taking a test for which he has registered, *you should be prepared to make the necessary arrangements for testing under competent supervision and comparable examination conditions every properly registered candidate who reports to your center* [emphasis added].[13]

Of course, this wording had allowed the practice of segregated testing, and for the time being Cameron wanted it dropped altogether. In the revised letter to SAT center supervisors, as Cameron had explained to John Hills, there would be no paragraph of any kind about segregation or desegregation. Instead of including a cautionary message, similar to those included to letters to LSAT or other ETS test center supervisors, a message that Cameron and others knew could devastate College Board testing in the South, Cameron would deal with center supervisors individually.[14]

In a document dated July 26, 1961, which was probably written by Crane and titled "Special College Board Desegregation Procedures," the author outlined a series of steps for Cameron's involvement in setting up new test centers in the South. A key component was Cameron's commitment to visit each existing center located in the hard core states of Alabama, Florida, Georgia, Louisiana, Mississippi, and South Carolina. Cameron would develop a report form that he would complete following each visit and then circulate to specified ETS personnel. Crane and others at ETS provided Cameron with additional questions to ask supervisors, questions about their policies and procedures apart from those involving desegregation, particularly those concerning test center security, something that ETS and the College Board of course took as seriously as they did all other aspects of testing integrity. With its questions about the testing of black students placed within the context of other testing concerns, the report form appeared less inflammatory. The school visits were to begin in August 1961.[15]

Cameron supported the procedures forwarded to him by Crane. He made a point of reminding Crane that the College Board trustees had prohibited the transportation of test candidates from the site for which they had registered to another site, but had not specifically prohibited the testing of black candidates in separate rooms in established centers. Cameron expected that the College Board and ETS would have to tolerate this practice temporarily in the hard core states. Part of Cameron's plan was to "force" immediate desegregation only in certain metropolitan areas, as had been done in Atlanta. In most other areas, Cameron and his staff would "negotiate" with centers over time to achieve desegregation. Not allowing testing in separate rooms, in Cameron's opinion, would present "a rather grim job of trying to find centers in federal buildings, armed forces installations, and so forth, in most regions within the six hard core states." (At this time, Cameron was still including Florida in the group of hard core states, hence his reference to six states rather than five.)[16]

Meanwhile, another issue involving the testing of black candidates had arisen—ETS staff had discovered several clear breaches of test security at black high schools in Georgia. In these cases, center supervisors had either not returned test materials on time or had failed to return some materials altogether, with the result that ETS had been unable to score the tests on a timely basis. ETS inquiries into these security breaches revealed that the test supervisors involved, most of whom were new to their duties, had simply not understood their responsibilities adequately. In one case, a supervisor had delegated the return mailing of test books, and the tests had languished in a storeroom for months. In another, the tests had been returned to ETS via first-class mail rather than private carrier, and this seemingly minor deviation from approved procedure caused a significant delay in test processing. Obviously, these new supervisors needed additional training, which provided another reason for visiting the centers. Since by this time Cameron had accepted the responsibility for most things having to do with test administration in the hard core states and since, unlike the College Board, ETS had no regional offices, all center visits no matter what their purpose became part of his job.[17]

Cameron and his colleagues at the College Board and ETS agreed that it was not feasible for Cameron to visit each center himself. Nor would it be possible for his staff to provide much support since they were nearly overwhelmed with the growing demand for College Board services in the southern region. Cameron would have to have assistance, especially in Georgia which, with its dual center system, had 120 centers. Turning to two of the men he had met with in Atlanta in January 1960, L. H. Pitts and Ben W. Gibson, Cameron proposed that he hire them as consultants to visit the Georgia centers. Pitts, a black minister and educator, had recently left his job as executive secretary of the Georgia Teachers and Education Association to fulfill his lifelong ambition of becoming president of Miles College, a small, black liberal arts college in Alabama. A native Georgian, Pitts had been groomed by his boyhood hero W. M. Bell to succeed Bell as president of Miles. According to Cameron, Pitts's new job involved a "drastic" cut in pay from his salary with the Georgia Teachers and Education Association. The ETS consultant stipend ($50.00 per day), in addition to Pitts's concern about education for blacks in Georgia, motivated Pitts to accept the consulting position, a job he would perform while on leave from Miles.[18]

Cameron was pleasantly surprised when Pitts accepted the position. It was important to Cameron that a respected black educator visit the black test centers, and Pitts, especially because of his new position as president of a well-known black college, was highly qualified. His main task would be to impress upon center supervisors the necessity of following ETS test administration guidelines to the letter. In order to give equal scrutiny regarding the impartial testing of all candidates, Pitts also was to learn how the black high schools would handle the testing of white students who might be assigned to centers in their schools. Cameron met with Pitts at Miles College in September, and later that month Pitts traveled to the ETS campus in Princeton for a day of training on test administration policies and procedures.[19]

Pitts favorably impressed the ETS staff members he encountered during his visit to their campus. In a telling remark that reflected the lifetime of racism he had experienced, Pitts stated that his mission as a consultant was "to impress upon everybody concerned that, in handling ETS's and the College Board's affairs, it [was] not good enough for his performance to be up to the standard of his white counterparts; it must be better." In addition to the forty-five black high schools serving as test centers in Georgia, Pitts was also asked to visit one black high school in Hatties-burg, Mississippi, and another in Birmingham, due to concerns over test security. Both had failed to follow correct procedures in returning tests to ETS. With the numbers of black students taking the SAT expected to in-crease, it was imperative that all test administrators understand and prac-tice accepted test procedures. ETS equipped Pitts with a site visit form, modified according to Cameron's instructions, and a list of the centers he was to visit.[20]

While the list of specific centers is long forgotten, it is still possible to draw some conclusions about conditions at the Alabama, Georgia, and Mississippi schools Pitts visited. Compared with the rest of the country, southern states spent far less educating their citizens. In 1950, Georgia's per pupil expenditure was only 60 percent of the national average. Ala-bama students fared less well at 50 percent, and Mississippi's expendi-ture was only about 30 percent of the national average. Funds allocated to black schools fell short even of those levels.[21] Far from being "equal" to schools for white students, black schools suffered from a history of in-adequate funding, and of course it was this overt disparity that had led to the overturn of *Plessy* in 1954. In the early 1950s, once the NAACP began suing school districts against segregation, some districts moved hurriedly to mitigate the disparity. In Atlanta, where the per pupil expenditure for whites was more than twice that for blacks, officials hastily erected new facilities in hopes of saving the "separate but equal" system mandated by the *Plessy* decision. These were dubbed "Supreme Court Schools" by understandably cynical black residents.[22] In Georgia, this almost frantic reparation became something of a pattern when Governor Herman Tal-madge raised $200 million in additional funds for education through a special sales tax, allocating a disproportionate amount to upgrade black education. Such isolated efforts did little to overturn decades of neglect; nor were they ultimately effective in preserving the institution of "sepa-rate but equal" schools.[23] The schools Pitts visited, like nearly all schools for black children, were underfunded and understaffed, with class sizes often much too large for effective instruction. It was little wonder that the overworked and underprepared teachers and administrators had not followed through on their ETS test center duties; these were simply not a priority.

Ben Gibson, liaison officer between colleges and universities and the board of education for Atlanta public schools, also agreed to act as a consultant for the College Board's Southern Regional Office and became responsible for visiting most of the existing test centers at white schools and colleges in Georgia. Gibson, an Atlanta native and Emory College graduate, had begun his career as a Fulton County (Atlanta area) high school guidance counselor prior to working for the Atlanta board of education. Like Cameron, Gibson was a World War II veteran, having served as a navy pilot. He was known among his associates for his "powers of persuasion" that reportedly had been valuable in his work with Atlanta schools and Georgia colleges and universities. While described by friends as an intellectual, Gibson could comfortably slip into the role of a "good old boy." Although Cameron may not have realized it at the time, his choice of Gibson to act on behalf of the Southern Regional Office was inspired— the persuasive and affable Gibson would prove himself a match for the most dedicated segregationists.[24]

Ben Gibson did not run from an argument; nor did he press too hard. In an entry written in his personal journal in the late 1940s, Gibson recorded his exchange with some acquaintances having to do with black voting rights in Georgia. "Of course, I do not argue too ardently with my farmer friends. . . . They know that I believe a Negro should have the unobstructed right to vote. They know that I am a Liberal. Every now and then we exchange sharp remarks, but it is hard for men who hunt and fish together to engage in political and economic discussions." Gibson made his case without alienating his friends, a trait that would serve him well in his work for the College Board.[25]

On July 17, 1946, the day that Eugene Talmadge defeated James Carmichael in the 1946 Georgia Democratic gubernatorial primary, Gibson, a supporter of the moderate Carmichael, wrote that he had been disappointed to see so few blacks at the polls. He explained the reluctance of rural blacks to push for their right to vote by appearing at the local polling places: "Their relationships with the white men are too direct on farms to run the risk of the subtleties of disapproval." Gibson hoped

that at least some urban blacks, taking advantage of their relative ano-
nymity, would turn out to vote. Talmadge, an ardent segregationist, had
"set people in Georgia afire with resentment against the Negro." Gibson
recorded sadly: "It is impossible to discuss rationally the Negro as a human being with most people in Georgia."[26]

Several days later, on July 26, Gibson was stunned by the lynching of
two black ex-servicemen and their common-law wives in nearby Monroe,
Georgia, and wrote, "My soul as well as my mind is troubled." Even while
he hoped for justice, Gibson felt a "depression of shame." He rightly feared
that justice for the four black victims would not come. "No white man
will open his mouth against another about this wanton slaying of four Negroes." Should a white man actually be brought to trial, Gibson could "en-
tertain no hope of his conviction." Gibson was correct in his prediction.
No one involved in the Moore's Ford lynching, as it came to be called,
was ever identified, despite years of intense investigation by state and
federal agents. There is no question that this incident had a lasting effect
on Gibson. Knowing only a few men who openly supported improvement
in the lives of black people, Gibson often felt isolated and frustrated.
Still, he was not without some measure of hope: "The hearts of white
men must undergo the subtle change that all hearts are capable of before
we can begin to solve this racial problem." Gibson's reflections indicate
that he had undergone such a change. Whether he believed then that
the overwhelming "racial problem" had a solution is not known, but in
taking on his new responsibilities at the College Board he must have
believed that he could contribute in some way.[27]

Cameron drafted a detailed description of Gibson's new job. By talking in person with school personnel, Gibson was to learn if a center had
ever tested any black candidates and, if so, under what circumstances
those candidates had been tested. He was then "to develop a feel for the
situation" and, if necessary, advise supervisors that they would no longer be allowed to test candidates in separate buildings. If the supervisor
responded that he or she would not be able to comply, then the center
would be closed "subject to the provision that testing facilities must be
reasonably accessible to all candidates." Cameron reminded Gibson that
in Georgia most black candidates could be expected to choose centers lo-

cated in black schools and colleges. As a result, the numbers of black students electing to take the SAT at white institutions would be relatively small, except where centers had been desegregated, notably in Atlanta. At nearly every test administration in a limited number of white centers, a few black students could be expected to appear due to a center's being convenient, through error, through reassignment for lack of capacity, or because the candidate wanted to create a "test case."[28]

Cameron and his College Board and ETS colleagues dreaded the possibility of test cases and their potential for publicity. Should a test case lead to a protest being filed in court, according to Cameron, "both the school and the CEEB [College Entrance Examination Board] would be vulnerable. This could lead to a court order for the desegregation of the school; it could also force the CEEB to have *only* desegregated centers, leading to a great deal of inconvenience to all concerned." Cameron recognized both the negative side of the threat of test cases as well a possible benefit. He emphasized this point to Gibson. "In view of these facts, it seems only sensible [for the schools] to avoid any possible controversy by being prepared to accommodate any candidate who shows up, and to test all impartially."[29]

Cameron recommended that Gibson not inform test supervisors of his planned visits. The element of surprise would reduce the chance of publicity about the desegregation efforts and forestall the opportunity for, in Cameron's words, "the construction of mental defenses" on the part of the supervisors. According to Cameron, his own usual procedure of "just dropping in" on supervisors had worked well. He added that Gibson could expect to be taken to see the principal and/or the superintendent. Keeping the desegregation effort out of the public eye was very important to the success of Cameron's plan. Ever since his conversation with John Hills following the AACRAO meeting in Miami, he had been in discussions with the College Board and ETS about the designated individuals in each organization who needed to know what was going on.[30]

Cameron included one positive event in his letter to Gibson. University System of Georgia chancellor Harmon Caldwell, probably at the suggestion of John Hills, had recommended to the board of regents that all state colleges and universities be "urged" to test all candidates regardless of race. Gibson, in his role at the Atlanta board of education, was likely well aware of this development.[31]

The College Board trustees met at the Board's offices in New York on December 14, 1961. Significantly, Henry Chauncey made no mention of test center desegregation in his report. Perhaps he knew the project was well in hand. Instead, Cameron reported on that project and answered the trustees' questions about his progress. Cameron felt compelled to remind the trustees, a predominantly New England group, that the South viewed by many as a "mixture of sand, scurvy, and sowbelly" was not the only South that existed. While that archetypal South was certainly still a reality in many areas, Cameron also saw an emerging region "of increased vitality, accompanied by changes in the public conscience." Cameron noted that despite the "pockets of continued fanatical resistance, the South as a whole has accepted the challenge of the latter half of the twentieth century, and is trying to meet it." This was, in Cameron's opinion, true for education if not in politics, and he believed that the College Board Southern Regional Office was aiding schools through its guidance counselor workshops and a variety of supporting materials and publications, especially those promoting college attendance.[32]

With regard to center desegregation, Cameron made several points. The one perhaps of greatest importance to the trustees was that, with the exception of those located in the hard core states, most testing centers in the remaining seven states covered by the Southern Regional Office were desegregated, operating with few reported problems. A few exceptions remained in Virginia and Texas. Even in the hard core states a few desegregated centers existed, despite the fact that state laws expressly prohibited the mixing of races. In those instances "desegregated testing depends almost exclusively on the prejudice and/or fear of the person ultimately responsible for the school or college concerned." Cameron reported that efforts to desegregate test sites would be "materially aided by the fear that incidents growing out of testing may lead to orders for the desegregation of schools"—a reference to the threat of test cases. Their desire to avoid racial "incidents," those that involved black students being turned away from centers at white schools, would motivate school officials to quietly desegregate their centers, in Cameron's opinion.[33]

Cameron added that problems created by security breaches at a few black high schools had somehow become known to several white school administrators. While the breaches in security had been unfortunate, they were proving to be an additional motivation for white schools and colleges to desegregate their own centers rather than entrust white students to testing at black institutions where testing conditions might be substandard. A positive development that Cameron included in his report was that during the current year there had been fewer complaints about racial incidents at southern test centers than in any other recent year. He attributed this improvement to the desegregation of schools in North Carolina, the establishment of centers at black high schools and colleges in Georgia, and the desegregation of the Atlanta centers. Cameron reminded the trustees that improvement had occurred despite the fact that, driven by the SAT requirement established by the board of regents, the number of candidates from black high schools in Georgia had more than doubled, increasing from 473 during the 1959–60 academic year to more than 1,200 in the following year.[34]

During a question-and-answer period following his report, a trustee asked Cameron when he predicted that all centers would be completely desegregated. He wisely replied that it was impossible to say. Cameron was then asked if any new segregated centers were being established and, even though he and others had agreed that some segregated centers might have to be opened temporarily under certain conditions, he replied that they were not.[35]

It is clear from other sections of Cameron's report to the trustees that he and his staff were working diligently to advance the College Board's programs in the South. Programs for high school guidance counselors were a priority, and in black high schools Cameron's office faced particular challenges in meeting the demand for counselor workshops. Due to lack of funding and inadequate counselor training, the state of college guidance at most black high schools in the South was below average, and there was much work to be done to inform black educators about college readiness and application. Black counselors were enthusiastic participants in College Board workshops, perhaps in part because Cameron and his staff were often their only link to predominantly white colleges and the new opportunities for their students that those colleges held. Another area that required Cameron's attention was the college admissions process throughout much of the South, which lagged well behind the rest of the country in terms of selectivity and procedures for admitting students. The College Board could help southern colleges and universities become more selective through the appropriate use of the SAT, thereby supporting a process that would admit only those students who would succeed academically. One institution with this emerging need was private Centenary College in Shreveport. By 1962 the college's admissions committee had decided they could no longer rely solely on high school transcripts in deciding which students to admit. Variances in grading practices among the school districts whose students applied to Centenary College impeded the admissions process to the extent that J. Howard Allen, director of admissions, supported adding the SAT as a requirement. Even with the state-supported colleges and universities leaning toward the ACT at the time, Allen preferred the SAT and was willing to "stand alone."[36]

Cameron mentioned competition from the ACT program in his report. In Texas, it appeared that by 1963 the College Board would test about two-thirds of college-bound high school students. Perhaps in response, midwestern ACT, according to Cameron, was attempting to sell its product by "loudly acclaiming" its "equalitarian nature," a derogatory, indirect reference to the College Board's roots in the private institutions of the Northeast, by offering summer make-up tests, and by charging less for its test. Cameron also mentioned his efforts to work with United Negro College Fund (UNCF) member institutions to adopt the SAT. Led by Fisk University, where Stephen J. Wright was president, four black colleges had recently decided to use the SAT. The College Board, Cameron reported, was conducting test validity studies at Fisk designed to "identify elements which may improve the prediction of college success among such culturally deprived groups." While black students as a group typically scored lower than their white counterparts on the SAT, most of the black colleges for which validity studies had been conducted were able to show a "remarkable" correlation between the test scores and the students' academic performance in college, confirming the potential usefulness of the SAT in admissions decisions involving black applicants.[37]

Ben Gibson and members of Cameron's staff continued visiting test-ing centers throughout the rest of 1961 and into 1962. L. H. Pitts, the Miles College president, also made his assigned visits, though little is known about the outcomes. Cameron continued to struggle with how desegregating test centers could best be accomplished. Without the ex-ecution of some creative ideas, it would be a very slow process.

Shortly after the meeting of the trustees in December 1961, Cameron had received discouraging news regarding the potential for desegregating the centers in Albany, Macon, and Savannah, Georgia, where each re-spective board of education had voted that Negro candidates could not be tested at white schools. Providing for adequate testing capacity in those three cities was a top priority. Cameron voiced his concerns to Richard Pearson, a College Board colleague, and offered Pearson two ideas for moving the desegregation process along. First, he again broached the sub-ject of moving test centers to federal facilities where they could operate on a totally desegregated basis. Aware that the College Board's prestige in national education circles afforded considerable influence in Washing-ton, Cameron suggested that in procuring those facilities his office could "expect cooperation in most cases only if we have directives from above" and speculated that Vice President Lyndon B. Johnson, who chaired the Presidential Committee on Equal Employment Opportunity, might be the person to contact. Cameron had already asked a friend to help him arrange a meeting with the vice president. Another possibility, Cameron wrote, was to approach national security advisor McGeorge Bundy, Presi-dent John F. Kennedy's special assistant for national security affairs, about the use of federal facilities.[38]

The second idea Cameron offered Pearson was the possibility of form-ing a College Board committee to whom Cameron would report peri-odically and from whom he would garner assistance to "go as fast as we can" in desegregating the centers. The structures of both the College Board and ETS allowed for and relied upon the work of advisory commit-tees, so Cameron's idea was not original. He believed that establishing a committee would also assure the College Board trustees that the South-ern Regional Office was sincere in working steadily toward desegregat-ing the centers. At least one ETS trustee, William C. Fels, president of

Bennington College in Vermont, already had registered his impatience with the pace of Cameron's progress. Cameron's initial idea for the committee's makeup was that it should include representatives from ETS and the College Board, possibly trustees, as well as southern black leaders and a representative of the Southern Regional Council, a pro-desegregation association comprised of black and white educators, journalists, and church and civic leaders.[39]

Pearson's colleagues at the College Board agreed that Cameron should present the idea to the trustees at their March meeting. Pearson left the question of how to pursue the use of federal facilities solely up to Cameron, suggesting that it might be a good idea to approach both Vice President Johnson and McGeorge Bundy.[40] Cameron made his recommendation to the trustees at their March 14–15, 1962, meeting at the College Board offices in New York, reminding them again that resistance to desegregation had "stiffened considerably" in many areas of the South during the last few years and that progress in at least some of those areas would be determined by his ability to establish centers at facilities outside the control of school districts. The trustees voted to authorize board chairman Frank D. Ashburn, headmaster of The Brooks School, North Andover, Massachusetts, to establish "a special committee on examining center policy" and charged the committee with re-examining the Board's policy on center desegregation, studying the progress that had been made, and considering any changes needed in the policy or its implementation. The committee was to report back to the trustees "at an early date."[41]

Before Cameron could turn his attention to recommending individuals to Ashburn for membership on the special committee, he set to work with Joseph Terral of ETS crafting the wording of the paragraph about testing all candidates that was to be included in letters to be sent to test supervisors in August at the beginning of the 1962–63 testing year. Apparently, Cameron's earlier reluctance to send such a letter had abated. He and Terral decided that the paragraph would read as follows:

> The test application does not in any way indicate the race of the candidate, who himself chooses a center from the list in the bulletin of information. You should be prepared, therefore, to admit and seat all candidates. If you cannot do this, please notify us.[42]

Both men considered first sending the letter to a limited number of centers so as to test reactions, but finally agreed to forgo this step and send the new paragraph to the "whole caboodle" of supervisors.[43]

By the middle of April 1962, Cameron had developed a list of four categories of the several committee members he planned to recruit—"a northern trustee [College Board]; a southern trustee; a prominent southern Negro educator; a southern liberal leader, familiar with factors involved and an active worker for desegregation." Cameron briefly considered two other categories: someone representing "a more conservative southern point of view" and a "knowledgeable non-partisan." He thought that Goldwater Republican and textile heir Howard H. ("Bo") Callaway might be a candidate for the southern point of view position, but wisely changed his mind about that category, confiding in a colleague that "there is not now much in the way of middle ground in the South." Later, Cameron would appreciate his decision to exclude Callaway. Cameron believed that Reed Sarratt of the Southern Education Reporting Service (SERS) would be the most likely person to fill the role of the "knowledgeable non-partisan," but there is no evidence that Cameron ever approached Sarratt about serving on the committee. In his letter to Pearson, Cameron noted that Sarratt's position at SERS was probably "too sensitive" to allow his participation. Sarratt's contribution to the College Board's desegregation project would have compromised the signature unbiased status of his organization.[44]

Those who agreed to serve on the committee were Arthur Howe Jr., dean of admissions and student appointments at Yale University (a "northern Trustee"), who, at the request of College Board president Edward Noyes, would serve as chairman; J. Alton Burdine, dean of the College of Arts and Sciences, University of Texas (a "southern Trustee"); Leslie W. Dunbar, executive director, Southern Regional Council (a "southern liberal leader"); Ralph McGill, publisher, *The Atlanta Constitution* (a "southern liberal leader"); William L. Pressly, president, Westminster Schools, Atlanta (a second "southern Trustee"); and Stephen J. Wright, president, Fisk University, Nashville, Tennessee (a "prominent southern Negro educator"). For Cameron, Wright's membership on the committee was essential. College Board president Edward Noyes wanted to add a public school representative but feared that doing so would mark that person as a segregationist and place him in a dangerous position within his community.[45] The new committee members were asked to attend one meeting per year and to make themselves available at other times to advise the staff and trustees.[46]

Cameron's impressive committee of leaders represented a range of experience regarding their involvement in desegregation. Of course, their personal backgrounds and vocations varied as well. Committee chair Arthur Howe had spent nearly all of his life in New England and since 1953 had served as the head of Yale's board of admissions. Howe was probably the committee member most removed from the challenges of desegregation. In his position at Yale, Howe recruited and admitted the "well-rounded" man, one with both "brains and character" and most likely to make a positive contribution to society. He presided over an admissions process that gradually evolved to include a pool of applicants more varied than the traditional circle of private secondary schools. While Yale had long admitted a few outstanding black applicants, it did not begin actively recruiting black students until 1961.[47]

J. Alton Burdine, one of Cameron's "Southern trustees," was a relative newcomer to the College Board and was probably influential in the decision of the University of Texas to require the SAT and the College Board English Composition Test in its admissions process. Since the state of Texas was years ahead of the hard core states in desegregating its public schools, colleges, and universities, Burdine may have been more detached from the current challenges of desegregation than other southerners serving on the committee.[48] A native of Mississippi, he held a Ph.D. from Harvard University and had earned both his bachelor's and master's degrees at a segregated University of Texas.[49] But by 1958, when Burdine became dean of the College of Arts and Sciences, the University of Texas had been admitting black students for several years, beginning with the admission of Heman Sweatt to the university's law school in 1950 and the admission of three undergraduates in 1955. By 1956, the University of Texas had enrolled more than one hundred black students in its undergraduate programs.[50]

One of Cameron's "southern liberal leaders," Leslie Dunbar, was deeply involved in desegregation as head of the Southern Regional Council (SRC), an interracial, Atlanta-based organization that supported desegregation in the schools and beyond. With approximately 80 grass-roots groups—called Human Relations Councils—operating in most southern states, the SRC supported local actions to move the process of school desegregation from the courts into the schools and communities themselves. Southern Education Reporting Service (SERS) director Reed Sarratt significantly named the SRC "the leading organization opposing segregation."[51] Prior to joining the SRC in 1951 as director of research, Dunbar taught at Cornell University, Smith College, Mount Holyoke College, and Emory University. He was promoted to the position of executive director of the SRC in 1961. Dunbar once observed that what was remarkable about southern liberals was their "long sustained refusal . . . to repudiate the South. . . . Few liberals have acted out their beliefs. They do not try to enter their children in Negro schools, do not usually refuse to eat in segregated restaurants or worship in segregated churches. . . . The general conformity of the liberal to social practices which he opposes is a mark of his dogged refusal to alienate himself from southern society." Of course, Dunbar himself was an exception to his own definition of a southern liberal, openly acting out his beliefs through his work with the SRC.[52]

Newspaper publisher Ralph McGill, another "southern liberal leader" and certainly the most well-known member of Cameron's committee, shared Dunbar's views on southern liberals, and, also like Dunbar, he made his views on race widely known. McGill writes of the southern liberal, "The often cruel injustices of the rigid formula of race may have offended him and aroused him to open opposition." Nevertheless, McGill felt that the southern liberal was "held" by his region, unable to be unattached. McGill recognized all of the South's problems, especially its struggle with matters of race, and, even as he found himself increasingly at odds with the many facets of massive resistance, continued to work hard to change people's minds.[53]

Historian John Egerton describes McGill's metamorphosis from a "mainstream white Southerner" to a southern liberal. Following the *Brown* decision, McGill, who had previously believed that the South should and would solve its own problems without intervention from the federal government, saw that the only side he could take was the side of the law. Finding that the "middle ground had eroded away," Egerton writes, "he landed firmly on the 'radical' side of law and order and nonviolence, the side of Martin Luther King and virtually all black Southerners." McGill would then write frequently about the "chloroforming myths" of white supremacy and "separate but equal." Edgerton knew McGill personally and speculated that one of his most important contributions was demonstrating "the capacity of white Southerners to change." "If he [McGill] could change," Edgerton writes, "if he could do the right thing, maybe the rest of us could too."[54] By the time McGill agreed to serve on the College Board committee, he had won the 1959 Pulitzer Prize for journalism and was syndicated in more than three hundred newspapers.[55]

As headmaster of the private, elite, and firmly segregated Westminster Schools in Atlanta, William Pressly, Cameron's second southern trustee, was sheltered from the challenges of public school desegregation occurring on his doorstep. During the troubled fall of 1961 when Atlanta public schools began desegregating, Pressly felt the impact of that historic occasion only in the sizable increase of applications from the children of white parents determined to avoid integrated schools at any cost. Across the South, desegregation was a boon to private schools. Pressly's board of trustees did discuss desegregation during a meeting in 1961 but took no action. The possibility of desegregation would not be raised again formally until 1964, and, with Pressly's urging, the trustees finally agreed to desegregate, enrolling the school's first black students during the 1966–67 academic year. This event distinguished Westminster Schools by making it the first independent, non-church-affiliated school in the Deep South to desegregate.[56]

Stephen Wright was the lone black member of the committee. As president of Fisk, he had supported the peaceful student sit-ins in Nashville stores during the spring of 1961. Civil rights leader John Lewis, a Fisk student and sit-in participant, writes: "[President Wright] was the first black college president in the country to take such a stand. We were euphoric."[57] Wright saw himself as part of a new movement among black people—especially the young, a movement that required taking a more direct approach to improving their status. In Wright's view, this new approach was the result of three "bitter" lessons learned by blacks in the years following World War II. First, "the white South would never voluntarily dismantle the Jim Crow system." Second, despite "good race relations," whites would never find blacks "ready" to assume full citizenship. Third, "the only effective way to change [the Negro's] status was to employ with vigor and imagination the instruments of pressure": the courts, the vote, economic power, and "protests of a variety of types." Wright believed that these lessons had spawned a "new Negro" of the South.[58]

Wright also strongly believed that education was essential to improving the lives of southern blacks who, in turn, would help build a stronger country: "The nation will be the beneficiary of the talents and genius of many thousands of young Negroes who, under the [current] system, either fail to be developed or atrophy. This is a luxury which this nation in these demanding times cannot afford." Ben Cameron recognized that Wright, the only committee member he knew well, would make an important contribution in efforts to desegregate the test centers.[59]

Wright lent his support to the College Board because, in his own words, "it took its responsibility to desegregate itself seriously. . . . It took seriously the opportunity to assist in the admission of black students to institutions of higher education all over the country, as a matter of fact. Of course it was one of the few organizations that had contact with both higher education and secondary schools across the nation." Acknowledging the College Board's unique and influential position in education, Wright viewed his service on Cameron's committee as an opportunity to expand access to higher education for black students. An additional motivation for him to serve may have been his concern, one he shared with Cameron, that some states were implementing the SAT to keep black students out of their white institutions.[60]

As Cameron prepared for the first meeting of the committee—scheduled for October 1, 1962—he was cognizant of the dismal pace of school desegregation in the hard core states. Alabama, Mississippi, and South Carolina remained segregated at all levels. In Georgia, Atlanta schools had begun their second year of desegregation, with 44 black students attending school with whites. In Louisiana, only New Orleans Parish schools, now in their third year of desegregation, were desegregated, with 107 black students attending white schools. Cameron's meeting was held at the Westminster Schools with committee members Howe, Dunbar, Pressly, and Wright present. Burdine and McGill were unable to attend. Also present were College Board vice president and treasurer George H. Hanford, Joseph Terral of ETS, and Cameron. Cameron had briefed the committee members in a comprehensive, confidential report mailed to them in advance of their meeting. The report consisted of background material on the desegregation project and his suggestions for future action. In his report, Cameron wrote that he had made some progress. While he had closed a few testing centers due to their unwillingness to go along with the new policy, a few other centers had decided to cooperate and were testing all candidates without any discrimination. But, Cameron added, "there is little indication of increased moderation in most of the hard core area." One area that did show promise was Florida, which Cameron had previously counted among the hard core states. A center in Jacksonville had been closed following white parents' protesting the presence of black candidates at their children's school, but other centers in that city had agreed to test under desegregated conditions, and no serious problems had been reported. Florida's schools were desegregating relatively rapidly, aiding Cameron in his efforts to provide desegregated centers in all parts of the state and allowing him to drop Florida from his hard core state list. Five states remained—Alabama, Georgia, Louisiana, Mississippi, and South Carolina—and he summarized the status of center desegregation in each state for the new committee.[61]

Cameron called the test center situation in Alabama where schools remained totally segregated "contradictory." The two main "trouble spots" were Montgomery, where, according to Cameron, "the influence of the state government is strong," and Birmingham, which was "ruled in all racial matters by a highly irrational police commissioner." Montgomery, the state's capital, had been the site of the successful 1955–56 bus boycott inspired by Rosa Parks. White reaction against that success as well as against the *Brown* decision ran strong in Montgomery, center of the state's pro-segregation government. John M. Patterson, Alabama's governor from 1959 to 1963, had proclaimed, "If any school in Alabama is integrated, it will be over my dead body."[62] The situation in Birmingham may have been worse. There, Eugene "Bull" Connor, the "highly irrational" police commissioner Cameron referenced in his report, had distinguished himself during the May 1961 Freedom Ride by granting a mob of Ku Klux Klansmen fifteen undisturbed minutes during which they were allowed to beat the freedom riders, seriously injuring several, before Connor's policemen finally arrived. Questioned later about the delay, Connor professed that his men had been unavailable because they were spending Mother's Day with their families.[63] In May 1963, Connor would become internationally known and immortalized in black-and-white photographs and film when he set his policemen, police dogs, and high-pressure water hoses on teenagers and even younger children participating in the Children's Crusade march.[64]

Montgomery's only testing center was located in the city's board of education offices. Black candidates were tested there, while white candidates were led across the street to a public junior high school, thereby, according to Cameron, allowing officials to evade "the letter of the law of prohibition of the transportation of [Negro] candidates to a separate building."[65] In Birmingham, Phillips High School, a white public school, had served as a test center for years, quietly testing both black and white candidates without incident, although Cameron acknowledged that in most instances black candidates had been tested in separate rooms there. When Police Commissioner Connor, now police *and* education commissioner, learned of this situation, he immediately banned black students from entering the white high school, and, apparently, no one opposed his order. Black candidates were now being tested at Parker High School, the black school whose students would later participate in the 1963 Children's Crusade organized by Martin Luther King Jr. and others. Since Bull Connor's ban, no black candidate had been assigned to white Phillips High, but some white students had been assigned to Parker. In keeping with state laws separating the races, white students had not been allowed to enter the black school.[66]

In contrast to Montgomery and Birmingham, testing without discrimination was usual in many of Alabama's small towns and rural areas. Of course, the number of black candidates was quite small, and some centers had had no black candidates. Cameron noted that many centers in small

Alabama towns, those communities where massive resistance had not yet taken hold, had "traditionally tested all candidates together with no difficulty." One unidentified center supervisor did complain about having to test "out-of-town Negroes," a sentiment that would be repeated in other hard core states. It seems that to a segregationist the only thing worse than a Negro was an out-of-town Negro.[67]

At the time of the meeting of the new committee, October 1962, South Carolina, where schools also remained segregated, had only one public high school that had tested black candidates impartially for any length of time. The College of Charleston center and the Spartanburg center, located at a Naval Reserve Training Center, were the only other desegregated centers in the state. When the center supervisor in Camden learned that a student from a black high school was scheduled for the May 1962 SAT, he advised ETS that he would not be able to test the student. ETS responded that the center would be closed. The supervisor's board of education "immediately" granted him permission to operate on a desegregated basis, and Cameron stated that, to his knowledge, this was the first case in which a school board had given its official permission to desegregate a center. He found the incident "remarkable" and a hopeful sign.[68]

The centers in New Orleans, all located in private or parochial schools and colleges, had operated on a desegregated basis for years. However, in Shreveport, which Cameron believed to be the most racially troubled spot in Louisiana, black candidates were being transported from white Byrd High School to black Booker T. Washington High School. At the same time Cameron noted that a number of centers outside New Orleans were testing without discrimination. The only report of trouble at a test center during the past several years had involved white candidates who had arrived late on the day of the test and had been reassigned to a black school for testing.[69]

In his report, Cameron again did not spare his home state of Mississippi, the third state continuing complete school segregation. Probably referring to the troubles brewing over the University of Mississippi's desegregation, in which his segregationist father, a federal district court judge, was playing an obstructionist role, Cameron wrote, "Particularly at this point in time, a native Mississippian feels the less said the better." As far as the College Board was concerned, Cameron stated, "Mississippi might almost be ignored." Only 1,267 College Board examinations had been administrated in the entire state during the previous test year; and, while the total number of candidates tested in the South had risen 67 percent during the previous two academic years, the number for Mississippi had remained stagnant. Even worse, the number of candidates from black high schools had dropped by more than 50 percent. Cameron was unable to explain the statistic for black candidates, having expected an increase to accompany colleges' ongoing talent searches for gifted black students and the simultaneous implementation of SAT requirements at private black colleges. The highest number of black candidates tested on any given test date during the previous year in all of Mississippi was seven, and a total of only twenty-six black students were known to have taken the SAT in the state that year. There had been no reported racial incidents at any center that had tested black candidates, but, given the small numbers, Cameron did not find that surprising. At least two centers had tested on a desegregated basis, but far more common was the practice of testing black and white candidates in separate rooms in the same building. Should their numbers increase substantially, Cameron expected that this benign situation would change.[70]

Cameron's negative assessment of race relations in his home state was based on facts and not on his own biases. With the highest percentage of blacks of any state, Mississippi was, according to historian Joseph Crespino, "the poorest, least urbanized southern state." Crespino finds Mississippians "atypical" not only of their fellow countrymen, but also of southerners generally. The state, Crespino writes, "lacked the moderating influence of business leadership that existed in cities such as Atlanta." As a result, Mississippi would instead claim another kind of leadership—in its intense support of segregation, particularly in the level of violence perpetrated by whites against both black and white supporters of desegregation. It is no surprise that the White Citizens' Council movement originated and flourished in Mississippi, continually suppressing any progress toward racial equality.[71]

Cameron saved his report on Georgia until last, judging the situation there "more complicated and more challenging than that in any other state." He reminded the committee members that, since 1957, all of the state's public colleges and universities had required the SAT for admission, the only state system of the five hard core states with such a requirement. While the SAT requirement had been enforced "rigorously" at the white institutions from the first, it had only recently been enforced at the black institutions. That fact, plus the gradual improvement in college guidance at the black high schools, fostered by Cameron and his staff, was responsible for the large increase in black test candidates in Georgia (then totaling 1,779), giving Georgia more than 10 times the number of black candidates in Alabama, Mississippi, or South Carolina, and nearly 8 times more than those in Louisiana. Because of several racial incidents at Georgia test centers and because of the increase in the number of black candidates, Cameron explained, the College Board and ETS had established a dual center system in Georgia, opening a center for black students in nearly every community that had a center for white students. Cameron admitted that this decision had probably been "unwise" from the standpoint of eventual center desegregation. However, the dual system had allowed testing to occur without any reported complaints from black students. On the other hand, a white student who reported for testing at Emory University's desegregated center in Atlanta left the March 1962 SAT administration, refusing to be tested in the same room with a black student. Complaints from whites rarely occurred, but this incident probably reminded Cameron of the potential for future challenges.[72]

Of the 129 test centers now in Georgia, the 52 in white high schools were the most problematic for Cameron. All but one of the schools were public, and Cameron had learned that not one would "routinely" test black candidates, "either in the same room, or in a separate room in the same building." One of the 52 schools would accommodate "an occasional possible Negro candidate in the same room," and 28 would test an occasional candidate in a different room in the same building, usually the principal's or guidance counselor's office. Four schools had "routine arrangements" to test black candidates in a separate building—this arrangement having been developed prior to the days before dual centers were established. Seventeen schools stated emphatically that they "would not test Negro candidates under any circumstances." Six schools evaded altogether Cameron's question about their testing practices, and he concluded that it was likely that they would not test black candidates. Cameron's attempt to gain the support of the office of the Georgia state superintendent of education in the College Board's efforts to desegregate centers had been "met without sympathy." Cameron, speaking candidly to the committee, was not optimistic about test center desegregation in Georgia, especially in smaller communities and rural areas, "within the next few years."[73]

Complicating the situation in the hard core states were three possible developments that Cameron reported. First, and most important, was the likelihood that more black students would soon register for the SAT, meaning that the potential for racial incidents at the test centers could increase. Second, the U.S. Navy was negotiating with the College Board for the use of a College Board testing program for high school students interested in its Naval Reserve Officer Training Program, beginning in 1965. The navy of course would insist that test centers be desegregated. Finally, the Coast Guard Academy had asked the College Board to guarantee that no test candidate be discriminated against due to race. The other service academies, which allowed for testing of their candidates on military bases, had not yet expressed similar concerns. Cameron believed this situation was due to the fact that the service academies, with their requirement of congressional nominations, placed a de facto limitation on potential black candidates from the South.[74]

Cameron's report to the new committee included his idea for accelerating the process of desegregating test centers: establishing centers outside the public secondary school systems—in military installations, other federal facilities, white colleges and universities, black colleges, parochial schools, and churches. Cameron expected that military and other federal facilities were the most likely to be able to accommodate significant numbers of candidates.[75]

The Special Committee on Examining Center Policy opened its first meeting on the morning of October 1, 1962, with a general discussion of Cameron's report, which they had studied in advance. The positive aspects of Cameron's facts and figures produced the optimistic consensus that "complete desegregation can be achieved in the foreseeable future." Committee members also agreed that any public announcement of the effort to desegregate the centers should be postponed until "a policy of complete desegregation of testing centers can be fully enforced." There was also general agreement that their efforts should focus only on desegregating test centers and would not extend to "reforming Southern Education." The committee noted that moving toward desegregating the centers involved financial sacrifice on the part of the College Board—increased staff expenses and probably lost revenues—and the "sacrifice of convenience on the part of some candidates," referring to the closing of centers that would not comply, causing students to travel long distances. Even greater sacrifices might be expected in the future.[76]

The committee's discussion moved from the broad and general to the specific and detailed, reflecting the diligence of the group. The corporate culture of both the College Board and ETS demanded thoughtful and thorough work, and the special committee followed that pattern, carefully crafting two documents that would undergird Cameron's task. Members first reviewed the procedures the College Board and ETS had put in place with regard to the Southern Regional Office assuming responsibility for most test center functions in the hard core states and agreed that those arrangements were appropriate for the time being. The committee then reviewed the policy statement that the College Board's trustees had approved at their March 1961 meeting:

> The first responsibility of the College Entrance Examination Board is to provide for the testing of all candidates under standard, equitable conditions. The Board will, however, make a definite and specific effort in all areas to assure that all testing centers be equally accessible to all candidates without regard to race when this can be accomplished without definitely jeopardizing the Board's ability to test all candidates.[77]

The committee shortened and strengthened the trustees' policy and voted to recommend the adoption of the resulting "precept" as an internal policy to replace the one the trustees had approved in March 1961. Hanford's and Cameron's very detailed notes reflect that the conversation around modifications to the original policy was important and painstaking, consuming much of the meeting. The resulting new policy read as follows:

> It is the responsibility of the College Entrance Examination Board to provide for the testing of all candidates under standard, equitable conditions. Conditions cannot be considered "standard" or "equitable" if any discrimination against a candidate within a testing center is made on the basis of race, color, or national origin.[78]

Cameron's and Hanford's notes on the changes to the original policy explain several key points that reveal the thoughtfulness of the committee's recommendation. For example, the phrase "within a testing center" was included so that all rooms used for administering the tests, including restroom facilities, would be covered. Lunchroom facilities were also discussed, but, probably because ETS's Terral was present and familiar with ongoing difficulties in the matter of lunch facilities for black LSAT candidates, the committee decided that dining facilities were "not a necessary adjunct to [an SAT] testing center." The word "religion," which one might have expected the committee to include in reference to discrimination against candidates, was intentionally omitted because the College Board did in fact operate special "Sunday centers" for candidates "whose religious beliefs prevent testing on Saturday."[79]

The committee then revised Cameron's seven-part plan, editing it severely and eliminating three steps altogether—having judged them to be superfluous—with the following four-part result:

1. Determine regularly the conditions under which all Negro candidates are being tested.

2. Refuse to establish any new testing centers which are not operated in conformance with stated policy.

3. Close any testing center at which it is established that a candidate has not been treated in accordance with stated policy, and where negotiations fail to produce the assurance of future compliance.

4. Seek to establish now *[sic]* additional centers which will be desegregated in areas where separate centers now exist for whites and Negroes, so that the separate centers for both races may be closed.[80]

Again, Cameron's and Hanford's careful notes explain the reasons for the changes. The changes to the second part, which prohibited the establishment of new centers that would not comply, were probably the most striking and generated the most discussion. The new version allowed no exceptions to the policy of refraining from opening new centers which would be operated on a segregated basis. The committee wanted to prevent at least one possible strategy of resistance, that of a white school cleverly circumventing desegregation altogether by establishing a center solely for its own students. This could be accomplished by first estimating the number of students from the school who would be likely to take the tests and then indicating that the school's testing capacity (number of available seats) was that same number, in effect barring any students from outside the school from being tested there. Enabling such a situation would put the College Board and ETS in the position of allowing the school to "purchase immorality" through manipulation, and the committee wanted no part of that. It also agreed that any College Board member college that wished to establish a center "would be subject to the same limitations," meaning that it could not limit the test administration to its own, presumably white, students. The third part of the plan, closing a center where unfair treatment of black students had occurred and might continue, allowed time for negotiating with a school for future conformity to the policy. Georgia's dual center policy motivated the committee to include a certain amount of flexibility.[81]

The College Board's competitor, ACT, referred to not by name but as "another testing program," entered the discussion at this point. The committee considered the possibility that the proposed desegregation policy might well lead colleges and universities to choose the ACT over the SAT; however, they believed that the southern education community as a whole accepted that within a very few years school desegregation would progress at least to some degree, and testing programs would have to be operated under desegregated conditions. The committee's position was significant and perhaps optimistic, as was their stated "immediate goal" of "*providing opportunities* [committee's emphasis] for all candidates in desegregated centers by 1965." The committee's ambitious, "long-range goal"—they did not hazard to name a year—was "assuring that all centers will be operated on a non-segregated basis (that is, all centers open to all) [committee's parentheses]."[82]

Cameron's original plan had included the word "gradually," that is, "so that the separate centers for both races may be *gradually* closed." Committee members wanted to infuse the plan with a "sense of urgency," and so removed the word.[83]

Finally, the committee recommended changing the wording in the widely distributed College Board bulletin regarding special arrangements for candidates who might have to travel more than seventy-five miles to a regular center. Instead of stating that special centers *would* be arranged in that case, the sentence would read that the College Board would "attempt" to establish special centers for candidates who would otherwise have to travel more than seventy-five miles to a center. In making this change, the committee provided for the fact that, given the strong wording of the recommended new policy and plan of action, ETS simply could not promise a desegregated center within the seventy-five-mile requirement as it had in the past.[84]

Committee chairman Arthur Howe adjourned the meeting at 3:45 p.m., and Cameron must have felt a sense of relief and accomplishment. He had gained the backing of an informed and distinguished group that had spent valuable time carefully hammering out an official policy statement and a plan of action. Now when he faced school officials, he would do so with an added sense of confidence.[85]

The meeting minutes omit two of the most important events that occurred that day. First, by virtue of becoming a member of the special committee, Stephen Wright, Cameron's choice for the "Southern Negro educator" position, had been empowered to act for the College Board in seeking alternative test sites. Undoubtedly, Wright was intrigued by the section of Cameron's report that suggested the use of military installations, and it is possible that he and Cameron had discussed that idea prior to the committee meeting. The second event not covered in the minutes was a brief, informal discussion about the use of federal facilities that took place among Cameron, Wright, Howe, and Hanford after the others left. Wright thought he could be helpful there. Wasting no time following the meeting, and without assistance from either Vice President

Johnson or McGeorge Bundy, Wright, acting with the knowledge of his colleagues, telephoned a longtime acquaintance, James C. Evans, a black civilian assistant to the secretary of defense. Wright's call set off a series of conversations and actions that would give the College Board and ETS a powerful alternative to school-based test centers.[86]

Establishing Test Centers at Military Bases, 1962–1963

It is in the national interest for the Defense Department to cooperate with the College Entrance Board in making suitable testing facilities immediately available.
—Norman S. Paul, assistant secretary of defense in a memo to the undersecretaries of the army, navy, and air force, February 19, 1963

You fellows must be up against a stone wall in Mississippi!
—Lieutenant Colonel Robert T. Larkin, Columbus Air Force Base,
Columbus, Mississippi, in a conversation with Ben Gibson, April 17, 1963

Appointed by President Franklin D. Roosevelt to advise government officials on ways to improve race relations in the armed forces, James C. Evans had spent most of his career devoted to that task. By 1962, he had become, according to Stephen Wright, "one of the two or three most influential blacks in the Federal government." Evans would soon direct that influence to the College Board's test center desegregation efforts. Evans, a Tennessee native, earned bachelor's and master's degrees from the Massachusetts Institute of Technology and, in addition to working for the Department of Defense, taught engineering courses at Howard University.[1] Evans responded positively to Wright's telephone call about the use of federal facilities as testing centers and began looking into the matter. Within a few weeks, he had considered various possibilities and commu-

nicated those to Wright in a letter. Writing in a style that Ben Cameron
would later refer to as "circumlocution," Evans skillfully steered away
from the use of military bases. Instead, he suggested that it "might" be
a good idea to consider other federal facilities in the vicinity of current
test sites, especially "those coming within the purview of the Department of Justice," and also that the U.S. Office of Education "might" be
able to "reveal channels for elimination of segregation in facilities used
for administering the Examinations." In addition, Evans speculated that
"various State and Federal Government agencies . . . might" be able to
help locate facilities that could be used on a desegregated basis.[2]

Those multiple "mights" probably didn't strike Stephen Wright as particularly encouraging; however, Evans did assure Wright that he supported
the College Board's efforts to desegregate its testing centers. Reminding
Wright of his (Evans's) work in race relations at the Department of Defense, and especially his efforts on behalf of the "Private Pete" program
for the "illiterates" of World War II, Evans conveyed his willingness to
help the College Board and asked Wright to react to his several suggestions. Evans enclosed with his letter a quote from James M. Meredith,
who earlier that year had become the first black student to enroll at the
University of Mississippi. Meredith's quote had appeared in the November 10, 1962, issue of *The Saturday Evening Post,* and read, "Certainly my
Air Force days were the most influential times of my life. I served in
nothing but integrated units. It seems to me the integration of the armed
forces is one of the most important things that has happened to the Negro in the United States."[3]

Evans took pride in the role he had played in the desegregated armed
forces, and rightly so. Described by historian Alan L. Gropman as a "be-
hind-the-scenes fighter," Evans was immersed in investigating individual
cases of racial discrimination in the military, especially in the air force.
Moreover, Gropman credits Evans with influencing President Harry S.
Truman to issue his 1948 Executive Order, the historic document that
announced the requirement of equal treatment and opportunity for all
members of the armed services. Evans's office was also the destination
for complaints from black servicemen about their treatment away from
their bases. Following the *Brown* decision in 1954, Evans's complaint

files began to expand considerably. Servicemen hailing from all over the country who found themselves stationed in the South became increasingly frustrated and angered by being forced to send their children to inferior segregated schools, which according to federal law by that time should have been integrated. Gropman, who had examined Evans's complaint files, describes them as existing "by the hundred weight," the thickest being those containing complaints about discrimination in off-base housing. The voluminous files dealing with school segregation problems ran a close second.[4]

Complaints about school segregation continued to flow into Evans's office well into the 1960s, and not all involved schools located off-base. In Charleston, South Carolina, the military had built a school for dependent children only to bar the children of black servicemen from attending. Instead, these children were bused to black public schools many miles away. This case was one of dozens absorbing Evans's attention at the time he and Wright became involved in assisting the College Board. Evans's intimate knowledge of racial discrimination against servicemen and their families may have been responsible for his attempt to direct the College Board to alternate federal facilities. Or, he may simply have been testing the College Board's resolve.[5]

Wright immediately forwarded Evans's letter and its enclosure to Ben Cameron, who answered that he planned to act on Evans's suggestion about the U.S. Office of Education.[6] Cameron surely took special notice of the James Meredith quote, being painfully aware of his own father's role in blocking Meredith's attempts to desegregate the University of Mississippi. Judge Cameron, an ardent segregationist, had fought Meredith's admission through every possible legal maneuver, much to the dismay of his fellow Fifth Circuit Court judges. Eventually, Supreme Court Justice Hugo Black silenced Judge Cameron's opposition, and the case to desegregate the University of Mississippi proceeded toward its eventual, though troubled, success.[7]

Judge Cameron's behavior in the Meredith case was consistent with his earlier stands regarding the desegregation of public schools. His first dissenting opinion as a member of the Fifth Circuit Court, written in 1956—two years following the first *Brown* decision—promoted the idea that local boards of education should be allowed to desegregate schools, free from the involvement of the federal courts. Judge Cameron's subsequent dissenting opinions consistently followed along those lines.[8] Despite the fact that they "disagreed on everything," the younger Cameron loved his father and claimed that he was not a racist.[9] This assertion, in the context of the times, is not implausible. Upon Judge Cameron's appointment to the Fifth Circuit Court, President Eisenhower remarked that the judge had been given "the endorsement of the NAACP."[10]

During the summer of 1962, at a critical point in the Meredith case, the younger Cameron attended a meeting in Atlanta with Fisk University president Stephen Wright and Benjamin Mays, the distinguished president of Morehouse College. While waiting to cross a street, the three men simultaneously spotted a headline on the front page of the *Atlanta Journal:* "Cameron Again Denies Admission." A perplexed Wright remarked that he simply couldn't believe that his liberal friend Ben Cameron was Judge Cameron's son, and a resigned Cameron could only be amused at Wright's disbelief.[11]

The disagreement between father and son on the subject of desegregation became known in a very public way when stories about each appeared simultaneously on the front page of the *New Orleans Times-Picayune.* The two stories revealed that Ben Cameron had ruled against a recent desegregation effort *and* that Ben Cameron was in New Orleans giving a speech promoting school desegregation. Upon discovering this juxtaposition of two Ben Camerons and their conflicting views on desegregation, the judge wrote to his son, requesting that he call himself Ben F. Cameron Jr. in the future. The judge enclosed a signed, blank check to cover the cost of revised calling cards and stationery. Ben Cameron Jr. did as his father requested. Their social and political disagreements troubled both men, and it is to the credit of each that they worked to keep those disagreements from fraying family ties.[12]

In early December Cameron and Richard Pearson of the College Board discussed Evans's suggestion of pursuing nonmilitary federal facilities through the Department of Health, Education, and Welfare. Pearson believed that instead they should stick to their idea of military bases, and Cameron agreed. The two determined that they would travel to Washington as soon as possible to make their case to Evans and any other Department of Defense officials whom Evans might suggest.[13]

Meanwhile, the College Board trustees met at Tulane University on December 13 and 14, 1962, and passed, word for word, the two resolutions of the Special Committee on Examining Center Policy, as Cameron's committee had come to be called—the internal policy that disallowed segregation on the basis of race, color, or national origin, and the four-part directive to the staff.[14] Cameron's report to the trustees included his estimate that by charging his staff with the desegregation plan, the trustees were committing the Southern Regional Office to allocate one-fourth to one-third of its energies over the next two years to the desegregation efforts. For the first time, Cameron proposed a schedule and a budget for the desegregation project, telling the trustees that after an initial two-year effort, another three to five years would be required to reach the goal of all centers being desegregated. "Substantial" desegregation of testing centers would be accomplished by 1965. In making this commitment, Cameron stated that he was "completely conscious of the amount of work involved." "But," he continued, "I am convinced that it is both worthwhile and necessary." Cameron estimated that the total direct cost of desegregating the test centers would approach $100,000, a considerable sum. With finances in mind, he reminded the trustees that the success of the College Board's ongoing negotiations for use of the SAT by the service academies depended upon assurances that the tests would be offered only at desegregated centers.[15]

Cameron announced an addition to his staff. Ben W. Gibson Jr., originally hired as a temporary consultant in 1961, recently had accepted Cameron's offer of a full-time position with the Southern Regional Office. One of the many positive things Cameron had to say about Gibson was, "As a native Southerner, Mr. Gibson will be of special assistance in our negotiations for the desegregation of testing centers." Ben Cameron could not have chosen a better partner.[16]

A few weeks after the December 1962 trustees meeting, Ben Gibson shared with Ben Cameron his thoughts about how best to establish new centers in the hard core states, with special attention to the use of military bases. It was imperative, according to Gibson, that the College Board gain direct authorization from officials in Washington before approaching individual base commanders. Gibson feared that if a base commander, acting without direct authority from the Department of Defense, should open a test center, complaints from the local community's "segregation leaders" would eventually reach that community's congressman, who would object strongly and publicly. Gibson believed that "a messy situation" would develop, in turn jeopardizing the use of any military base in the South. Gibson also raised the possibility of establishing test sites in Catholic and Episcopal schools since their governance structures allowed them the flexibility to be more liberal than the public school systems.[17]

Cameron and Richard Pearson arranged to meet with James Evans and his colleague Stephen S. Jackson, a special assistant to the assistant secretary of defense for manpower, in Washington, D.C., on January 16, 1963. Bypassing Evans's suggestions about the Office of Education, Cameron stated in a letter to Evans that the purpose of the meeting would be "to discuss with you, and possibly Judge Jackson, ways in which we might enlist the assistance of the Department of Defense in implementing our policy of non-segregation in our testing centers." Cameron reminded Evans that all three service academies held memberships on the College Board and that this fact might "give our request added weight." Cameron enclosed a copy of the College Board's newly approved policy statement on test centers.[18]

Cameron and Pearson's meeting at the Pentagon lasted most of the day. Talking first with Evans and then with Jackson, the two men "received sympathetic attention," and departed with an agreement that they would formalize in writing their request for the use of military bases as test centers. Wasting no time, Cameron and Pearson drafted the request on their return trip, by train, to New York. Pearson immediately informed his superiors, College Board president Frank Bowles and vice president George Hanford, about the meeting and reminded them that if military bases were to be used during the current year, the College Board would have to move quickly.[19]

Evans reported on the meeting to Stephen Wright, remarking that the trustees' decision to move against racial segregation was "reassuring." He reminded Wright of the dismal situation with regard to the small number of black youths who were able to gain admission to the service academies (one-third of 1 percent). Even though test center desegregation would not alter that grim situation, Evans was pleased. For him, the trustees' action represented "the removal of one more barrier to equal opportunity." Coming from someone with Evans's experience, that was praise indeed. Evans also gave Wright his personal assessment of Ben Cameron. First, tactfully noting that Cameron had a "strong and proud family background in Mississippi," Evans remarked that Cameron had shared with him his experiences in a segregated navy during his service on Okinawa during World War II. In Evans's view, Cameron's subsequent observations of an integrated military had "contributed to his strong conviction in the direction of equality of educational opportunity." The successful integration of the military, Evans added, had facilitated the extension of equal opportunity to civilian organizations.[20]

The College Board's official request to the Department of Defense was communicated in a letter to Norman S. Paul, assistant secretary of defense, from College Board president Frank Bowles. The College Board asked that military facilities be made available, in the United States and abroad, under three circumstances or conditions:

1. When satisfactory civilian facilities are not accessible;
2. Where military facilities can adequately accommodate such testing centers, and arrangements for their use may be agreed upon with local commanding officers, upon request from the College Entrance Examination Board, or the Educational Testing Service, acting upon its behalf;
3. It is established policy to use local teachers and other civilian personnel for the administration of College Board examinations. Continuation of this policy is contemplated in this request.[21]

Cameron and Pearson supplied supporting information about the College Board, emphasizing its ongoing relationship with the military. Not only did the College Board test more than 17,000 young men annually for admission to the service academies, but it also held memberships on various boards and panels related to the service academies. In addition, service academy officials had served as College Board trustees and committee members. Next, Cameron and Pearson emphasized that the

Bureau of Naval Personnel was considering using College Board tests to help it select candidates for the Navy ROTC program and would require desegregated test centers. A final point was that military facilities had been used as test centers in the past and, in fact, were being used currently as a matter of convenience for applicants to the service academies and members of the armed forces or their dependents and as a service to local communities, primarily through the use of reserve armories.[22]

Should the Department of Defense agree to provide test facilities on bases, Cameron and Pearson suggested that they consider two options. The first stipulated that a policy regarding the use of military facilities as test centers be established "as being in the national interest," and that this policy be published in order that College Board and ETS representatives could refer to it in their discussions with commanding officers. The second option, and the one chosen, eliminated the publication of the policy and outlined a plan for notifying by letter the commanding officers of a specific list of twenty-six military bases located in the five hard core states. The individual letters would inform the commanding officers of the policy directly and ask for their cooperation in establishing centers.[23]

The Department of Defense moved with surprising speed. Stephen Jackson met with George Hanford at the College Board's New York offices on January 28, 1963, just twelve days after his meeting with Cameron and Pearson at the Pentagon, to confirm the plan. Only a few additional details were required before it could unfold, and Cameron was asked to provide those—the schedule of test dates for 1963–64, the normal hours of administration, and the number of candidates, number of centers, and maximum number of candidates tested by state at any administration during the previous year.[24]

Only one week later, on February 4, Assistant Secretary of Defense Norman S. Paul issued a memorandum to the undersecretaries of the army, navy, and air force about using bases as test centers. Paul, acting on Cameron and Pearson's suggestion, wrote that it was "in the national interest" for the Defense Department to work with the College Board in providing desegregated testing facilities "immediately." Stephen Jackson wrote to Bowles a few days later to say that the commanding officers of the twenty-six bases in the five states were being notified about the policy and the likelihood of their being contacted soon by College Board representatives.[25]

On March 11, Cameron sent a letter to the twenty-six base commanders, enclosing a copy of Stephen Jackson's letter to Frank Bowles. He advised each commander that should the College Board fail in its ongoing efforts to desegregate centers near his base a representative of the College Board might be contacting him. Cameron indicated that the situation was complicated by the fact that he needed a list of centers by April 1, if at all possible. ETS was pressing Cameron for center location information in order to meet their April 8 bulletin publication deadline.[26]

The next day, March 12, Jim Buford, a member of Cameron's staff whose usual assignment was supporting the work of colleges and universities, called on Colonel Frank Elliott, wing commander at Barksdale Air Force Base in Shreveport, Louisiana. If the pace of school desegregation was slow in New Orleans, it was "glacial" in Shreveport, according to historian Adam Fairclough. He writes, "The *Brown* decision marked the beginning of a relentless campaign by Shreveport's ultrasegregationists to silence the heresy of interracialism." A lawsuit to desegregate Shreveport's schools would be filed in 1965. Two years later, only a handful of black students were enrolled at white schools, and a protracted series of efforts and counter efforts lasted for years. At the core of white supremacist sentiments in Shreveport was its White Citizens' Council.[27]

Founded in Mississippi in 1954, and self-described in a promotional pamphlet as "the modern version of the old-time town meeting called to meet any crisis by expressing the will of the people," the Citizens' Council movement attempted to put a respectable face on racism. Espousing nonviolence but using nearly every other conceivable method of coercion and intimidation, this regional organization presented itself as a "responsible" alternative to the Ku Klux Klan. Taking up the cry of "racial purity," the membership exploited segregationists' fears of intermarriage and the unthinkable—a black man and a white woman engaged in a sexual relationship, resulting in the "mongrelization" of humanity. In fact, Robert Patterson, the movement's founder, was allegedly prepared to sacrifice his life "to prevent mongrelization." It followed that maintaining segregated schools would be a key tenet of the organization. One Alabama Council member proclaimed that "Desegregating the schools will lead to rape!" While the influence and growth of the regional Citizens' Council movement peaked in 1956, its membership, which frequently included prominent business and civic leaders, still wielded considerable power in many areas of the South, including Shreveport.[28]

At Barksdale Air Force Base, Colonel Elliott and his staff welcomed Jim Buford and agreed to open a center. Cameron had hoped that either Centenary College or Byrd High School, both in Shreveport, would be willing to operate a desegregated center, but Buford's efforts with each had been unsuccessful. Centenary College, Louisiana's only independent liberal arts college, had operated a desegregated LSAT center in the past but balked at doing the same for the SAT. While Centenary president Joe J. Mickle and admissions director J. Howard Allen supported the idea of a desegregated center—Allen told Buford that he was sure that the faculty and students "would not react against the idea"—some members of the college's governing board were current or former members of the White Citizens' Council and had previously targeted Centenary College faculty thought to be racially liberal. According to Allen, the board "would certainly overrule him as soon as they learned of Negro candidates being accepted for testing." Allen's disclosure appears to be the first instance of the Southern Regional Office learning that their desegregation efforts might involve a confrontation with members of the White Citizens' Council.[29]

The influence of the White Citizens' Council was also a factor in the decision by J. H. Duncan, principal of Byrd High School, Shreveport, not to desegregate his test center. Duncan wanted to continue his practice of sending any black test candidates who appeared at his school to Booker T. Washington High School, a black school in that city. In his meeting with Jim Buford, Duncan rated the local situation with regard to desegregation "pretty bad." A "strong" White Citizens' Council was "very active" in Shreveport and could cause difficulties for the board of education if they allowed Duncan to desegregate the center at Byrd High. Duncan believed that his students would not "react negatively" to black students being tested with them, should the College Board procure a desegregated center at another location. Mrs. Raines, a counselor at Byrd and the school's test center supervisor, agreed to continue in that capacity if Buford could find another location and unless the school superintendent objected. He did. Another white school in Shreveport, Fair Park High, had housed a center for the first time during the December 1962 test administration. Fair Park's principal stated that he would not be able to operate a desegregated center; that, as a result, he realized he would unfortunately lose his center; and that opening a center at the Barksdale Air Force Base would be a satisfactory solution to the problem in Shreveport.[30]

On March 14, three days after Cameron wrote his letters to the base commanders, Ben Gibson set out to visit five of the nine military bases in Georgia. Gibson's first stop was Savannah, one of Georgia's most troublesome cities with regard to test centers due to both the large numbers of test candidates in the area and the total lack of progress on school desegregation. Gibson called on Hunter Air Force Base and Fort Stewart, where he was warmly greeted despite having arrived ahead of the letters of introduction from the Department of Defense and Cameron. At both bases, Gibson and the commanding officers discussed local segregation problems, which Gibson learned were the cause of serious personnel problems among servicemen. While integration was official armed forces policy, points of tension existed where the lives of black servicemen touched civilian life off-base. Military historian Morris J. MacGregor writes, "Black servicemen often found the short bus ride from post to town a trip into the past, where once again they were forced to endure the old patterns of segregation." As James Evans would have confirmed from his experience in reviewing complaints from black servicemen, two of the most problematic points of contact were off-base housing and public schools. Complaints from black servicemen, who generally had little control over their assignment locations, eventually spurred President John F. Kennedy, in 1962, to establish the President's Committee on Equal Opportunity in the Armed Forces. The committee set out "to improve equality of opportunity for members of the Armed Forces and their dependents in the civilian community, particularly with respect to housing, education, transportation, recreational facilities, community events, programs and activities."[31]

The president's committee, also known as the Gesell Committee after its chair, attorney Gerhard Gesell, soon discovered that in many parts of the United States, not only in the South, black servicemen and their families were often forced to live in areas relegated to blacks and that combined outrageous expense with terrible, unsanitary living conditions. Perhaps even worse, servicemen's children often had no choice but to attend black schools that were nearly always inferior to the white schools in the same town or city. Of course, servicemen from outside the South often found even the white schools inferior. Resigned to the fact that desegregated schools in Alabama, Georgia, Mississippi, and South Carolina would not be a reality in the near term, the federal government had determined that building on-base schools in those states was the only viable solution. The Gesell Committee reported: "To all Negroes these community conditions are a constant reminder that the society they are prepared to defend is a society that deprecates their right to full participation as citizens." There was no question in the minds of committee members that these conditions had a strong, negative impact on the morale of black servicemen. President Kennedy forwarded their report to Secretary of Defense Robert McNamara, who asked military base commanders in fifteen southern states to encourage the desegregation of schools in their areas. This was a well-intentioned but naïve request. According to Reed Sarratt of the Southern Education Reporting Service (SERS), "Such efforts as were made succeeded mainly in stirring the ire of southerners in and out of Congress" and strengthening their resistance to desegregation. At the time of Gibson's visits to military bases in 1963, Secretary McNamara was preparing to announce that he not only supported putting an end to discriminatory, off-base practices, including segregated schools, but also that he would support sanctions against communities that discriminated against blacks. Under McNamara's guidelines, any public community facility that discriminated against black military personnel would be classified as off-limits to all servicemen and their families, regardless of race. With southern congressmen and senators crying "economic blackmail," McNamara's idea was delayed and not actually implemented until 1967; however, the concept had been discussed well ahead of its publication, and many base commanders (and probably many community leaders) would have been aware of its threat in the spring of 1963.[32]

Colonel Daugherty, the commanding officer at Hunter Air Force Base near Savannah, was especially sympathetic, as he and Gibson were both well acquainted with the principal of Savannah High School, Howard F. Moseley. Since beginning his work for the College Board, Gibson had found nearly all test administrators, principals, and superintendents in Georgia schools to be welcoming and polite, and many had expressed their desire to cooperate with the College Board, even when faced with boards of education and/or communities unsympathetic to desegregation. Moseley proved to be a remarkable exception. Gibson first visited Savannah High School on September 22, 1961, a short time after taking the temporary consultant position with the College Board. In his meeting with the school's assistant principal and test administrator, Martha Coleman, he learned that she was willing to test black students who were assigned to Savannah High. Then Principal Moseley joined the conversation, and, according to Gibson, upon hearing Coleman agree that she would test black students at Savannah High, "he [Moseley] did not go up in smoke, but in flames." Responding to Coleman's statement, Moseley exclaimed, "No! Positively no! Not in this school!" and then "with great arrogance, really lectured me [Gibson]." In his tirade, Moseley ticked off his points about what should be done with regard to testing: ETS should determine the race of candidates (the implication being that segregated testing could then easily be implemented); Georgia should engage a testing agency that would provide segregated centers (meaning ACT); if a black student should appear at his high school he would evict him—"If he didn't leave, I'd call the cops. They'd handle him."[33]

Moseley grudgingly conceded that his high school would probably have to integrate soon, perhaps even by the following fall, 1962. A biracial community group supporting desegregation had been in negotiations with the board of education. But even after that event occurred, Moseley emphatically stated, he would not allow the testing of black students at his school. Presumably, Mosley meant black students attending other high schools. Gibson remained calm throughout his one-hour meeting with Moseley. The strategy that Cameron had outlined for Gibson and other Southern Regional Office staff members meeting with school officials for the purpose of discussing desegregated centers was to arrive at a school or college unannounced, to locate the test center supervisor, to bring up the need for desegregating the center, and to "help him talk through his problem." Under no circumstance was the College Board representative to become offended, even if offensive remarks were made about the College Board, the trustees, or the representative himself. Each College Board representative was instructed not to leave the school until he had restored the good humor of the official, who might have become "hostile or resentful." Commenting on this strategy in a summary report for the trustees, Cameron referred to it as "a quiet crusade of persuasion" and recalled that "It took a little better than two hours of listenin' and talkin' to get one official 'in a good humor.'" Either by following Cameron's strategy or by relying on his own wisdom, Gibson was determined to leave Savannah High School only after Moseley had calmed down. Gibson turned the conversation to other matters, and, once Moseley learned that Gibson was from Atlanta, and not a "Yankee," "Moseley felt some better towards me."[34]

In November 1961, weeks after Atlanta schools began their slow process of enrolling black students, Gibson had written to Cameron about his time on the highways and byways of Georgia, driving from school to school to learn about testing conditions for black students, "tipping his hat to every fiftieth pine tree" on the lonely back roads of southeast Georgia. He reported that most of the school officials he had met were willing to "face up to" the fact that desegregation was coming to Georgia schools. Furthermore, they respected the College Board, its examinations, and its other programs. By singling out Savannah High and Moseley in his 1961 report, Gibson underscored how difficult that meeting had been, even though the two men had parted on fairly good terms. For Moseley, learning that Gibson was from Georgia had seemed to be a "sweetening" factor, and Gibson predicted that in the future he would "drawl and drop my 'g's' more than normal" in his dealings with Moseley and other difficult officials. One hundred years after the Civil War, Yankees and organizations and ideas perceived as being "Yankee" still remained unpopular with many southerners.[35]

The testing situation at Savannah High School was a classic example of the massive resistance to mandated school desegregation. Until the prior 1960–61 school year, black candidates had been tested at the school without any known incident. Perhaps at that time Moseley was not yet the school's principal, or perhaps the center supervisor did not disclose this practice. Gibson, in filing his report to Cameron on his meeting with Moseley in 1961, had reasoned that there was "No point in closing [the center at] Savannah High because Moseley is arrogant, but because his arrogance could be troublesome." Gibson feared that if the College Board closed the Savannah High School center, the board of education would retaliate by closing centers at the other high schools in the district, including the black high school, thereby creating a situation that would make it difficult for any Savannah area student to be tested locally.[36]

Gibson did not visit Moseley during his trip to the two bases near Savannah in March 1963, but it is very likely that he had in mind the possibility of closing the Savannah High School center while meeting with military base officials. Gibson next headed for Albany to call on the commanding officer at Turner Air Force Base, part of the Strategic Air Command. The base gate sentry was skeptical about Gibson's mission, but once Gibson showed him a copy of Stephen Jackson's letter, typed on Department of Defense letterhead and with a return address announcing Jackson's position as special assistant to the assistant secretary of defense, "he [the sentry] became greatly impressed and agitated." The sentry had cast Gibson as a high-level official from the Department of Defense, and Gibson was very well treated when he arrived at the base commander's office. Gibson enjoyed this mistake for a few minutes, experiencing a "flurry of welcome." After he corrected the sentry's error, he was introduced to the base personnel director who explained what it would mean actually to use a strategic air base as a test center. First, should an emergency arise (the October 1962 Cuban missile crisis was offered as an example), it would become impossible for civilians to be allowed on base.

The same would be true during a practice drill. Second, the base's planes routinely flew on Saturdays, when College Board exams were scheduled, and, as Gibson, himself a former naval aviator, ruefully noted, "a jet bomber taking off does not enable serenity to flourish." Aside from those two not insignificant concerns, the base officials agreed that they could accommodate a test center.[37]

Gibson visited Albany High School that same day, March 18, 1963. For months Albany had been the focal point of a struggle among several civil rights organizations, contributing to NAACP executive director Roy Wilkins's concluding that 1962 was "perhaps the lowest moment for the civil rights movement during the Kennedy years."[38] In 1961, the Student Non-Violent Coordinating Committee (SNCC), a group of young civil rights activists with initiatives in the segregated southern states, established the Albany Movement as a natural outgrowth of their Southwest Georgia Project, which had originally focused on civil rights in rural counties. Recognizing the importance of Albany politics in the region, and taking advantage of volunteers it recruited from the student body at black Albany State College, the Albany Movement made several demands on the city's leaders, including fair employment and the desegregation of public transportation. SNCC organized large demonstrations in support of their demands. These attracted the attention of Martin Luther King Jr., who traveled to Albany in December 1961 to lend his support, and his involvement there resulted in his being jailed. Subsequently, the Albany Movement collapsed, but it is credited with providing the Southern Christian Leadership Conference (SCLC), led by King, with a new sense of purpose and some key lessons in organization and planning. Unfortunately, Albany's citizens were left with a community that was more divided than ever.[39]

Of his visit to Albany High School, Gibson reported that "Until all the trouble, fomented internally by James Gray, editor of the *Albany Herald*, and externally by Martin Luther King, Jr., McNabb [Albany High principal] tested Negroes and whites in the same room . . . for two or three years with no opposition." According to McNabb, following "the trouble," the community had "raised 'hell'" because he had tested black and white students together. The board of education, reacting to community pressure, ordered McNabb to stop desegregated testing and send black test candidates to the board of education building for testing. Once Albany State, a public black college, became a test center in December 1961, black candidates routinely took the College Board exams there.[40]

Gibson learned from McNabb that prior to what he called "NAACP pressure and [its] resulting turmoil," the board of education, along with a racially mixed community group, had entered negotiations that were to result in the integration of Albany's public schools. These negotiations had since been suspended. From information he received during his visit, Gibson determined that "the big stumbling block in Albany is James Gray, editor of the *Albany Herald*." White leaders were now afraid to negotiate with the local black leaders because of their fear of the "editorial hatchet" wielded by Gray. Principal McNabb indicated that Albany's black leaders were holding back on pursuing integrated schools only until the community had a "respite from all outside agitation." Gibson strongly recommended that the Southern Regional Office give Albany some time in terms of establishing a desegregated center, stating, "If we close the center in Albany, I think we will open up old and deep wounds and really help no one."[41]

Within three weeks of Gibson's visit, a suit was filed in U.S. District Court, requesting that all public schools in Dougherty County (including Albany) become racially integrated. Two of the suit's plaintiffs were the children of William G. Anderson, president of the Albany Movement. Those filing the suit requested that the defendants be required to develop a desegregation plan, rather than have such a plan dictated by the court.[42] Referring to the fact that the school board would be able to craft its own school desegregation plan, Gibson forwarded to Cameron a clipping from the *Atlanta Constitution* about the suit with this note, "The alternative described in the above news item implies that Principal McNabb was correct in saying that all Albany needed was a period of quiet in order to negotiate some of its racial problems. Let's not close Albany center for any reason while a plan to desegregate schools is being worked out." On March 18 Gibson also visited Fort Benning, located near Columbus, Georgia, where he was made welcome and was assured that providing a testing center there would be possible.[43]

On March 21, Gibson interrupted his tour of Georgia military bases to call on Maxwell Air Force Base near Montgomery, Alabama. James Buford, the member of Cameron's staff who had visited Shreveport, Louisiana, had been assigned the duty of visiting two other Alabama bases, Fort McClellan and Fort Rucker, later that month. But because Gibson had already traveled to Maxwell in January and had established contact with Dr. James C. Shelburne, director of the Air University, and Dr. Kenneth Groves, director of evaluation, he was the likely person to make the trip to Montgomery. Gibson's purpose in his earlier visit had been to learn more about the air force officer training program and how College Board programs might be useful to it, and to learn how the base's leaders might respond to a request to use one of their facilities as a test center. Shelburne and Groves had been enthusiastic about cooperating with the College Board in providing a desegregated center. Shelburne was, in his own words, possibly "too enthusiastic" about the prospect of hosting a desegregated test center. Fed up with the racial turmoil in Montgomery, he told Gibson that he would like having the center at the base "for no other reason than to discomfit the stupid authorities in Montgomery."[44]

When Gibson returned to Maxwell Air Force Base on March 21, he presented to the sentry a copy of Stephen Jackson's letter to Frank Bowles as a means of identification. At Turner Air Force Base in Georgia, Gibson had enjoyed being mistaken for an upper-level official from the Pentagon; at Maxwell, he was amused to be introduced as "president of the College Board." Air University director Shelburne took up where he had left off in January, telling Gibson that the Montgomery center should in fact be relocated to Maxwell—that "somebody needs to do something positive [about desegregation] in Montgomery." Shelburne asked if Gibson had exhausted his efforts with Montgomery school officials, with Huntingdon College, and with the Catholic high school, and Gibson assured him that he had. While public schools in Birmingham, Huntsville, Mobile, and Macon County were moving, under court order, toward desegregation that fall, Montgomery lagged behind by one year. Shelburne then turned Gibson over to Groves, the university's evaluation director, to make the necessary arrangements. Before leaving Montgomery, Gibson telephoned Walter McKee, the superintendent of Montgomery schools, to advise him about his visit to Maxwell Air Force Base. McKee responded by saying that if it was necessary to move the center he was glad that it would be located at Maxwell. Gibson assured McKee that the only problem the College Board had with the Montgomery center was that it could not test on a desegregated basis and that they would be making a decision about moving the center shortly.[45]

James Buford visited the Redstone Arsenal in Huntsville, Alabama, on March 27 and Fort McClellan and Fort Rucker on the next day. His visits went smoothly, and Cameron must have been pleased at the responses Gibson and Buford had gotten so far. Selma schools remained segregated, and the Selma center was one that Cameron knew would have to be dealt with, but he put off sending a staff member to nearby Craig Air Force Base until later. No record can be found of a visit to Breckley Air Force Base, also in Alabama, even though it had been one of the bases suggested by the Department of Defense.[46]

On March 27, Gibson summarized the test center situation in Georgia. He analyzed the testing needs of each area of the state in terms of the anticipated number of test candidates at each center and was disappointed to see that the seating capacity offered by military bases in key areas was not sufficient to allow the Southern Regional Office to close centers that would not operate under desegregated conditions. As a result, his "tentative" advice to Cameron was that they not disturb the testing situation in Georgia. Gibson believed that they should continue the dual test center system in Georgia until more of its school systems desegregated. He also pointed out that they needed to continue to call on University System of Georgia colleges and universities for the purpose of learning if they were in fact following Chancellor Caldwell's directive to operate test centers on a desegregated basis. If so, some centers that wouldn't desegregate could be moved to those locations. Gibson was particularly concerned about the College Board's ability to test all candidates in the Columbus, Macon, and Savannah areas in December 1963, due to the anticipated heavy volume.[47]

Determined to meet the ETS April 8 publication deadline, Gibson resumed his visits to Georgia bases and on April 2 met with officials at Robins Air Force Base near Macon, where he was pleased to learn that he could count on their cooperation. Robins had adequate facilities for a center and might be needed in the future since Macon's size and central location made it a critical site for testing. On April 4, Gibson returned to Hunter Air Force Base in Savannah to meet with new base commander, Lieutenant Colonel J. R. Caferella. Again, Gibson's visit went well.[48]

On April 11, Cameron, agreeing with Gibson that they should leave the centers in Georgia alone for the present, but wanting to preserve the option of using military facilities in the state, wrote the commanding officers of all Georgia bases. To those Gibson had visited, he expressed his appreciation for offers of cooperation and stated that testing problems in their areas did not "warrant our calling on you immediately for facilities." To those base commanders whom Gibson had not visited, he explained that "At the present time the problem of desegregated testing is not acute in [your] area," but that if conditions changed, he would advise them and send a representative to their bases.[49]

Having so far dodged altogether any publicity about efforts to desegregate test centers, Cameron was probably chagrined a few days later when he read an article published in the April 10, 1963, edition of *Air Force Times*, forwarded to him by a friend. The headline announced "Services to Offer Facilities for College Tests in South," and the article accurately reported the College Board's new testing policy and the Defense Department's willingness to make base facilities available in southern communities where integrated testing was impossible. It even listed the specific air force bases that were standing by to help. A similar article appeared at about the same time in the *Army Times*. Fortunately for Cameron, his staff, and the numerous school and military base officials who were doing their best to cooperate quietly with them, civilian newspapers did not pick up the story. Cameron's view on publicity remained firm. In addition to his fear of exposing cooperative officials to ridicule, Cameron's distaste for boasting contributed to his position. Any public "protestations of righteousness" about their position on desegregation were, in his opinion, "likely to be self-defeating."[50]

Gibson, having finished his rounds of visits to military bases in Alabama and Georgia, headed to Mississippi, where he called on the commanding officers at air force bases in Biloxi, Columbus, and Greenville.

Consistent with his earlier experiences, the commanding officer at Keesler Air Force Base, Biloxi, with whom Gibson met on April 16, had no prior knowledge of the Department of Defense authorization. Still, he assured Gibson that the College Board would be able to establish a center at the base, although the capacity for the numbers that could be tested was not what Gibson had hoped it might be.[51]

On April 17, Gibson arrived at Columbus Air Force Base, Columbus, Mississippi. Unlike other base commanders Gibson had visited, Lieutenant Colonel Robert T. Larkin was well prepared, anticipating a meeting with a College Board representative. Larkin sympathized with Gibson's cause, apologized for the small size of his classrooms, and "extended with pleasure" the base's facilities, explaining that he realized that "You fellows must really be up against a stone wall in Mississippi." Larkin's assessment was correct. When the 1963–64 academic year began that fall, only the state of Mississippi would maintain its totally segregated public school system.[52]

The next day, April 18, Gibson met with Colonel N. H. Roberdeau, commanding officer at Greenville Air Force Base, Greenville, Mississippi, who also extended his full cooperation. He then showed Gibson a copy of the *Air Force Times* article, which Gibson had not been aware of until that moment. Roberdeau was understandably concerned about publicity, confiding in Gibson that the mayor and other Greenville politicians would look into the test center matter once they learned the center had been moved to his base. Gibson assured the colonel that the College Board had no plans to publicize the center. Roberdeau also asked that Gibson confirm the outcome of the final negotiations for a desegregated center in the Greenville schools prior to establishing the center at the base. He predicted that Gibson's request would be denied. Roberdeau enjoyed good relations with many Greenville leaders and believed that if he did receive complaints from the community he would be able to handle any "discussion" quietly. Following his meeting with Roberdeau, Gibson telephoned W. G. Thompson, assistant superintendent of the Greenville public schools, who assured Gibson that the only way to test black students in Greenville was to have centers at both the white and black high schools. This would involve opening a new, segregated center at the black high school, and

Thompson volunteered to call the principal there. However, Gibson explained to Thompson that the College Board, in keeping with its policy and procedures, would not do that. Instead, the College Board would move the center to Greenville Air Force Base. Thompson acknowledged that the tests could certainly be given on a desegregated basis there.[53]

Because of a complex situation with regard to testing in Jackson, Mississippi, high schools, Gibson and Cameron had decided that it would be best to use Millsaps College, a private, Methodist college, as a test center and had received permission to do so from the president of Millsaps, H. E. Finger Jr. Believing that the testing situation was under control in Jackson, Gibson did not visit any military facilities in that area during his April 1963 trip to Mississippi. Because of increasing racial tensions, circumstances in Jackson would deteriorate in only a few months, upsetting Southern Regional Office plans for the December 7, 1963, administration of the SAT in that city.[54]

Cameron had agreed to research the possibility of testing at military bases in South Carolina, but there is no evidence that he visited the bases in person with the exception of the marine corps base at Parris Island. Cameron's schedule had become increasingly challenging, both professionally and personally. He was traveling a great deal for the College Board, and, when he was at home in Sewanee, Tennessee, his time was increasingly taken up with a desegregation matter taking place literally at his doorstep. Cameron and his wife were then the parents of two school-aged children who attended public school in the local, segregated school district. Cameron presided over a biracial civic group whose aim was to pressure leaders of the town of Sewanee to integrate its schools, but whose efforts had been unsuccessful.[55]

Due to constraints on his time, Cameron's communication with military base officials in South Carolina, where not one public school had desegregated, took the form of letters and telephone calls instead of personal visits. However, he did personally call on officials at many of the centers in South Carolina schools during March and April 1963, driving around the state in a rental car for more than three weeks before returning home. South Carolina had followed Georgia's lead in requiring the SAT for applicants to its state institutions, which meant that the volume of candidates to be tested was substantial. Cameron sought help from an acquaintance, President Robert C. Edwards of Clemson College (later Clemson University), who, in January 1963, had desegregated his institution by admitting its first black student, Harvey Gantt, under federal court order. According to Cameron, Edwards hadn't wanted to be forced to desegregate Clemson College, but, once the court ruled, he was determined that Gantt's enrollment be handled peacefully. Beginning in 1961, Edwards and other state leaders, particularly businessmen, had quietly laid the foundation for racial change. Edwards himself had worked closely with the Greenville community and other areas near Clemson, calling on business leaders and civic groups to support the college's desegregation. Those who had expected at Clemson the violence of the University of Mississippi were disappointed.[56]

The level of cooperation South Carolina officials extended to Ben Cameron was unmatched by the remaining four hard core states, and Clemson University president Robert Edwards was the key. In encouraging Edwards's support for desegregated test centers, Cameron fully exploited the prestige of the members of his Special Committee on Establishing Center Policy, including their names and professional titles, in a letter to Edwards. Favorably impressed, Edwards then promoted the idea of desegregated testing at a meeting of South Carolina's public college and university presidents. He also introduced Cameron to the president of the state Chamber of Commerce and other business leaders who agreed to speak to school board superintendents on behalf of desegregating the centers. Finally, Edwards approached Governor Donald S. Russell about Cameron's plan, and the governor quickly gave his endorsement.[57]

Reactions among South Carolina school officials to the idea of center desegregation varied. The superintendent in Spartanburg was supportive, offering to work with his colleagues around the state. The Columbia superintendent hesitated at first, but agreed in the end to cooperate only because the Spartanburg district had desegregated its centers, a clear example of the influence school officials had on each other. The Sumter school system superintendent, L. Currie McArthur, proved to be one of the most challenging to convert. Cameron and McArthur spent an entire day arguing face to face with no agreement in sight. Then, once Cameron returned to Sewanee, the superintendent, adamantly wanting to keep his center, called him almost daily for two weeks trying to convince Cameron to allow their center to remain segregated by offering options that did not satisfy Cameron. Superintendent McArthur's objections continued for months. At one point in his correspondence with Cameron, McArthur included the following inflammatory paragraph in a draft of a memorandum he threatened to send to his board of education, even while acknowledging that the board should comply with the College Board policy:

> The Board of Trustees of Sumter City Schools would under no circumstances wish to adopt a position indicating any sympathy with forced interjection of alien customs. The act of the College Board in directing its regional representatives to make this requirement of examining centers is arrogant, fatuous, and reprehensible. It is predictable that, even when we make every effort to lessen the consequences on our students of each race, this unjustifiable act will place our students of each race under sufficient stress to have a pernicious effect upon the circumstances under which the students stand the examination.[58]

Cameron stood firm, using his tactic of quiet persuasion, and continued to respond to McArthur's objections with great patience, understanding, and solid information on testing. The threat of moving the center to nearby Shaw Air Force Base, where Gibson had arranged for the December administration of the test, was the strategy that finally defeated McArthur and his board.[59]

At one point in early April, during his difficult negotiations with South Carolina school representatives, Cameron was tempted briefly to depart from the guidelines established by the special committee and consider a temporary solution—offering white students who did not want to be tested in the same room with black students the opportunity to be tested in a segregated environment. This would be accomplished by establishing a "closed" center at a white high school, meaning that the high school would test only its own students. Within a few days of acknowledging that he was considering the idea, he rejected it. He wrote to Clemson's

President Edwards: "We regard this expedient to be very undesirable." If white students absolutely insisted on taking a college admissions-related test in segregated circumstances, they could choose to do so under the established College Board Institutional Testing Program. This arrangement was normally offered as a mechanism for special administrations of College Board examinations on college campuses only for that college's own applicants who for a variety of reasons had not been able to take the test at a regularly scheduled administration.[60]

By early May 1963, Cameron completed his South Carolina "campaign" for desegregated test centers, and for the most part his results were encouraging, with many school officials changing their earlier official positions on desegregation and agreeing to abide by the College Board's policy. One of the several school districts that refused to desegregate its center completely was the Beaufort system, where black students were tested in separate rooms at white Beaufort High School. J. M. Randel, the Beaufort school superintendent, in consultation with his board, asked Cameron to move the center to the Marine Corps Recruit Depot at Parris Island when that alternative was offered. Randel agreed to allow the test supervisor from Beaufort High to continue to function as center supervisor for the new center at Parris Island.[61]

Cameron also closed test centers in several other South Carolina locations, resulting in the loss of prestige to the schools and inconvenience to their students. Among those were centers in Clinton, Conway, Laurens, Newbury, and Winnsboro. The specific situations with regard to desegregation were undoubtedly unique to each school, but Cameron recorded a pattern. Typically, the school principal or superintendent confided that he and his faculty would be willing to desegregate their testing center, but that their governing board and/or community would not. In many communities, boards of education officially voted against the idea, and Cameron's contacts reported those negative outcomes with regret.[62]

During the next several weeks, following visits by Buford, Cameron, and Gibson to military bases, ETS opened a total of eight centers in military facilities, six centers at military bases and two in other military facilities. All were near schools that had originally planned to administer the

College Board examinations in December 1963, but had failed to agree to operate their centers on a desegregated basis. In Alabama, centers were opened at Craig Air Force Base in Selma, following Ben Gibson's visit there in July; at Maxwell Air Force Base, Montgomery; and at Redstone Arsenal, Huntsville, which Gibson also visited in July. In Louisiana, Cameron opened a center at Barksdale Air Force Base, Shreveport, and also arranged to test candidates at Army Reserve Training Centers in Lafayette and Monroe. In Mississippi, centers were opened at the air force bases in Columbus and Greenville. ETS took these new arrangements in stride and enjoyed vicariously Cameron and Gibson's successes. Margaret Van Doren, ETS head for centers and supervisors, wrote a College Board colleague, "We celebrated over the military bases joining our other centers and will happily register late candidates without getting hives over them." Some of the arrangements to move centers were completed after the ETS publication deadline, so in addition to all the other formal procedures involved with opening and closing centers, Harold Crane, operational services division director at ETS, wrote to the principal of each school which had originally been scheduled to test on December 7, but which Cameron had decided to close. Crane informed the principals that the College Board would be using military installations as test sites on December 7, 1963, and that "at least some" candidates from his school would be assigned to a particular base. Candidates would receive maps of the base along with their tickets of admission, and Crane also enclosed maps with his letters to the principals. In this form letter, he made no mention of the reason for the center's being closed. In his personalized letters to each principal, Crane explained that his school's center had been closed because ETS had learned that it would not be able to operate under desegregated conditions and thanked him for his past support. Crane also advised the principals that if conditions changed at some point in the future, he would be happy to re-establish centers in their schools.[63]

Gibson's report on his July 25, 1963, tour of Redstone Arsenal, a U.S. Army Missile Support Command facility in Huntsville, Alabama, illustrates the peculiarities of testing high school students at a military base during the Cold War. The huge base, more than forty thousand acres, had at least three entrances, so it was entirely possible that some students would get lost. Gibson hoped that the map that someone on the base planned to prepare would take care of that problem. It was imperative, Gibson was told, that candidates "cannot, must not, get off the prescribed route on the base." Redstone Arsenal personnel described the base as "very restricted" with "very alert" security officers. Students would sit for the tests in Rocket Auditorium, a venue equipped with four hundred "plush" seats and located immediately next to the Propulsion Laboratory, a highly restricted area "with one narrow entrance manned by two heavily armed guards." Students staying on base after the SAT for the afternoon Achievement Tests would not be able to eat lunch in the base cafeterias because they were closed on Saturdays. Instead, a mobile canteen would be deployed from the PX to Rocket Auditorium. Gibson wrote that base leaders had received an official directive from Third Army Headquarters informing the Army Missile Support Command that it needed to do its best to support the College Board. Impressed by the considerable effort being made to operate a first-class test center, Gibson confided to Cameron that the directive from headquarters must have been "one potent document."[64]

Meanwhile, as a follow-up to the Gesell Report, base commanders in Louisiana—including the commander at Barksdale Air Force Base in Shreveport—under orders from the Pentagon, sent letters to local school districts requesting descriptions of their school desegregation plans. Negative reactions followed. In Washington, Louisiana's congressional delegation denounced the military's involvement in school desegregation as "semi-dictatorship" and "Gestapo." In Shreveport, the American Legion executive committee "unanimously condemned" the Gesell Report as well as the order from the Pentagon for its implementation. As a preemptive strike, upon learning of the request for information, at least one school district official advised the navy that children of personnel based in that community would no longer be allowed to attend local schools.[65]

Having met the immediate challenge of securing centers for the December 7, 1963, test administration, Cameron and his staff directed their attention to other matters, including two issues related to desegregation.

First, Cameron needed to counter a College Board proposal to publicize their desegregation efforts. Second, Cameron and Gibson began preparing for their "march through Georgia," an exercise they hoped would lead ultimately to the elimination of Georgia's dual center system, ending segregated testing in that state.[66]

The March through Georgia and a Setback in Mississippi, 1963–1964

School desegregation came to cities other than Atlanta as Georgia public schools opened their 1963–64 terms early in September. Savannah desegregated under court order and Athens did so voluntarily.

Mississippi public schools opened the fall term still segregated . . . in [some] areas, schools opened in August and will close [temporarily] when cotton picking begins.
—*Southern School News* (September 1963)

In July 1963, George Hanford, vice president and treasurer of the College Board, forwarded to Ben Cameron a memorandum from Charles M. Holloway, director of information services, soliciting ideas about publicizing the College Board's policy on desegregated testing. Having firmly established that their work must be done quietly, Cameron and Gibson must have found Holloway's interference irksome. Holloway wanted the College Board publicly "on the offensive" regarding the civil rights movement. Publicizing their progress in this area would, in his opinion, "put the Board on public record at a critical time." He reminded his colleagues that College Board representation at a recent White House meeting on civil rights highlighted the Board's "immediate involvement" in that area and expressed his support for issuing a public statement that fall.[1]

After discussing Holloway's position with Ben Gibson, Cameron shared his own views with Hanford and Edward Noyes. While he agreed that the ongoing work to desegregate test centers had put the College Board "on the side of the angels," Cameron stood "firmly opposed to any gratuitous public announcement of either our policy or of the desegregation of testing centers we have been able to accomplish." Furthermore, Cameron would remain opposed until the "climate" in the South changed sufficiently to remove from that announcement any "news value."[2]

Cameron had two reasons for disagreeing with Holloway's position. The first was "purely practical." Describing ongoing negotiations for desegregated centers in some communities as being "delicate" and "tenuous," Cameron feared that a public announcement at this time could "easily reverse completely" all that had been achieved and all that he hoped could be achieved by early 1964. Cameron's second reason, he wrote, was "perhaps less compelling" than his first, and more personal: "I object strongly to anyone's extolling his own virtues." Cameron explained he was suspicious of anyone who did so.[3]

Gibson concurred. Many of his contacts in schools, not to mention Colonel N. H. Roberdeau at Greenville Air Force Base in Mississippi, had expressly stated that they wanted no publicity. Gibson had spoken with Noyes and Hanford also and told Cameron that they had given him "the distinct impression that they understood and sanctioned the necessity of quiet negotiations." In making his point about doing their job quietly, Gibson adopted his "good old boy" role and quoted a "grizzled," black hunting companion from Georgia: "White boy, all that yappin' you are a-doin' ain't gonna help them dawgs ter ketch that rabbit a damn bit." Noyes and Hanford squelched Holloway's idea and allowed the Southern Regional Office campaign to remain "quiet" as far as the College Board itself was concerned.[4]

The desegregation of test centers stayed on the minds of those at the very top of the College Board. In March 1963, Frank Bowles, long associated with both the College Board and ETS and now between terms as College Board president, asked Richard Pearson, College Board executive vice president, whether the College Board trustees should solicit help from member schools and colleges, those selected to represent high schools and higher education on the College Board, in providing testing facilities. Pearson then asked Cameron, "Do you know of any cases where either member colleges or member schools have refused to provide desegregated testing facilities?" Cameron did. Although two member colleges had agreed to begin testing candidates under completely desegregated conditions and there were other member colleges in the South that had routinely operated desegregated centers, "quite a few" had refused his requests to establish testing centers on their campuses "because of the possibility of Negro candidates." Two test supervisors who represented their colleges as voting members of the College Board administered tests in two segregated centers located in public high schools. Cameron was in the process of closing one of these centers, unless the local school board allowed the school to change its policy. As for the second school, which as yet had been assigned no black candidates, Cameron was monitoring the situation for further developments.[5]

Cameron reported that the situation in member secondary schools differed from that in member colleges in that there were fewer problems with the latter. He had closed testing centers in two member schools, one that had just been approved for College Board membership, and one that had recently let its membership expire, perhaps due to the desegregation policy. Cameron believed that the first school would probably decline membership now that its center had been closed. He suggested to Pearson that any discussion about establishing a policy specifically directed to member schools should be left to the Special Committee on Examining Center Policy, which he thought would meet within the next several months. Pearson apparently agreed with Cameron. It would be more than two years before the College Board formally addressed this sensitive question.[6]

Frank Bowles also involved himself in the plans for the "march through Georgia," which Cameron and Gibson expected to launch in the fall of 1963. Part of their strategy for success included securing desegregated test facilities at University System of Georgia colleges should their efforts to desegregate secondary school centers fail. The continued support of the system's board of regents was critical, and Cameron expected to approach system chancellor Harmon Caldwell to let him know about his staff's upcoming visits to the presidents of system institutions. At the suggestion of John Hills, director of testing and guidance for the system and a supporter of school desegregation, Cameron asked Bowles to write to Howard H. "Bo" Callaway, one of the system's most influential regents and, coincidentally, Bowles's cousin, to seek his support.[7]

Bowles, who had returned to his role as president of the College Board but had just announced his plans to join the Ford Foundation, wrote to Callaway at once and advised him of the gradual progress the College Board was making in quietly desegregating test centers. Bowles described the College Board policy as nothing more or less than putting the organization "in general compliance with court actions on the matter of integration." Giving the military establishment high marks for its cooperation in providing centers for the upcoming testing year, Bowles saved his highest praise for school administrators and local boards of education willing to abide by the new policy. Bowles attributed the College Board's success to "the fact that we have worked absolutely quietly on this matter, have permitted nothing to come into the papers, and have held firmly to the one principle that students taking the same tests are entitled to the same facilities and treatment." He advised Callaway that Cameron would be contacting him soon. In seeking Howard Callaway's support, Frank Bowles must not have understood the extent to which his cousin supported segregation. Callaway, who had political ambitions, so far had shrewdly avoided being labeled a radical segregationist.[8]

On October 15, Cameron met with Chancellor Harmon Caldwell to inform him of the strengthened College Board policy on desegregated centers. Although the revised policy required no action from the board of regents, which had already agreed two years earlier to cooperate with the College Board on center desegregation, Cameron reminded Caldwell of the policy and told him that during the current school year College Board representatives planned to "call on all testing centers in the state seeking compliance with the policy." Caldwell said he would share that information with the board of regents; he expected no resistance on their part.[9]

Two days later, Cameron met with Howard Callaway at Callaway Gardens, Pine Mountain, Georgia. It is not surprising that Cameron, having considered adding him to the special committee, was disappointed with Callaway's reaction, finding him to be "much less sympathetic" to the College Board's efforts than was his associate, Chancellor Caldwell. "Despite a letter from his cousin, Frank Bowles," Cameron found Callaway "very disturbed" by yet another example of an action to "ram integration down the throats of Georgia." According to Cameron, Callaway predicted that if the College Board continued in this vein, the board of regents would drop its SAT requirement for system institutions, or at least drop it for its black colleges where "they [the SAT exams] do no good anyway." Eliminating the requirement for black colleges would reduce dramatically the numbers of black test candidates, thereby, in Callaway's estimation, eliminating the need for desegregated centers. Callaway's warning was not to be taken lightly. The SAT requirement imposed by the board of regents was responsible for Georgia's large number of test candidates of both races, and losing Georgia as a client would have had a serious financial impact for the Southern Regional Office. Cameron, in keeping with his practice of persistent "listenin' and talkin,'" stayed with Callaway until he had thoroughly explained the College Board's position. At last Callaway agreed that he did not foresee any difficulty arising from the board of regents. In a letter to Chancellor Caldwell, Cameron wrote that he had met with Callaway but did not elaborate further. Cameron also informed the chancellor that as of October 1963, forty-five centers in Georgia (approximately one-fourth of centers in the state) had agreed to operate in accordance with the College Board policy on desegregated testing.[10]

On October 17, while Cameron was meeting with Howard Callaway in Pine Mountain, Georgia, staff members at the ETS campus in Princeton were compiling an official list of centers that had been closed due to noncompliance with the desegregation policy. In Alabama, four centers had been closed; in Louisiana, two. Mississippi and South Carolina each had lost eight centers due to noncompliance with the policy. No center in Georgia was yet listed as having been closed for refusing to comply, but that situation would change soon.[11]

The reliance of the College Board on the dual testing center arrangement in Georgia and the fact that all test centers in the Atlanta area were desegregated had bought Cameron some time in Georgia. Because no black students were being turned away from centers there, Cameron had not been required to intervene on their behalf. The existence of the dual center system had allowed time for the College Board staff, primarily consultants Ben Gibson and L. H. Pitts, to make initial, fact-finding visits to nearly every center in the state. Their visits during the 1961–62 academic year and the good will that had typically resulted from their courteous and helpful conversations laid the foundation for the relationships Cameron and Gibson would rely on in their Georgia campaign during 1963–64.[12]

It is easy to see why Cameron and Gibson referred to their efforts in Georgia in terms of a military exercise. School segregation was their formidable enemy, and they would need a solid strategy to ensure victory. But their situation was far from hopeless. The two men had allies in many schools and colleges; they had prepared a fallback position in Georgia's military bases, should their efforts to secure testing sites in some schools fail; and they had the benefit of their past successes. In planning exactly how he would proceed, Gibson carefully traced a map of the state, dividing it into thirteen sections according to the distances candidates would have to travel to centers offering ample seating capacity and also, in his opinion, capable of operating desegregated centers. (Perhaps in an effort to avoid bad luck, Gibson did not designate any area with the number XIII, instead labeling the Athens area "XII," and skipping to "XIV" for Atlanta.) He then created spread sheets, listing by area each town or city and any schools and colleges that served as test centers, along with the number of candidates tested during the last two years and seating capacity for the upcoming year. One column on the spread sheets provided a space for indicating if a center would have to be closed. For good measure, Gibson included a section for military bases, also listing those by area. Gibson listed a total of 158 schools and colleges where test centers were located in Georgia. Between September 1963 and May 1964 the itinerant Gibson visited nearly all of them at least once.[13]

During the summer of 1963, Cameron decided that in most cases he and Gibson would have to include superintendents and/or boards of education, along with principals, in negotiations for desegregated centers. In at least one instance, a principal had acted without proper authority from his superiors, and this had created difficulties. As a result of this new requirement, Gibson's visits would be extended to allow time to visit both the schools and the board of education offices in each town or city. Ultimately, the objective was to have no segregated centers, black or white, remaining in any of the hard core states by the time the December 1964 tests were administered.[14]

Cameron also decided that the Special Committee on Examining Center Policy would not meet during the fall of 1963, as he had planned. In a letter to Arthur Howe, chair of the committee, Cameron explained that "It seemed rather foolish to convene the group to tell them that, for all practical purposes, our centers are desegregated everywhere except in Georgia." Cameron confidently assured Howe that within a few months he would be able to report that all testing centers would be "open to all candidates for the testing year 1964–65." The committee's official purpose in the future, in Cameron's opinion, would reside in advising Cameron in three areas: the "public attitude" of the College Board regarding center desegregation, the continuation of the committee's existence, and the ongoing "surveillance" of test centers with regard to desegregation. Cameron believed that committee oversight of center surveillance would be required "for some time." Cameron did not mention an unofficial purpose—he would still be able to reference the stature of his committee members in supporting the College Board's policy, as he had done with good results in South Carolina. Howe agreed that the committee need not meet that fall; instead, he and Cameron would plan for a meeting in February 1964, at which time, Cameron projected, his and Gibson's "work in Georgia" would be "completed, or virtually completed." In fact, Cameron's prediction about the Georgia timetable proved too optimistic, and the committee did not meet in February.[15]

Gibson's strategy for scheduling his visits across Georgia is not clear, but records show that, unlike General Sherman, he chose to begin his march in Savannah. Eight Savannah schools and colleges housed test centers, and Savannah High School, led by Principal Howard F. Moseley, had one of the largest seating capacities of any center in the state. Perhaps Gibson wished to allow plenty of time for establishing an alternate center should Moseley fail to cooperate, or perhaps he simply wanted to get his visit with the difficult principal behind him. However that may be, Gibson made Savannah High his first stop, arriving at the school on September 23.[16]

Earlier that month, fifteen black students had desegregated Savannah High School, and when Gibson arrived the atmosphere at the school was still palpably tense. On the first morning of school desegregation, television cameras and a crowd of angry whites greeted the students, shouting "two four six eight we don't want to integrate." Ulysses Bryant, one of the fifteen, later recalled the verbal and physical abuse he and the others suffered throughout that school year, including threats of lynching. Once, Bryant was even attacked and knocked unconscious while at school. Despite the extensive academic preparation and training in nonresistance they had received from the Council on Human Relations and the NAACP, the students were simply unprepared for their openly hostile reception and what followed. Years later, several in the group reflected that they would not have agreed to transfer to Savannah High had they known how difficult their experiences would be. It was obvious to Bryant and his black classmates that Principal Moseley "didn't want us there." Unfortunately, this kind of harsh treatment was not unique to Savannah High School and was exhibited not only by white students and their parents but also by white teachers and administrators in schools throughout the South.[17]

Three plainclothes policemen met Ben Gibson at the Savannah High School entrance, and one of them escorted him to Principal Moseley's office. The conversation between the two men began cordially enough with Moseley explaining that the new black students were not faring well academically. Three had already left the school because they couldn't keep up with the heavy academic workload. These particular students held after-school jobs and would have had to quit them in order to schedule adequate time for study. Moseley shared the black students' test scores and other admissions information with Gibson, who confided in his report to Cameron his own concern about the remaining twelve students' potential for academic success at Savannah High School. Moseley, surely unnecessarily, reminded Gibson that he was a "staunch segregationist," and speculated that schools across the South should have accepted a small number of very qualified black students immediately following the 1954 Supreme Court decision, thereby following the letter if not the spirit of the ruling. Moseley reasoned that if the schools had acted at that time, "the NAACP wouldn't have had a leg to stand on in court." "The Niggers, the ones that wanted to try our schools out," Moseley declared, "could have done so; and I believe all the trouble could have been avoided."[18]

Gibson then explained the reason for his visit, pointedly asking Moseley "if he could or could not test Negro and white candidates together." In response to his question, Gibson "got the Moseley blitz." "If you don't leave us alone," Mosely exploded, "I'm going to get up at the next First District Principals' meeting and recommend that the State of Georgia go to the ACT [the American College Testing program]. The ACT isn't pushing anybody around." Gibson quietly replied that it was Moseley's "privilege" to make whatever motion he wanted at the meeting, but that he could hardly characterize Gibson's question "pushing" since he had allowed Moseley nearly two years to answer "a very simple question." Moseley then calmed down. "I'll tell you what. I'll try. You know how I feel about this thing. You know that it can't be advertised that we'll test anybody and everybody who shows up. If you'll be patient and not push me, I'll try to test the Nigger and white candidates together. But if we're invaded by a horde of Niggers, you know I can't run [test] everybody together." "I don't trust your Yankee outfit," Moseley fumed. "You want to push us too fast down here. Now if you say anything about this school being open to Niggers for College Board tests, I'm not going to try. . . . You'll just have to leave me alone."[19]

Finally, Moseley declared his apprehension about an "outside crowd" of black students coming to his school, explaining to Gibson, "Now, I can test *my* Nigger students with my white students." At this point center supervisor Martha De Witt joined the meeting, and Moseley told her, "We will try to test the candidates at the Board tests together, but I'm reserving the right to back out if that Yankee crowd loads a bunch of Niggers on me." Gibson patiently agreed to give Moseley some additional time to work things out.[20]

That same day, September 23, Gibson also met with O. L. Douglass, principal and center supervisor at Beach High School, a black high school that had served as a test site for a few years. During the previous year, 1962–63, the center at Beach High School had tested a total of 171 candidates, all black. The only white candidate that Douglass could recall testing at the facility was an airman from Hunter Air Force Base, who had taken the test during the 1961–62 test year. Gibson's meeting with Douglass was cordial, and Gibson recommended to Cameron that Beach High School, which would continue to be prepared to test all candidates on a desegregated basis, be retained as a center for the foreseeable future.[21]

The next day, September 24, Gibson called on Thord Marshall, the new superintendent of Chatham County (Savannah) Schools. Marshall, a former superintendent of schools in Fort Lauderdale, Florida, had chosen a challenging time to become superintendent in Savannah, arriving just when a few white schools were enrolling their first black students. Discussing with Gibson the process of integrating two white public high schools (Savannah and Groves), Marshall explained that the two situations were very different. Howard Moseley, in Marshall's estimation, had let his emotions get the better of him and was having problems. On the other hand, Donald Gray, the principal of Groves, the second white high school, had carefully prepared both students and teachers for the arrival of several black students on the campus. As a result, Groves High, contrary to fulfilling everyone's anticipation that an "explosive situation" would develop there, had instead become "the quiet school." Marshall further explained that "Moseley, by just being Moseley, had gotten the press down on him and needlessly had complicated the problem." Marshall encouraged Gibson to continue to be patient with Moseley, believing that together they could "bring him around." Allowing Moseley to be responsible for closing the center, in Marshall's view, would be "playing into his hands."[22]

Gibson next called on Donald Gray, the principal of Groves High School. During their meeting two years earlier, Gray had impressed Gibson as being a thoughtful, caring man whose students "must take pride in him." In 1961, Gray had told Gibson that should black candidates be assigned to his school for testing he would not turn them away, but that he would have to test them in a separate room to avoid trouble. At the time, Gibson had been concerned for Gray, fearing that there would be "repercussions" from the community against the principal should it become known that Gray actually allowed black students to enter his segregated school to be tested. During their September 1963 meeting, Gray continued to impress Gibson favorably. Gray was "very proud of the way his [white] students had measured up to the responsibilities of attending a desegregated school in a community that is vociferously opposed to desegregation." Yet, Gray was not overly sanguine, confiding in Gibson that "acceptance of the Negro students as ordinary Groves students" was a "distant" goal of his. Unfortunately for the black students at Groves, their principal did not appear supportive of them. While Gray had avoided the protests that greeted the black Savannah High students, his new pupils reported sensing his dislike for them.[23]

Jenkins High School, a white public school, was also on Gibson's schedule for September 24. Its assistant principal, Adam Andrews, was the center supervisor for a new center at Benedictine Military School, a Catholic institution that presented no difficulties with regard to desegregation. Jenkins High, which as yet had had no black applicants, also served as a test center. Gibson met with Jenkins's center supervisor, who was apprehensive about possibly being identified by the community as the person responsible for "desegregating" Jenkins through the simple act of allowing black students to be tested there. Andrews, the assistant principal, on the other hand told Gibson that he did not foresee any problems.[24]

Savannah was the location of two University System of Georgia institutions, Armstrong College (white) and Savannah State College (black). On September 25, Gibson's final day in Savannah, he called on both colleges. During the preceding summer term, Armstrong had become integrated through the enrollment of one black male student who, Gibson was told by center supervisor Nellie Schmidt, had made the Dean's List. Schmidt did not anticipate any problems related to testing black and white students together. This belief was a departure from what Foreman M. Hawes, president of Armstrong, had told James Buford, Southern Regional Office staff member, during a 1962 meeting. At that time, Hawes had expressed concern about desegregated testing on his campus and stated his need to check with the board of regents before committing himself on that point. Hawes also had a local board of directors, and Buford, who described racial prejudice in Savannah as "monolithic" in his 1962 report to Cameron, believed that Hawes's hesitation stemmed from his fear of a negative reaction from his local board. The subsequent integration of several of the system's colleges and universities, beginning with the University of Georgia in January 1961, meant that center supervisor Schmidt could now state with confidence that there likely would be no problem with desegregated testing at Armstrong.[25]

On September 25, 1963, the day of Gibson's visit to Savannah State, the board of regents voted to allow the first white student to enter the historically black college. Savannah State representatives assured Gibson that their testing center was open to all candidates. Among officials he met with that day was Martha Wilson, the test supervisor for Savannah State who earlier that year had been involved in the lunch facilities dispute with Layton Wolfram at ETS, resulting in Wolfram's censure for inappropriate racial language. There was apparently no mention of that incident during Gibson's visit. Gibson also met with Savannah State acting chief administrative officer T. P. Meyers, who was leading the college until the arrival of a new president. A harried Meyers was coping with everything from the "residual effects" of the previous year's campus demonstrations (in which Martha Wilson's "lunch-less" charge Bobby Hill was an active participant) to academic problems associated with the college's lack of selectivity in its largely open door admissions practices. Gibson offered Meyers assistance from the College Board in predicting students' academic success. This would have aided Savannah State's academic counselors, but the overwhelmed Meyers, whom Gibson found in a demoralized state, had no enthusiasm for committing himself to yet another task.[26]

St. Vincent's Academy, a Catholic girls' school, was likely Gibson's final stop in Savannah, and, in sharp contrast to his experience with the discouraged Meyers of Savannah State, he found nothing wrong with the morale there. As principal of St. Vincent's Academy, Sister Mary Fidelis, according to Gibson, was someone "who knows what she is doing, why she is doing so, and how to get things done." Gibson found her "bright," "brisk," and "twinkly"—someone "who gets right down to business." Gibson had met with the principal earlier that year as a result of her request to establish a center in her school. Because she could offer a capacity of five hundred seats in a vital area of the state, Gibson had been quick to respond to her request. The rarely effusive Gibson had been enchanted by his visit to St. Vincent's and the tour of the school that Sister Mary Fidelis herself had conducted. "Sister Mary Fidelis seemed to fly up the stairs," Gibson recorded. "I took them two at a time in order to hear her comments on a variety of subjects. We swept into a lab. . . . Sister Mary Fidelis floated down the steps."[27]

Perhaps most impressive to Gibson during his spring 1963 meeting with the nun was her strong stand in favor of desegregation. Earlier that year she had broken an unwritten Savannah law by inviting all Catholic schools in the area to an educational program at her school. Students from a black Catholic school had attended, and their presence had raised the ire of some of her students' parents. Sister Mary Fidelis was unflappable. "My parents only really squawk *before* an integrated event," she explained. "After it has been done, I just tell them it was done and to quit trying to interfere with their children's broad education. After all, I run St. Vincent's." She saw no problem with operating a desegregated center, and Gibson had been happy to establish one at her school.[28]

On September 25, Gibson found Sister Mary Fidelis "her usual bright, brisk, benevolent self." She was pleased to tell Gibson that her school was now "slightly" desegregated, having enrolled one "very fine Negro girl" as the result of the bishop of Savannah's directive that Catholic schools there desegregate beginning that fall. Predictably, some of St. Vincent's parents had reacted by withdrawing their daughters from St. Vincent's and enrolling them in a co-ed school. "Now," she told Gibson, "you would have loved the fireworks. Mothers! The big argument [against integration]. Intermarriage. I asked them, 'Pray tell, in a Girls' School? Intermarriage?'" The mothers, according to the nun, "got to thinking, 'You know that Girls' School, St. Vincent's, really has no boys.' So they sheepishly called to know if I would take their daughters back." Sister Mary Fidelis had agreed that the girls could return, under the condition that the parents "change their tune at home. Quit talking nonsense to your daughters."[29]

As the starting point in Gibson's travels across Georgia, Savannah presented contrasts, not only in attitudes about desegregation, but also in terms of institutions—black and white, secondary and higher education, public and private. Savannah High's Moseley represented the most challenging attitudes that Gibson and Cameron would encounter, while Gray, Douglass, and Sister Mary Fidelis represented the most cooperative. Some administrators did want to cooperate with the College Board but were afraid to. Armstrong College president Hawse's concerns about his local board's reaction reflected a situation they encountered repeatedly. The schools and colleges in Savannah had begun to desegregate, and that city represented what was happening all over Georgia and the South. Gibson left Savannah and traveled to the southwest corner of the state, intending to visit centers at two public high schools in Bainbridge— Bainbridge High (white) and Hutto High (black). There is no record of the visit to Hutto. At segregated Bainbridge High, Gibson met with Principal J. W. McAllister, who told Gibson that he believed his center could be desegregated by December 1964, Cameron's deadline for center desegregation. Gibson agreed to check back with McAllister in a few months. The center at Hutto High School was testing so few students that Gibson recommended in his report to Cameron that it be closed, at least for some of the test dates, since Bainbridge, the white school, would likely be able to accommodate all candidates.[30]

Gibson's next recorded center visit, on September 27, was to Albany, not far from Bainbridge, where he again met with Principal Harold McNabb. The lawsuit to desegregate Albany schools was still in federal court, but the only remaining issue appeared to be timing. McNabb predicted that the date would be September 1964. With that fact in mind, Gibson recommended that the College Board not insist on an immediate answer from McNabb regarding testing in December 1964. Instead, testing would continue at both Bainbridge High School and Albany State College, a black college in the state university system. Gibson returned home to write reports on his first busy week of activity in the "march."[31]

Meanwhile, Cameron remained heavily involved in efforts to desegregate the school district in Sewanee, Tennessee, where now only his daughter Anne attended public school. Attempts to reason with the school board had failed. In Cameron's words, "You couldn't get any response. We'd go to their meetings and stand up and make statements and they would just sit there like Norman Rockwell paintings." When Cameron, acting in his capacity as president of a pro-integration civic organization, sent a series of formal petitions supporting school desegregation to the board of education by registered mail, a board representative diligently signed for each document, but the board never once responded. Giving up on this course of action, Cameron's organization then threatened the board with a lawsuit. Years later, Cameron recalled, "Well that [the lawsuit] was all right to them. They weren't all that against it [school desegregation]. It's just that they could not survive and take action voluntarily." If a court told the board they would have to desegregate their schools, that would be different—their hand would be forced, and they would not face retaliation from segregationists in the community.[32]

Cameron and his wife, along with five other couples—two black and three white—sued the local school district in early summer 1963 for the desegregation of local schools. The suit was handled through the NAACP legal defense fund and was one of very few cases in which white families participated in a suit for school desegregation. It was a difficult time for Cameron and his immediate family. News of the lawsuit broke in Tennessee newspapers on July 3, and the stories played up the role of the white plaintiffs. That same day, Cameron, who had been away from home attending a lengthy College Board institute in Virginia, was on leave for the July 4 holiday and had scheduled some dental work in Nashville. With six of his teeth pulled, Cameron drove back to Sewanee feeling "sort of miserable." Arriving home, Cameron learned of the newspaper stories and immediately telephoned his brother Winston, a Mississippi attorney, to ask his advice on how to handle their father's reaction when he learned about the Cameron lawsuit. Cameron apologized for his slurred speech (the result of his dental surgery) and explained the loss of his teeth. Anticipating the crisis that would occur when the judge learned about his son's desegregation activities, Winston joked that it was too bad that Ben had wasted his money paying a dentist—"you could have come down here and I'd have knocked them out for you." The brothers agreed that Ben should write to their father at once, which he did.[33]

Judge Cameron's reply to his son's letter opens a window on a changing South. More than nine years after *Brown*, in the face of a steady stream of court orders in favor of integration, even a determined segregationist could see that the Jim Crow South would not survive forever. Judge Cameron wrote to his son that while the news of the lawsuit "grieves me just as the twitting I have received from some judges since they learned . . . of the divergence in our attitudes . . . I have no censure for you." Judge Cameron maintained his position that his son was wrong in his attitudes about desegregation, but added significantly, "I am sure your views are sincere and are based upon the light you are given to see. The fact is that we live in different worlds and maybe it takes folks like you and folks like me to keep fighting for the truth, that it may, in God's good time, be found." The judge asked his son to reassure granddaughter Anne, in whose name the lawsuit had been filed and who was worried about her grandfather's reaction to it, that he was very much looking forward to her upcoming visit. And he told his son he was sorry about his teeth.[34]

Throughout the remainder of 1963 and into 1964, the suit consumed much of Ben Cameron's time. The federal court judge ruled in favor of the plaintiffs, and Anne Cameron, along with other white students, would be allowed to attend the black school for the duration of the school year. In subsequent years, according to the ruling, the black and white schools were to be combined to form a "unitary," desegregated county system. Cameron, finding the timetable for this solution unsatisfactory, met with the judge to ask his permission to negotiate a different solution with the school board. Wanting the unitary county system to be created at once, Cameron argued that this could be accomplished by adding temporary classrooms to the white schools in order to accommodate both races. The school board agreed, with one stipulation—Cameron would have to raise the funds himself. Within three weeks, he and a friend had raised the required $60,000, all of it locally. The usually modest Cameron remarked many years later, "to be able to do that in a small southern town is something."[35]

Meanwhile, by October 1963, ETS staff had compiled their list of closed centers in the five hard core states. At that time they were not aware of something that had diverted Cameron and Gibson from their "march through Georgia" in early October. One of the centers ETS had listed as closed was Murrah High School, a white public school in Jackson, Mississippi. Central High School, also a public white high school in Jackson, was not yet on the official list of closed centers, nor was it on the official list of open centers.[36]

In April 1963, in preparation for a conversation with Cameron, Gibson put on paper some of his thoughts about the testing situation in Mississippi. First, to put the desegregation project in perspective, he recorded the total number of candidates, black and white, tested in the entire state during the previous three administrations of the test. It was only 1,149. Frustrated with the level of resistance to desegregation in Mississippi, a tired and exasperated Gibson then wrote, "It does not seem possible to desegregate any centers in this state" and then proceeded to offer Cameron three possible solutions to the impasse. The first was an arrangement whereby the College Board and ETS would temporarily authorize centers in white schools to give the tests only to their own students, an idea Cameron had considered briefly during his trip through South Carolina. All other students, including the very small number of black students, would be sent to out-of-state, desegregated centers in southwestern Tennessee and New Orleans. His second, even more extreme suggestion was to close all centers in Mississippi, sending all candidates, black and white, to out-of-state centers in Alabama, Tennessee, and Louisiana. While Cameron, also exasperated by the lack of progress in his home state, was probably tempted by these two ideas, he rejected both of them. Gibson's third suggestion, which Cameron approved on April 9, was to use military bases as test sites for most of Mississippi. In Jackson, a "closed" center (one that would test only that school's students—presumably white) had been considered, but Cameron and Gibson decided that they would negotiate instead with Millsaps College, a private, white institution.[37]

Millsaps was an obvious choice. An oasis of relative racial tolerance in the Mississippi desert of massive resistance, Millsaps College, though segregated, for decades had supported a dialogue between black and white moderates. Its partner in this endeavor was Tougaloo College, an integrated, historically black, Christian college located just a few miles away. Beginning in the 1930s, the faculty and students of these two small liberal arts colleges had met regularly to exchange ideas on the changing racial climate in the South and how they might nurture movement in the direction of racial integration. From 1954 until the mid-1960s, following the *Brown* decisions and prior to the 1964 Civil Rights Act, these exchanges became more likely to be held on the Tougaloo campus since mounting pressure from the White Citizens' Council and a similar organization, the Sovereignty Commission, succeeded in constraining Millsaps's overt participation in integrated activities. Sovereignty Commission personnel even manned a surveillance point at the entrance to Tougaloo, threatening white visitors as they arrived on campus. Tougaloo offered lectures and forums that brought to its campus famous Mississippians—Medgar Evers, Hodding Carter, and Eudora Welty—and pro-integrationist musicians—Joan Baez, Bob Dylan, and Pete Seeger. Millsaps faculty were known to attend these events. Edwin King, a Millsaps faculty member and Mississippi native, was impressed especially by the integrated pre-forum dinners customarily held at Tougaloo. Commenting on the racially mixed group attending the dinners, King remarked that at that time in Mississippi "Dining together was about as radical as you can do." As segregationists learned about these continuing biracial activities, they began a barrage of threatening phone calls and letters to Millsaps faculty and administrators.

Millsaps president H. E. Finger found himself in the difficult position of balancing his personal convictions in favor of integration with the very real and practical consideration of losing financial support from donor churches. In fact, between 1955 and 1966 the college's income from those sources declined by around $2 million, a large sum for the small college. While he accepted the reality that pro-segregationist forces would keep Millsaps a white college for the foreseeable future, Finger took an unyielding stand for academic freedom. Throughout his tenure as president, 1952–64, Finger defended his faculty's right and responsibility to foster in their students the curiosity to explore new points of view. Among other results, Millsaps faculty and students continued to participate in the Tougaloo forums. The White Citizens' Council and other segregationist groups identified Finger as an enemy of segregation and more than once threatened him with death if he continued to support desegregation.

Following the fall 1962 admission of James Meredith to the University of Mississippi, a Millsaps professor challenged her colleagues to desegregate their own college. During spring semester 1963, as a first step in this process, the Millsaps and Tougaloo faculties brought together racially mixed groups for cultural events on the Millsaps campus; integrating college facilities was a move toward integrating the college itself. It was at this juncture, in spring 1963, that President Finger agreed to provide a desegregated SAT test center on the Millsaps campus. The College Board's request aligned perfectly both with the goal of the two faculties to support integrated events at Millsaps and with Finger's own convictions.

Despite the mixed success of the integrated events hosted that spring at Millsaps—Tougaloo faculty were shocked when black participants were denied admission on several occasions and threatened to publicize similar events through the media, something that Millsaps wanted to avoid—and despite the escalating racial unrest in Jackson following the murder of Medgar Evers that summer, Finger continued to support the integration of Millsaps facilities, although somewhat reluctantly. Addressing his board of trustees in August, Finger clearly stated that it was "morally right" for Millsaps to seat its black visitors at college events; however, he honestly revealed his personal qualms about integrating Millsaps facilities when he continued: "I propose that we seat the Negroes. I hope they will not come. If they come, I hope they will be few in number. . . . I have not forgotten that we are operating an institution in Mississippi." Finger went on to say that the financial problem that this course of action would produce "*could* be acute." Moreover, should "unfavorable publicity" result, the college's "'image' problem *will* be acute . . . and enormously complicated [emphases added]." Still, Finger predicted that the college would survive the current challenge "if we are bold."[38]

Cameron arranged for the Millsaps center with Frank W. Lane, dean of faculty at Millsaps. By April 10, the day after his conversation with Gibson and concurrent with the biracial cultural events taking place at Millsaps, Lane, with his president's approval, had given Cameron a tentative agreement for a center. On May 6, Lane gave Cameron a definite commitment to operate a desegregated testing center beginning with the December 1963 administration, and the formal process of opening a center began. Cameron and Gibson turned their attention to other matters during the summer, and it was September before Gibson called on the principals of the two white public high schools in Jackson.[39]

W. M. Dalehite, principal of Central High School, had been unhappy to learn a few months earlier, in November 1962, that Murrah High School, a more affluent school and Central's "cross-town rival," also had been designated a College Board testing center. Fearing the loss of his own center and "a loss to the prestige of this school," Dalehite wrote to ETS to express his disappointment as well as his willingness to do whatever he could to retain his center, including expanding seating capacity, in case it was in fact under consideration for elimination. Dalehite, who learned about the addition of a testing center at Murrah by seeing that school listed in the new College Board bulletin, stated that he wished that ETS had contacted him about adding capacity at his school before negotiating with Murrah and subsequently opening a center there. He complained to ETS that Murrah test-takers were troublesome. Murrah students, who had always been "irked" that they had to take the College Board examinations at Central, a school they considered inferior to their own, were disrespectful of his school and the SAT. "They come [to the test center at Central] dressed in shorts and wearing hair curlers. They have attempted to smoke during tests and constantly have to be reminded of the no-talking policy." According to Dalehite, Murrah students frequently arrived late for testing, and some even had been turned away from the center for tardiness.[40]

In 1961, Cameron had advised ETS to keep the Central center open, pointing out that the school had been testing black students there for years, although in a separate room. At that time, counselor John Weems, a personal acquaintance of Cameron, had assured him that black test candidates were common at Central and had been tested without incident. While Cameron had appreciated this level of cooperation at the time, it was no longer enough. If Central continued the practice of assigning separate rooms to whites and blacks, Cameron wrote to ETS, the high school would lose its center.[41]

In August 1963, Principal Dalehite received a letter from Gibson, reminding him of the policy on desegregated centers. Dalehite responded that he was "dismayed" to receive yet another letter from the College Board on this subject, assuring Gibson that his school had "never turned any one away because of color or race. We seldom administer a test wherein all candidates are white. I cannot understand the reason for continued concern." Dalehite had not interpreted Gibson's letter correctly, believing that testing black students in the same building but in separate rooms met the College Board's requirement of desegregated conditions.[42]

Shortly afterward, on September 3, Dalehite was informed in a letter from Harry Crane, director of operations at ETS, that his center had been closed. Dalehite had anticipated this event, as his school was not listed in the new College Board bulletin. Once again, he was understandably disappointed that he had learned indirectly about his center's status. When Gibson visited Central on September 10, a visibly angry Dalehite "flourished" a document in his face. It was Crane's letter, which, in Dalehite's opinion, "didn't say a thing." Dalehite told Gibson that he had been testing black candidates for years in a separate room. He had never turned one away and had "never had one to complain. On the contrary, I've had them to thank me for the courtesy I've always shown them." The obstinate Dalehite complained to Gibson that the College Board was "trying to hurry us too fast in Mississippi." Dalehite had discussed the entire situation with Kirby Walker, Jackson's superintendent of schools, who recommended that the centers at both Central and Murrah should be closed in light of local resistance to desegregation generally. Dalehite told Gibson, in confidence, that the school board had always been aware that Central was testing black students, but had previously "turned their collective backs" on that fact.[43]

Dalehite described to Gibson the considerable current racial unrest in Jackson, reminding him that NAACP field representative Medgar Evers had been murdered there only three months earlier. Racial tensions in Jackson had never been higher. Dalehite predicted that any school desegregation in Jackson was at least two years away. After learning that Gibson had secured a test center at Millsaps, Dalehite warned him: "When the word gets out that Central students and Murrah students are going to be tested in the same room at Millsaps College with Negroes, a lot of the [white] students won't go." Dalehite went on to say that he knew President

Finger well, and that he "was headed for trouble. Your test center at Millsaps is heading for trouble." Dalehite was warning Gibson about the situation, he said, only because of Superintendent Kirby Walker's high regard for Ben Cameron.[44]

Gibson met with Murrah principal James Merritt the same day and learned that the local board of education had refused to authorize the operation of a desegregated center. Merritt pointed out that no black student had yet appeared to be tested at his school, nor would one be likely to appear. He also warned Gibson that, should the facilities at Millsaps become unavailable, Tougaloo College, the only other test site in the area, would not be an option for white candidates. They absolutely would not enter a black institution to be tested. Merritt and Gibson were joined by guidance counselor Helen Carter, who, according to Gibson, was very supportive of College Board programs. To illustrate to Gibson how strongly the parents of Murrah students resisted desegregation, she told him that recently they had reacted angrily to an educational film that featured a black student. This incident had made her wary of showing a new College Board film that also featured black students. Upon hearing about the existence of the film in his school, Merritt became agitated. "The blood rushed in a red panic to his face and he could not bear to look at me for a minute," Gibson wrote. "Merritt must be really afraid of his conservative parents."[45]

Gibson had done his best to maintain positive relations with the two principals whose centers he would close, hoping that once Jackson schools became integrated the centers could be reopened. For the moment, the testing situation in Jackson seemed under control with a center secured at Millsaps College, and he and Cameron could concentrate on Georgia. However, on September 25, while Gibson was in Savannah, and only fifteen days after his meetings at the two Jackson high schools, Marjorie Wheat, a member of the Southern Regional Office staff, took a call in Cameron's absence from the Millsaps College president. A noticeably upset President Finger had just learned that the Jackson school board was at that moment readying a public statement to explain why the College Board had closed its centers at the two white high schools and to reveal that Finger had agreed to operate a desegregated center at Millsaps. As a result of the threat of publicity, a threat similar to one Finger had underscored in his address to his trustees just one month earlier, Finger wanted Millsaps College removed immediately from the list of centers. He had even taken the initiative of securing an alternate location at the local Veterans Administration hospital. Finger assured Wheat that he would provide the test supervisors for the center. Wheat called Finger later in the day to tell him that Cameron would be back in the office that afternoon. She also wanted Cameron to ask him, provided "he wasn't [still] having hysterics" as she explained in a note to Cameron, if his decision to close the Millsaps center was final. Wheat had learned in the meantime that the VA facility seating capacity was very likely inadequate.[46]

In his afternoon telephone call, Cameron found Finger to be "extremely apologetic" about withdrawing his agreement to operate a desegregated center. Having given the matter a great deal of thought, Finger had decided that the publicity that the memo from Superintendent Kirby Walker's office would generate would undermine his college's current efforts to begin quietly desegregating its own student body. Cameron also talked to Superintendent Kirby Walker both that day and the next regarding the memo Walker was preparing to release. At Cameron's urging, Walker decided to give the memo only to white test candidates, listing the VA facility as the new test center and omitting any references to Millsaps College and President Finger. Walker assured Cameron that as yet no public statement had been made. Although not explaining directly why the centers at Central and Murrah high schools had been closed, the final sentence of Walker's memo to white students noted that "the policy of the Trustees of College Entrance Examination Board now requires that pupils be seated in the testing centers without regard to race, color, or national origin."[47]

On October 8, 1963, Gibson interrupted his march through Georgia itinerary and returned to Jackson to determine if the VA facility might be adapted for testing now that Millsaps had withdrawn. Though the administrative head was very willing, his facilities lacked sufficient seating capacity and possible availability. ETS had determined that it would need a capacity of at least 225 seats in Jackson for the upcoming December 1963 testing, and the VA could accommodate only 100. Gibson proceeded directly to the Army Reserve Training Center, where he met with Major E. E. McCafferty and Lieutenant Colonel Oliver Hord. There he secured seating capacity for 130 candidates, available by December. Hord told Gibson that he had a local board of supervisors, made up of civilians who advised him on community issues, but he did not believe they would object to the College Board using the training center.[48]

Gibson next visited the Navy Reserve Training Center ,which could accommodate up to 100 test candidates, thus raising the total capacity to 230, 5 over the required number for testing in Jackson. Russell Levanway, a psychology professor at Millsaps, had agreed to President Finger's request that he serve as test supervisor, and Gibson met with him on October 9. Levanway was very willing to supervise the tests, "provided his job as center supervisor [was] not complicated by *one word* of publicity that he would be acting in that capacity." Gibson assured him that it was not College Board or ETS practice to identify center supervisors by name and finalized arrangements for Levanway to supervise the center at the Army Reserve Training Center. William Bolick, another Millsaps faculty member, had also, at Finger's request, agreed to supervise the examinations at the Naval Reserve Training Center, but was unable to meet with Gibson during October 1963.[49]

Gibson, in his effort to maintain a positive relationship with the Jackson public schools, spent three extraordinary hours, from 8:00 a.m. to 11:00 a.m. on October 10, with Kirby Walker, the Jackson superintendent of schools. Walker had carefully mapped the morning's itinerary to enhance Gibson's "education" on race relations in Jackson. At their first stop, a coffee shop in the heart of the business district, near the Governor's Mansion, Walker ushered Gibson into a "back room" for an 8:30 a.m. meeting of the Double X Club, "a men's club of 20 persons, doctors, lawyers, insurance executives." Walker, a member of the club, informed Gibson that the group was "the heart of the [Jackson] White Citizens' Council."[50]

The Double X Club ("XX"), Gibson learned, owned a clubhouse on the Mississippi River, about sixty miles from Jackson, where Walker had gone fishing just a day or two before with other members. The two main topics of that morning's conversation were, Gibson reported to Cameron,

"The best bug for bream and how to fire that damn Nigger cook we got at the club house at Eagle Lake." Another "minor controversy" was where they should place a second refrigerator at the house. Walker then escorted Gibson to the post office, another local gathering place, where they met "several more arch conservatives." There Gibson heard President John F. Kennedy's name mentioned "with vigor" (referring to Kennedy's famous use of that word) and also "well decorated with profanity." While at the post office, Gibson was introduced to a young lawyer, attaché to a federal judge and leader of a moderate group attempting to keep the public schools open in the face of threats of integration. The young man told Gibson that Jackson's leaders, with the exception of some ministers, were "unmovable" regarding segregation.[51] Given the local influence of the Citizens' Council, some of whose members Gibson had just met, this assessment came as no surprise. Walker and Gibson then drove to the administration building for the black public schools. Walker and other white administrators were segregated in a building in one location, while the director of Negro education and his assistants, all black, were housed in another building across the city. The two staffs never met with each other, and the black administrators did not visit Superintendent Walker's office. Walker next took Gibson to sections of Jackson where blacks and whites had been "pushed together," where there had been riots and slayings following the Medgar Evers murder in June, just four months earlier. The two also drove to NAACP headquarters. Describing his host in a report to Cameron, Gibson wrote, "Walker is a slick talker. He tries to needle, to set you up for a kill, to tell you in one school that a teacher was beaten with bottles and cut with knives; to show you where a car with a white driver was bullet riddled."[52]

In response to Walker's question of whether Gibson was willing to enter some of the more troubled parts of the city, the unflappable Gibson replied, "I'm game. Are you?" During their tour, Gibson probed Superintendent Walker about his thoughts on the civil rights movement. For example, how did Walker deal with black teachers who "wish[ed] to do their part *as American citizens* [Gibson's emphasis] to gain civil rights for Negroes and to desegregate schools?" Walker told Gibson that he advised such teachers that if they weren't willing to work in a segregated system, he could help them find employment in another district, presumably out of state since at that time no Mississippi schools had been desegregated. He alleged that he didn't have any teachers who wanted to work both in Jackson and in a desegregated system. Walker told Gibson, "You can't come in here and understand us. You've got to live here."[53]

Walker tried to explain the power structure in Mississippi, stating that it was composed of a very few men who had prospered under the current racist system. "Why expand the charmed circle?" he asked. He admitted that he felt hopeless about the future of public schools in Mississippi in the short run. Local boards of education would close schools in order to avoid desegregation. On a topic even closer to Gibson's interests, Walker stated that he had considered making public the policy on desegregated test centers because parents "need to know what you all are up to, and that the public schools are not having anything to do with it." He also wanted the public to know about Millsaps College's cooperation. Fortunately for the College Board and the college, Walker had not carried through on his earlier threat. Nevertheless, he predicted, "The College Board will have it rough in Mississippi, maybe before December. The papers are just biding their time." Given the long-standing tradition of racism promoted by the *Daily News* of Jackson—Reed Sarratt, historian and Southern Education Reporting Service (SERS) director, dubbed one *Daily News* editor "the loudest of the segregationist editorial voices" in the Deep South—Walker's assessment was likely correct.[54]

Gibson then told Walker about the plans in motion to administer the tests in "federal facilities," though apparently not naming them, and Walker thought that such a strategy would cause "less rustling in the pews" among segregationists. Closing his memorandum to Cameron, Gibson wrote, "I do not like to form a severe opinion of a man on short observation, but I do believe I was in the company of a guileful man for three hours today and who will later tell his Double X cronies that they had coffee with an integrationist or worse. . . . He [Walker] sends his best regards to Ben Cameron." Gibson left his meeting with Walker with the worry that the superintendent still might carry out his threat to publicize the College Board's plan to desegregate test centers, even though it no longer directly involved the public school system or Millsaps.[55]

Exploring every possibility for testing in Jackson, Gibson next assessed two religious establishments that sponsored schools, the Catholic and Episcopal dioceses, where Gibson had good reason to believe he would be received with understanding. In 1954, shortly following the *Brown* decision, the Catholic International Council, the National Council of Churches, of which the Episcopal Church was a member, and the Synagogue Council of America announced their support of school desegregation. In the intervening years, many denominations took even stronger positions, expanding their support of school desegregation to encompass a wider range of civil rights issues and at the same time considering how their organizations should interact with black followers. While their leaders adopted and issued public statements about policies in support of desegregation, local clergy, especially members of Protestant denominations in the South, generally responded with silence to both *Brown* and the resulting resistance to school desegregation. Reed Sarratt writes, "No matter what the convictions of their minister might be, the members of almost any church shared the prevailing sentiment of their local community on segregation. The minister who stepped out of line did so at his peril." Ministers who spoke out in favor of desegregation lost their positions, sometimes suddenly. In January 1963, several months prior to Gibson's visit to Jackson, twenty-eight mostly young Methodist ministers in Mississippi had taken the bold step of publicly condemning in their "Born of Conviction" statement both racial discrimination and the possible closing of public schools as a means of forestalling desegregation. Sarratt writes, "Retaliation was swift and severe." Those who spoke out against them included members of the Mississippi Association of Methodist Ministers and Laymen (MAMML), an organization formed in the mid-1950s for the purpose of opposing integration, counter to the position of the national church. It is not surprising that MAMML's membership overlapped that of the White Citizens' Council. MAMML in turn published its "Methodist Declaration of Conscience on Racial Segregation," upholding the position that the church should remain segregated. Three of the twenty-eight ministers immediately were struck from their churches' payrolls, and at least fifteen, unable to withstand the social pressure, eventually were forced to relocate to other states.[56]

In what was surely a change of pace after his morning with Superintendent Kirby Walker, Gibson spent the rest of the day in Jackson calling at the offices of two bishops, one Episcopal and one Catholic. Bishop Jack Allin of the Episcopal diocese of Mississippi, with whom Gibson was already acquainted, was out, so Gibson left a message with Allin's secretary who assured Gibson that the bishop was very interested in College Board matters. Bishop R. O. Gerow of the Catholic Natchez-Jackson Diocese, whom Gibson was meeting for the first time, was unfamiliar with College Board tests or programs. But the elderly bishop was well versed in the opposition to desegregation. As early as 1951, Gerow had declared that racism had no place in the church and had expressly forbidden discrimination in the seating of black people in churches under his authority. Following Medgar Evers's murder earlier that year, Gerow became even more outspoken against the problem of segregation, which he unquestionably viewed as a moral one. In a statement Gerow issued two days following the murder, he wrote, "We need frankly to admit that the guilt for the murder of Mr. Evers and the other instances of violence in our community tragically must be shared by all of us." Gerow followed his words with action, stepping up his involvement with a biracial group of ministers and traveling to Washington to meet with President Kennedy on July 17, just five days after Evers died. Gerow would continue fighting racism, becoming active with the interdenominational Committee of Concern in response to the widespread burning of black churches in Mississippi and, in 1964, the integration of Catholic schools in that state. Gerow explained to Gibson that he believed the school situation in Mississippi to be, literally, "explosive." Gibson asked if the church would help the College Board, explaining that bishops in Georgia and Alabama had offered Catholic school facilities as test centers and that Bishop Allin earlier had helped establish a center at All Saints School in Vicksburg.[57]

Bishop Gerow then told Gibson about his own, as he saw them, failed efforts toward racial justice in Jackson and the rest of Mississippi. Referring to the "Born of Conviction" backlash, Gerow "had seen two Methodist ministers and one Episcopal minister forced to move," and currently two other congregations were trying to oust their ministers due to their "outspokenness" on civil rights. Only St. Peter's Church had desegregated, with a handful of black people attending Mass. Beyond that, there was absolutely no desegregation. The bishop told Gibson that he would consider his request and recommended that in the meantime Gibson should meet with Father Joseph Koury, his advisor on education.[58]

Gibson met with Father Koury the next day. Once Gibson explained the College Board's goal of desegregating test centers, Koury wanted to know what having a center would mean in practical terms. He, like Gerow, was discouraged about the church's lack of progress in promoting racial justice. While Koury did not immediately agree to recommend to Bishop Gerow that they accommodate a center during the current year, he asked that Gibson write to him about setting up a center for 1964–65.[59]

In retrospect, Gibson's October 1963 trip to Jackson was probably one of his most unsettling experiences in Mississippi, if not in all the Deep South. It also may have been the occasion of an incident he later related to Ben Cameron. Police cars frequently followed him as he traveled in that state. On one of Gibson's trips to Mississippi, probably his trip to meet with Walker, "within a very short time [of his arrival] a couple of police cars" began following his rental car "wherever he went," Cameron recalled. "They never bothered him. They just stayed behind him. I suspect maybe they were there to protect him." When Gibson checked in at the airport to leave, according to Cameron, "a nicely dressed civilian came up to the counter beside him and said, 'Have a good trip, Mr. Gibson.'" Gibson had never seen the man before and said nothing, just looked at him. "The guy pulled out his identification; he was FBI. So he had been following him around too, or following the Jackson police around," Cameron speculated.[60]

Back in Sewanee, Tennessee, Cameron wrote to James Evans at the Pentagon apprising him of the situation in Jackson and of the arrangements Gibson had made to test candidates at the Army and Navy Reserve Training Centers there. He asked Evans to arrange for some sort of official "backing" to be sent to both commanding officers there so they could be prepared to deal with any potential local pressures. The same day, October 16, Cameron wrote Evans a second letter, a summary of College Board activities related to military bases during the year, and thanked him for his help in securing such "magnificent cooperation." Cameron made one more request of Evans—that no further publicity be given to the fact that centers had been established at military bases. Referring to the articles that had appeared in the *Army Times* and the *Air Force Times* earlier that year, he told Evans how surprised he had been that the articles had not been picked up by civilian newspapers.[61]

Evans was seriously ill and did not respond to Cameron's request. Instead, others had temporarily taken on his duties and provided Cameron with the support he needed by contacting the military facilities in Jackson. One of Evans's assistants wrote to Cameron in late November to let him know that Evans was recuperating, although slowly, and that the date of his return was still unknown.[62]

Cameron arranged his schedule so that he could join the march through Georgia in Macon, between his meetings with University System of Georgia chancellor Caldwell and regent Howard Callaway. Like Savannah, Columbus, and, to some extent, Albany, Macon was of strategic importance to the College Board due to its central location and large seating capacity. Cameron met with Julius Gholson, superintendent of Bibb County (Macon) schools, and learned that the situation with regard to school desegregation in Macon was similar to that in Albany—school officials were awaiting the outcome of a court decision to force them to desegregate their schools. Gholson asked Cameron for more time. The superintendent did not foresee any problem with desegregated testing once the tension of the current situation subsided and once he knew which schools would be desegregated first. He expected that he would be able to operate desegregated centers by the following fall. Because black students could continue to be tested at the black high school, B. Hudson High, Cameron agreed to Gholson's request for more time.[63]

On his way back to Sewanee, Cameron called on Robert E. Lee, president of Georgia State College for Women in Milledgeville, an all-white college that would admit its first black student in 1964. Lee attributed the fact that Milledgeville had experienced very little "racial friction" to "an enlightened city government." He agreed to make arrangements for fully desegregated testing at the college. Cameron also met with Frank Lawrence, the superintendent of Baldwin County (Milledgeville) schools. Lawrence agreed that in keeping with the College Board's requirement that all centers admit all races, the two public schools, one white, one black, which served as testing centers in his district, would both be operated as desegregated centers.[64]

Ben Gibson returned to Georgia from Mississippi and continued his travels to schools and colleges, planning to visit Columbus first. In keeping with the policy of not announcing visits in advance, he had not scheduled an appointment and found that the superintendent was not available until later that week. So Gibson drove south to Edison, where he met with Harold McCarthy, principal of Edison High School, who adamantly told him that the local citizens and school authorities were "not going to permit any desegregation." McCarthy was resigned to giving up his center. Gibson tried to meet with McCarthy's supervisor, Superintendent Mitchell Conner, but he was out.[65]

The next day, October 22, Gibson met with school and college representatives in Adel, Pelham, Thomasville, and Valdosta. His visit with Valdosta State College president J. Ralph Thaxton went well. Thaxton and a local NAACP leader had worked together to integrate the college, and the first two black students had enrolled that September. The citizens of Valdosta, according to Thaxton, fortunately had "paid little attention to the event." Staffing problems had closed the testing center in the white high school a few years earlier. Pineville High School, the black public school in Valdosta, routinely tested black candidates.[66]

Gibson was learning that some principals and superintendents understandably wanted to keep both the white and black test centers in their districts open in order to keep the number of black candidates at white schools to a minimum, thereby reducing criticism from their communities. In Thomasville, Charles McDaniel, superintendent of schools, told Gibson that the school board had authorized him "informally" to desegregate the centers at both the white and black test centers, but if the College Board closed the center at the black high school (Douglass), he would be forced to close the white high school's center (Thomasville). Gibson agreed to the compromise since both centers would accept candidates from the opposite race and because the capacity that the white school provided was critical to accommodating large numbers of candidates in that part of the state.[67]

In Pelham, Superintendent of Schools D. D. Morrison wanted to cooperate, but he was not optimistic about the outcome. He would advise his board "that it would be better for local [white] candidates to remain at home, take the test with one or two Negroes, than go to Albany and have to take the test with several Negroes." H. A. Sessions, the Cook County (Adel) school superintendent, echoed Morrison's philosophy about white students being able to take College Board tests locally with a few black students rather than traveling some distance only to be tested with many more. Minimizing the number of black students encountered by white students appeared to be a last-ditch exercise in damage control. His school would be able to test on a desegregated basis, but any publicity by the College Board would be "most unfair" to him and his board. Publicity continued to be a major concern for both school administrators and for the College Board and ETS.[68]

Gibson met with Ray Bryant, superintendent of the Moultrie schools, the next day and must have been encouraged by Bryant's opinion that the College Board could begin offering tests on a desegregated basis by the December 1964 deadline, at Moultrie High School alone. Bryant thought that the center at the black high school (Bryant High) could be closed. Of course, this success pleased Gibson. He agreed to be in touch with Bryant in the spring to ensure that there were no problems. The superintendent of Crisp County schools (Cordele) told Gibson he would check with his board.[69]

The LaGrange school system superintendent, Belah Lancaster, "a very deliberate person," was frank with Gibson, stating that he was a "stubborn segregationist" and that, as a trustee of Mercer University, a private institution in Macon, he had opposed the admission of black students there "all the way." As a result of Mercer's becoming integrated, Lancaster explained, several benefactors had withdrawn their financial support. Consequently, he did not think there was any chance that his board would make the centers at the two county high schools, one white and one black, accessible to everyone. Drawing a parallel to the donor situation at Mercer, Lancaster emphasized that since the Callaway Foundation had donated $2 million to the school system, "no one would want to offend the foundation." (Gibson would hear a similar sentiment involving the Callaway

Foundation when he met with a principal in Manchester, Georgia, a few months later.) Lancaster also stated that some of the black leaders in La-Grange had told him that they also did not want integration. He agreed to talk privately with individual board members about center accessibility, and Gibson told him he would be back in touch in March.[70]

On October 25, Gibson returned to Columbus to meet with Henry Shaw, superintendent of the Muscogee School District, who explained that his district would be desegregating the twelfth grade beginning September 1964. Nevertheless, Shaw angrily told Gibson, "We are not going to throw open the test centers in our schools to just anybody." When Gibson calmly tried to reason with Shaw, the superintendent became emotional and then confided that a "tragic event" had occurred following a high school football game the previous weekend. Allegedly, four young black men had raped a white high school girl who had been parked in a popular lovers' lane with her boyfriend. The white boy had been locked in the trunk. The police believed that they had identified and arrested those responsible. The event had the entire community "torn up," according to Shaw. It was not a good time to negotiate with Shaw; Gibson told the distraught principal that he would be back in touch in September 1964.[71]

Gibson's meeting with William B. King, the new president of Georgia Southwestern College in Americus, on October 29, was disappointing, counter to Gibson's previous experiences with Georgia system colleges and contrary to the board of regents' recommendations. King told Gibson that, in his opinion, Americus was a "tinder-box," and that the College Board would be "most imprudent" to try to desegregate the center there. He asked for more time to comply. Although King believed that a qualified black applicant would probably be admitted to his college, he also believed that subsequently he most likely would have to close the college "in order to protect life and property" from local segregationists who would be enraged by its integration. Gibson did not pressure the new president any further, but he did discuss the matter with John Hills, his ally at the board of regents office. There would be new developments in Americus by the end of the year that would relieve the impasse. In the meantime, Gibson was satisfied that local black students could continue to take College Board tests at Sumter County High School, a black public school.[72]

While Gibson could not maintain the ambitious pace he had begun in Savannah in September, between November 1963 and March 1964 he visited most of the remaining test centers in Georgia, crisscrossing the state, dropping in unannounced, and talking with school and college officials about desegregating their centers. In the spring he followed up with principals and superintendents who had not been able to give him definite answers about desegregating their centers during the fall, and began the process of closing centers that would not comply with College Board policy. Cameron and Gibson closed approximately twenty centers in Georgia prior to the December 1964 test administration date.[73]

The outcomes of Gibson's visits varied. All eight Savannah centers remained open, including Principal Howard Moseley's Savannah High School. In Albany, the lawsuit to desegregate the schools dragged on through the summer of 1964, and the centers there were dropped from the official listing in the College Board bulletin. However, by the end of August, Harold McNabb, principal of Albany High School, advised Gibson that the tense situation there had eased to the extent that he would be able to operate a desegregated center at his school after all, and Gibson notified ETS that testing could resume in the previously closed center.[74]

Gibson visited Julius Gholson, superintendent of Bibb County schools (Macon), in March 1964, to follow up on Cameron's October meeting. Because of ongoing litigation involving school integration, Gibson's conversation with Gholson was confidential. Despite the unsettled outcome of the suit, Gholson agreed that all three public high schools in Macon would operate desegregated centers. Given Macon's significant seating capacity and its central location in the state, Cameron and Gibson were likely relieved.[75]

With centers assured in the high-demand areas where school desegregation appeared imminent, Gibson then turned his attention to schools that were still segregated and where resistance to desegregation and corresponding complex legal proceedings often placed in doubt its eventual occurrence. Gibson's return visit to Harold McCarthy, principal of Edison High School, was disappointing—McCarthy's superintendent would not allow a desegregated center. McCarthy regretted that he would lose his center and asked Gibson to keep in touch. He predicted that by the spring of 1965 the situation would have improved and he would be able to reopen his center on a desegregated basis.[76]

Gibson followed up his October meeting with H. Titus Singletary, superintendent of the Crisp County schools (Cordele), with a letter instead of a personal visit and was pleased when Singletary responded that his center would stay open, operating on a desegregated basis. The Crisp County board of education had brought the decision to a vote at their March meeting and passed a resolution that the center be continued.[77]

A March 1964 meeting with LaGrange superintendent Belah Lancaster, the self-proclaimed segregationist afraid of offending the Callaways, included more than an hour of fruitless "negotiating," according to Gibson. Lancaster would not budge from his position. He could not allow desegregated centers at either LaGrange (white) or East Depot Street (black) high school. Gibson closed both centers. Subsequent testing in the LaGrange area was held at LaGrange College, a private, white college in the planning stage of integration.[78]

Gibson contacted Henry Shaw, the superintendent in Columbus, by telephone in mid-March to ask if he would be able to maintain his test centers. Shaw told him that all three public high schools, one black and two white, would be able to test on a desegregated basis, but that if any "trouble" occurred in September, when school integration was scheduled to begin, he would have to cancel the centers for the December test administration.[79]

With regard to the situation in Americus, where Georgia Southwestern College president William B. King had told Gibson during their October meeting that it would be impossible to test all candidates together on his segregated campus, two interesting developments occurred. First, Gibson received two letters on December 13, 1963—one from John Hills and one from President King. Hills, who was well aware of the challenges Cameron and Gibson were facing, had brought up the matter of desegregated testing to King during a break in a meeting in Atlanta. Following that conversation, both Hills and King wrote to Gibson about a misunderstanding during their October meeting. King would, in fact, be willing to have a desegregated testing center on his campus after all.[80]

This news must have baffled Gibson, who had recorded that during their October meeting King had insisted that neither his college nor black Sumter High School, which had operated a test center for several years, "should be drawn into the battle" over desegregation in Americus, which he had described as a "tinder-box." Gibson left that meeting believing that King wanted to wait until December 1965 to begin operating a center in compliance with College Board and Georgia board of regents requirements. (If King thought Georgia Southwestern would be integrated by 1965, he was mistaken; his college admitted its first black student in June 1966.) Now, in his letter, King stated that he would operate a desegregated center, but both he and John Hills encouraged Gibson also to keep open the center at Sumter. Hills, an expert on testing, wrote that "it is important that such facilities which have been available to them [the black candidates], or chosen by them, in the past remain available to them in the future. No one should be forced into a testing situation which he may find awkward or unpleasant." Hills added that it would be "inhuman" to require black students to take the College Board examinations at the white college, where the experience "can be expected to cause suffering, anguish, embarrassment, or anger." Hills closed his letter to Gibson sympathetically: "Ben, I appreciate the difficulty of your task and that you would not have chosen it as your current activity." He offered to support Gibson's efforts in any way he could.[81]

The second, and possibly unique, development in Americus was one that Gibson learned of during a February 1964 meeting with J. L. Bozeman, principal of Sumter High, the black, public high school. At the January test administration, three white girls from nearby Dawson, Georgia, appeared at Sumter to be tested. Two of the girls were visibly upset to find themselves at a black school, but, according to Bozeman, the third girl told her companions, "We chose this center, and I am staying. You all can take the test somewhere else if you want to." The girl did stay, and Bozeman, who had already assured Gibson that all candidates were welcome at his school, observed that "the white girl took the test exactly like any other candidate."[82]

Principal Bozeman speculated whether the three girls had intentionally chosen his school on a lark, or whether they had simply selected a convenient school, not knowing it was black. In either case, Bozeman sympathized with their plight, telling Gibson that he thought it had been fine for the two who left to take the test somewhere else. He believed that they wouldn't have done well on the test under the circumstances. Sumter's guidance counselor and test center supervisor, Jo Maxye McKenzie, strongly disagreed. In her view, the girls should have been forced to take the test at Sumter High. Gibson, who may have wondered how the black counselor would have reacted if the situation had been reversed in terms of race, gently reminded McKenzie that any candidate could request a transfer to another center and that she would find instructions for doing so in the College Board bulletin.[83]

Gibson marched into a brick wall in Lyons, Georgia, a small community one hundred miles west of Savannah, in the form of Toombs County Superintendent H. D. Jordan, who emphatically objected to being placed in the position of arbitrating the College Board policy with his school board, which had returned "an unequivocal *no*" to the idea of operating the county's two testing centers on a desegregated basis. In Jordan's view, this situation made him, in the eyes of his community, personally responsible for closing the centers, when, in fact, it was the College Board who should be blamed. Closing the centers was "wrong," because "it did not suit most of the people in Toombs County, and because the local Board [of education] thought it would be wrong to acquiesce to an unsound policy."[84] Jordan then threatened Gibson. If the College Board closed the test centers, he and his board would present the board minutes (the ones that included the discussion on desegregating the centers) to the media in Augusta and Savannah—television stations, radio stations, and the press. He wanted the people of Georgia and beyond to know what the College Board was "up to" and would bet Gibson that any publicity on the closing of the Lyons centers would have "far-reaching effects."[85]

Gibson took Jordan's threat seriously. He recommended to Cameron that he explain to the College Board trustees "that publicity planned by Toombs Board of Education can unhinge commitments secured and negotiations now being conducted by superintendents with Boards of Education all over Georgia. Publicity of this sort could have wide influence in the South." There is no evidence that Cameron believed Jordan's threat should dictate College Board actions. Cameron adhered to his plan and closed both centers in Lyons prior to December 1964.[86]

In Georgia, Cameron and Gibson closed centers in Barnesville, Canton, Donalsonville, Edison, Elberton, Hartwell, LaGrange, Lyons, Manchester, Ocilla, Sylvania, Thomaston, Tifton, and Warner Robbins. Eight of Gibson's thirteen geographic areas of the state contained centers that had to be closed, with more closings occurring in Georgia's "black belt"— where the black population was higher and segregationists more prevalent—than in other sections of the state. The College Board did not have to resort to military bases in Georgia as it had in the four other hard core states. This was due to four factors: the desegregated Atlanta area centers accommodated a large number of black candidates; the temporary dual testing system provided a safety valve for a few volatile communities since black candidates in such communities would more likely choose a black center; the large and geographically dispersed system of colleges and universities in the state housed centers in key locations; and, finally, Cameron and Gibson brought dedication and a gift for quiet persuasion to their task.[87]

By the end of his march across Georgia and diversion into Mississippi, Ben Gibson was tired. His experiences in some school districts sometimes rattled and even frightened him, and he unquestionably bore the brunt of all the anger, fear, and frustration of school administrators and school board members toward the College Board. It was Gibson who personified the College Board and its policies to each superintendent, principal, and test center supervisor he visited, and it would have been nearly impossible for him not to be affected, not to mention exhausted, by many of his experiences. His Georgia colleague John Hills had noted that Gibson's efforts were taking a toll on him. As a result of his considerable investment of time, energy, talent, and emotion in the desegregation project, Gibson, in Cameron's opinion, had become overly involved in College Board and ETS testing issues unrelated to desegregation. As a result, the relationship of the two men became strained.[88]

By late summer 1964, even with the march across Georgia largely behind them, Cameron and Gibson still had a great deal to do in monitoring the difficulties of operating desegregated centers. The passage of the Civil Rights Act of 1964 in June triggered a new round of resistance to desegregation among die-hard segregationists, resulting in problems in schools that Cameron and Gibson had thought to be stable. In addition, school representatives with centers that Cameron and Gibson had closed made requests to reopen their centers; the constant threat of publicity continued to worry them; and Cameron would have to bring some new business to his special committee.

The Campaign Ends, 1964–1967

Number of black students attending school with whites in the
Deep South, 1963–64. 583.
—Reed Sarratt, *Ordeal of Segregation*

Number of black students attending desegregated College Board
Test Centers in Deep South, 1963–64. 2,500–3,000.
—Ben Cameron, Ben Gibson, reports

Ben Gibson did not take for granted that assistance from the Department of Defense would continue indefinitely. In early 1964 he wrote to Ben Cameron and Richard Pearson, the latter now serving as acting president of the College Board following Frank Bowles's resignation. Mimicking the formality of the political establishment, Gibson addressed his two superiors as "The Honorable Ben F. Cameron, Jr." and "The Honorable Richard Pearson" and reminded them that it was time to secure military base facilities for use as centers during the 1964–65 test year.[1]

Gibson suggested that they address their request to Alfred B. Fitt, James Evans's supervisor, and deputy assistant secretary of defense for civil rights. During Evans's long illness, Fitt had become the College Board's contact at the Pentagon. Gibson's draft of the letter to Fitt, enclosed for Cameron and Pearson's approval, requested continued use of all military facilities that the College Board had used during the current test year, with the exception of Barksdale Air Force Base in Shreveport, Louisiana.

The Barksdale test center would be moved to Centenary College, a private Methodist college that would admit its first black student in 1965.[2]

Cameron and Pearson communicated with both Evans and Fitt during the spring of 1964. Unlike James Evans, Fitt lacked enthusiasm for the military's involvement with the College Board desegregation effort. In March, he informed Pearson what he had learned through military channels about the racial situation in each of the cities where the College Board wished to continue testing at military facilities. Fitt indicated that the College Board might be able to move to civilian facilities in Huntsville, Alabama, and Beaufort, South Carolina, where Gibson and Cameron had set up test centers at the Redstone Arsenal and the Marine Recruit Depot, Parris Island, respectively.[3]

Fitt even optimistically anticipated "reasonable prospects" for setting up desegregated centers in Selma and Montgomery. He had sought no information on conditions in Jackson, as the military facilities there—reserve training centers rather than bases—fell outside his jurisdiction. Fitt encouraged Pearson to consider "whether the Board's policy of requiring integrated facilities is really served by moving the site from community to federally controlled property," a suggestion that left both Pearson and Cameron uneasy about the deputy assistant secretary's level of commitment to helping them.[4]

Hoping to learn more about Fitt's position, Cameron telephoned James Evans "to discuss with him again the Department's continued assistance." Evans told Cameron he would return his call and soon did so from a pay telephone outside the Pentagon. Evans had used pay telephones before when calling Cameron, and Cameron was never sure whether Evans was actually "scared" to talk to him, scared "to be seen" talking to him, or "was just trying to make it [their conversations] look more cloak-and-daggerish." Evans's unusual practice clearly intrigued and amused Cameron.[5]

If Evans's motive for leaving his office to return Cameron's telephone calls was unclear, his opinion about Fitt was not. While describing Fitt as a "dedicated individual," Evans reported that his supervisor often acted rashly, "rushing in" uninformed under various circumstances "regardless of the consequences." Evans believed that Fitt lacked an adequate understanding of the test center desegregation situation and that it was unlikely that Pearson or Cameron would be able to sway his opinion and gain his full support. Instead, Evans recommended that Cameron communicate with Edward L. Katzenbach, deputy assistant secretary of defense for education, and cease any direct contact with Fitt. Fortunately, once the persuasive Cameron had fully explained "the whole matter" to Fitt, he found the assistant secretary willing to support the College Board's efforts and involving Katzenbach was unnecessary. Cameron assured Fitt that he would continue to look for desegregated civilian facilities and that the College Board had succeeded very recently in securing a civilian facility in Jackson, Mississippi.[6]

That noteworthy success had come from Ben Gibson's efforts to gain the cooperation of Catholic Bishop R. O. Gerow, specifically through Gibson's conversations with Father Joseph Koury, education advisor to the bishop. After discussing Gibson's request for test facilities in Catholic schools in Mississippi, Gerow and Koury had judged the College Board test desegregation to be "in keeping with the Church's goals and policy." However, any decision to establish a specific test center would be made by the principal of each individual school.[7]

The Navy Reserve Training Center in Jackson was absent from discussions regarding testing facilities since Gibson had closed it after the December 1963 administration due to "sub-standard" physical arrangements, including poor lighting. On March 4, 1964, Gibson met for the first time with that center's supervisor William Bolick, whom Millsaps College president Finger had recommended. Bolick had been simmering since December, and not over the center's poor lighting. "Mr. Bolick is the most belligerent man I've met," Gibson reported to Cameron. "He did not invite me into his office. I had to stand in his doorway [during the entire exchange]. He bristled the whole time we talked." Bolick boiled over into an emotional tirade of complaints against Gibson, the College Board, and desegregated testing, declaring that "You [the College Board] don't know what you're doing. . . . You've got no right to put Negroes and whites together. . . . It just stands to reason the whites and the Negroes could not do their best" while seated in the same room. Bolick, who strongly disagreed with his moderate Millsaps colleagues on the subject of integration, demanded to know the reason behind the College Board policy on desegregated centers, and Gibson replied that the Board took the position that racial discrimination was immoral; "The Board simply believes any testing center should be open to any candidate." Bolick quickly retorted that it was impossible that a black candidate had ever actually been turned away from a test center in a white school. Becoming frustrated when Gibson cited specific instances where black candidates had indeed been turned away, Bolick next attacked the College Board tests themselves, insisting that they were fundamentally "invalid" and that the College Board kept its validity studies under wraps. Gibson calmly assured him that many studies were, in fact, published by the College Board and that he would be happy to send Bolick some of the publications that dealt with that issue.[8]

Bolick then angrily returned to the subject of desegregated testing, emphatically telling Gibson that the College Board had "no reason to test Negro demonstrators." Gibson calmly reminded Bolick that the College Board did not know the race of its candidates and certainly did not know if any candidates were "demonstrators." Bolick contended that Russell Levanway, his Millsaps colleague who had served as the supervisor at the Army Reserve Training Center, had in fact tested a "demonstrator" in December. Gibson asked if the candidate had actually demonstrated at the test center, and Bolick replied, "Well, he [Levanway] had a Negro candidate who had to ask questions about how to take the test—a lot of questions." When Gibson pointed out that any candidate had a right to ask questions about the test and that "asking questions is not customarily defined as 'demonstrating,'" the increasingly agitated Bolick retorted that "Well, if a Negro does it, that's what I would call it."[9] In Bolick's case, Gibson may have failed to follow Cameron's policy of leaving supervisors and other school officials in a pleasant mood. Gibson's subsequent meeting with Bolick's colleague Russell Levanway, only a few minutes later, was routine and cordial, with neither man mentioning a "demonstrator." Levanway's only comment to Gibson about testing black candidates was that he had expected more of them.[10]

In his June 1, 1964, letter to James Evans's supervisor, Alfred Fitt, Cameron formalized his request for centers at military bases, carefully explaining why the centers could not be moved to civilian facilities at that time. In Selma and Montgomery, Alabama, negotiations for desegregated centers were continuing, but Cameron feared that "the influence of state politics on local affairs," particularly in Montgomery, might overturn the progress he and Gibson were making. In Beaufort, South Carolina, the only schools with adequate facilities for testing were public schools under the control of a board of education that Cameron had not yet been able to persuade to cooperate. Cameron reminded Fitt that he and Gibson had been successful in securing civilian centers in Huntsville, Alabama, and in Shreveport, Louisiana. Cameron, perhaps getting into the "cloak-and-daggerish" spirit himself, uncharacteristically provided blind copies of his letter to Fitt, rather than standard ones, to James Evans as well as to his colleagues at the College Board.[11]

Fitt promptly granted Cameron's request. On June 4, he issued a memo to key representatives of the air force, army, and navy, stating that the Department of Defense would provide testing facilities at Craig Air Force Base in Selma, Alabama; at air force bases in Columbus and Greenville, Mississippi; at the army's recruiting station in Jackson, Mississippi; and at the marine corps training center at Parris Island, South Carolina. The centers would be available to support the College Board for test administrations through the spring of 1965. In late August, at the beginning of the 1964–65 school term, Cameron advised Fitt that the Beaufort, South Carolina, schools had voluntarily desegregated, making it possible for him to close the testing center at Parris Island. Cameron once again sent Evans a blind copy of his letter to Fitt. Within a few days, Evans wrote back, warmly opening his brief letter with "Dear friend Cameron."[12]

> The news of today [the progress Cameron had outlined in his letter to Fitt] seems favorable and I hope you feel rewarded for your perseverance. Increasingly, regulations are coming forth giving direct support from various government agencies to the programs and principles which you have been following. In this regard I hope to see you again next when you are in Washington.[13]

The government agency support to which Evans referred, and no doubt celebrated, was the result of the Civil Rights Act of 1964, which President Lyndon B. Johnson had signed into law on July 2. A legacy of the

Kennedy administration and later recognized as one of President Johnson's most significant accomplishments, the legislation had polarized Congress, generating the longest filibuster in the history of that body. Sweeping in its scope, the law confronted racial discrimination in hiring, banished Jim Crow laws in public facilities, and gave the attorney general the authority to sue public officials who supported de jure racial discrimination (discrimination based on state law), including officials in schools. Especially maddening to segregationists was the act's provision that schools and colleges that did not desegregate would lose federal funds, sometimes amounting to a significant portion of school and college budgets. At one point during the filibuster, President Johnson confided to Senator Hubert Humphrey of Minnesota, who was responsible for shepherding the controversial bill through the Senate, that should the legislation be signed into law, it would result in "mutiny in this goddamn country." The native Texan was not wrong. From its beginning, the landmark legislation had been linked to violence. Some have suggested that President Kennedy's first introduction of the bill on June 12, 1963, was a possible motive in the murder of Medgar Evers in Mississippi only a few hours later. That September, a black church in Birmingham, Alabama, was bombed, killing four young girls. The assassination of President Kennedy occurred in November 1963. Taken up by the Johnson administration, the ensuing debate on and actual passage of the bill in 1964 resulted in a new wave of violence, especially in Mississippi.[14] Historian James Patterson writes of the "bloody summer" of 1964, when both black and white activists participating in peaceful civil rights efforts in that state were beaten, shot, and even killed by extremists. Southerners also took their opposition to the Civil Rights Act to the polls. When Johnson ran for president that fall, he carried all but six states: Arizona, home state of Republican candidate Barry Goldwater, and the five states of the Deep South. Though Johnson was successful overall in Arkansas, North Carolina, Tennessee, and Virginia, most white voters in those states supported Goldwater, who had attracted segregationist supporters by withholding his support of the bill.[15] Historian George Musgrove writes that the result "effectively [created] a home for segregationists in the party of Lincoln." Despite the law's prohibitions of racial segregation in public accommodations such as schools, the difficulties of the College Board in desegregating its test centers were not at an end. On the contrary, probably even because of the new legislation, some communities across the South that had not yet desegregated their school districts stubbornly dug in their heels and refortified their resistance. Cameron and Gibson now faced the challenge of unexpected withdrawals by officials of centers who previously had been willing to operate on a desegregated basis, an echo of what they had faced in 1960.[16]

Natchitoches High School, Natchitoches, Louisiana, was one such example. Principal Dan Carr had agreed to operate a desegregated center in the fall of 1963, and had begun testing in January 1964. But in August 1964, one month after passage of the Civil Rights Act, Carr wrote to Harold Crane at ETS to explain that "due to the unrest within our community and the danger this unrest presents to our students, we feel that it is best for us not to sponsor a testing center for the College Board Admissions Test this year." Gibson recorded that the center had to be closed due to "back-lash" in the community, which now was being pressured by the federal government to integrate its schools. Disappointed about losing his center, Carr told Gibson that he hoped it could be reopened as soon as possible.[17]

The newest wave of resistance to desegregation took many forms and, ten years following *Brown v. Board of Education,* incredibly included an attempt to argue that "separate but equal" school facilities did not constitute discrimination under the Civil Rights Act. Representatives from the Department of Health, Education, and Welfare were engaged in a series of meetings with southern school officials to educate them about the act when this hackneyed argument was put forward. The Department of Health, Education, and Welfare representatives were not impressed and warned the school officials that federal funds would soon be withheld from schools and colleges found to be out of compliance. *Southern School News* published estimates of federal funding that could be lost by each southern state, calling the amounts "substantial." For the five hard core states, amounts ranged from $15 million in Louisiana to more than $26 million in Georgia.[18]

Another challenge, especially for Gibson, was providing continuing moral support to center supervisors willing to assume the risk of association with a desegregated activity in particularly resistant areas. In January 1964, a meeting with Ralph K. Tyson, director of testing at white Georgia Southern College in Statesboro, a small community in southeast Georgia, had reminded Gibson of the need to continue to proceed quietly in his dealings with colleges and schools in order to protect individuals who were supporting desegregated testing. Tyson reassured Gibson that the college itself had no problem in testing black candidates, but some whites in the surrounding communities clearly did. He related an incident prior to one test administration when two cars dropping off several black test candidates at the center's circular driveway were followed by two additional cars "containing rough-looking white men." They called Tyson, who happened to be nearby waiting for his assistants to arrive, over to their cars. He saw at once that the men were well-armed with rifles and shotguns. Their spokesman asked Tyson if he needed any help, but knowing exactly what the man meant, Tyson had played "dumb," asking "What do you mean 'help'?" The spokesman replied that the men were there "to haul the 'niggers' off if he needed any help." Tyson responded that he didn't need their help and quickly re-entered the test center, where he called the sheriff to ask that he immediately dispatch plainclothesmen to the campus by way of a back entrance. Before the lawmen could arrive, the white men drove away. However, the sheriff's men were able to trace them and later told Tyson that they were from a nearby community, one "noted for roughness and crudeness." At the time, Tyson reported the incident to no one besides the sheriff, not even Gibson. He feared that any knowledge of the incident or publicity of the fact that he was testing black candidates "could have set this whole section of Georgia off against the college and some elements of the white population off against Negroes."[19]

In the meantime, Tyson told Gibson, at subsequent test administrations several black candidates had requested that they be tested in a room separate from the whites. Tyson believed that when the few black students arrived at the center they felt overwhelmed by the very large number of white candidates, and, even though he and others had welcomed them, they were "uneasy." He confessed to Gibson that he wasn't always sure how to handle their requests but asked if he could simply continue to use his own judgment in seating candidates. Tyson's experience with black students' apprehensions about being subject to discriminatory behavior from white supervisors and/or students was one example of what the College Board would later call "hostile testing conditions." In these conditions, even though no overt discrimination might occur, black test candidates felt that the environment was inhospitable, something the College Board would contend with for many years to come.[20]

Seeking another perspective on racial tensions in the Statesboro area, Gibson telephoned R. H. Hamilton, the principal of William James High School, a nearby black school that also served as a test center. After assuring Gibson that he would test any white candidate who appeared at his school with a valid ticket of admission, he gave Gibson his personal analysis of the racial situation in Statesboro and largely agreed with Tyson's dire assessment. Hamilton advised Gibson to allow each center supervisor to manage "events" at test centers "quietly." Gibson wrote to Cameron that during his conversation with Hamilton he had felt that he "was being counseled with great sincerity" by the black principal "and that accessibility of centers to all candidates, particularly the center at white Georgia Southern College, was quite an accomplishment." And he advised Cameron that they should "leave this delicate accomplishment alone," suggesting that they should not insist that all candidates always be tested in the same room at the two Statesboro centers.[21]

As communities in the five hard core states either voluntarily desegregated their schools or were forced to do so by the courts or procedures arising from the 1964 Civil Rights Act, many center supervisors whose centers had been closed requested that they be reopened, and Gibson busily corresponded with both the schools and ETS. In order to track his and Cameron's progress, Gibson developed a spreadsheet on which he recorded each center that had operated during the 1962–63 test year, whether the center had closed or remained open, and the reason for any closings. He also recorded new centers, including those at military facilities. In October 1964, Gibson's spreadsheet was the basis of a report he made to George Hanford at the College Board. The report, Gibson wrote, would reveal "the impact of negotiations in terms of the Trustees'

Center Policy." Moreover, Gibson's report documents his and Cameron's success—both in desegregating test centers and in significantly raising the number of students taking the SAT.[22]

It is instructive to review by state the situation with regard to the number of center closings and the growth in testing by state. In Alabama, there were 16 test centers operating during the 1962–63 test year. Six centers were closed because they would not comply with the College Board policy. Of those 6, only Huntsville High School reopened during the 1964–65 test year. An additional school, in Dothan, closed due to noncompliance during that same year. The schools that remained closed were Parker and Phillips High Schools in Birmingham and high schools in Greensboro, Marion, and Montgomery. Gibson anticipated that for the 1964–65 year, given the 8 or 9 new centers that he was in the process of establishing, Alabama would have at least 20 centers, including 7 in colleges, 4 in black institutions, and 1 at a military base—a net gain of at least 4 centers. Despite Alabama's being an "ACT state," the number of Alabama students taking the SAT nearly quadrupled between 1959–60 and 1963–64 when more than 10,000 tests were administered in the state. The number of black Alabama students taking the test in the same period is not known, but it is reasonable to assume that it also increased substantially.[23]

In Georgia, the College Board and ETS began the 1962–63 test year with 139 centers. While arrangements were being made for tests for the 1964–65 year, 21 centers were closed due to noncompliance with the College Board's policy. A few other centers were closed for a variety of reasons, including lack of candidates and demolition of buildings. For the 1964–65 year, Gibson reported that there would be 138 centers, a net loss of only 1 center. While the number of centers in Georgia had stayed about the same, the total seating capacity had increased considerably— a change associated with the College Board examination requirement for admission to all state colleges and universities. Of the 138 centers that Gibson expected to operate in Georgia during 1964–65, 19 were new, including 5 in colleges and 1 at H. M. Turner High School, a black high school in Atlanta. Georgia remained the only state of the 5 where it would not be necessary to use military facilities as test centers. The number of test-takers in Georgia more than doubled to nearly 40,000 for the 1960–1964 period, with the number of black students tested increasing by more than one-third.[24]

Louisiana had 17 centers in operation during the 1962–63 test year. Four had been closed due to noncompliance, but Gibson opened 7 new centers during that year. With the subsequent closing of military base centers and the consolidation of other centers, 17 or 18 centers would operate during the 1964–65 test year, leaving the number of centers unchanged. Louisiana's test candidates doubled for the 3-year period, rising to more than 6,500. The number of black students taking the SAT in Louisiana after 1962, when 236 students from black high schools were tested, is not known.[25]

Like Louisiana, Mississippi began the 1962–63 test year with 17 centers. Twelve were closed for noncompliance, more than any of the other states proportionately and second only to Georgia, where 21 of 139 centers were closed. Three additional Louisiana centers were closed for other reasons. Gibson opened 7 new centers during 1963–64, including 5 at military bases or other military facilities. He estimated that 11 centers would operate during 1964–65, a net loss of 6 centers in Ben Cameron's home state. While in the other 4 states, the number of students taking the SAT doubled, tripled, or quadrupled, the total number being tested in Mississippi grew from 1,065 in 1959–1960 to only 1,493 in 1963–64. Students could easily be accommodated even with the reduced number of centers. The number of black students taking the SAT in Mississippi tripled between 1961 and 1964, but still remained very low at around only 80 students.[26]

Nine of the 29 South Carolina centers operating in 1962–63 were closed due to noncompliance. Three of the 9 centers had reopened for the 1963–64 year, and Ben Cameron had opened 4 new centers, including one at the Parris Island center. For the 1964–65 test year, the addition of several more centers raised the total number of centers to 30, a net gain of 1. After the state system initiated its SAT requirement for white colleges and universities, the number of test-takers tripled between 1959–60 and 1961–62, increasing from 3,600 to more than 11,000. Between 1961–62 and 1963–64, the number increased another 50 percent to more than 17,000. The number of South Carolina's black test candidates also tripled.[27]

Gibson's report on the impact of desegregating the test centers was incomplete. While records of precise numbers of black students being tested in the 5 states during 1963–64 could not be found, records do exist for 1959–60 and 1961–62 when 621 and 2,329 students from black high schools were tested, respectively. This almost fourfold increase was largely due to Georgia's new admissions requirement of the SAT for its state colleges and universities. By the 1963–64 academic year, the College Board must have been testing, all in desegregated test centers, at least 2,500 to 3,000 black students in the 5 hard core states. In sharp contrast, for that same 1963–64 period in the same 5 states, despite all efforts to desegregate schools, only 583 black students attended school with white students in formerly all-white schools—in Alabama, 21; in Georgia, 177; in Louisiana, 375; in Mississippi, none; in South Carolina, 10. These numbers demonstrate clearly the magnitude of Cameron and Gibson's accomplishment. Ten years after the *Brown* decision, out of a total of 636 school districts in the 5 states of the Deep South, only 11 school districts had desegregated, admitting collectively a mere 583 black children from a total of nearly 1.5 million.[28]

By October 1964, Cameron and Gibson had closed 52 centers in the 5 states, nearly one-fourth of the starting point of 218 centers. In nearly every case, they had given officials whose institutions housed the centers more than ample opportunity to comply, sometimes making multiple visits to a school or a superintendent's office over many months and always following up the visits with letters, phone calls, and/or College Board educational tools and programs. In a few cases in Georgia, they had allowed the dual center system to remain in place for the sake of expediency, so long as each center agreed to accommodate any candidate, regardless of race.[29]

They had purposefully avoided any publicity of their actions so as to minimize the risks to officials who had wanted to cooperate. They had written countless detailed memos and letters to their colleagues at the College Board and ETS to keep everyone current on center closings and openings. Cameron had made reports on their efforts to the College Board trustees at nearly every meeting since early 1961. Gibson, and to a lesser extent Cameron, had spent days and sometimes weeks at a time on the road, driving from one town to the next. Now, their task of assuring that each center would test all candidates in compliance with the College Board desegregation policy was nearly complete.

It is not surprising that two dedicated and bright professionals might disagree on at least some points of a common endeavor. Understandably, Gibson had begun thinking of himself as *the* College Board (and ETS) representative to schools in the five hard core states, and the school officials had likely begun to think of him in that way too. Because it sometimes became cumbersome for school officials to communicate with several different College Board and/or ETS staff members, for the sake of efficiency Gibson often had assumed responsibilities that were outside the scope originally assigned to him. By the end of the 1963–64 test year, clearly the most hectic of his tenure with the Southern Regional Office, Gibson no doubt was exhausted.

The year 1964 had been a particularly challenging one for Cameron as well. Judge Cameron's health continued to decline, and he died in Mississippi in April. The Fifth Circuit Court adopted a resolution recognizing the judge's service and his positive qualities—his courteous courtroom manner, intelligence, and devotion to the law—and also noted, diplomatically, that "He was fearless, unyielding and determined in the application of the principles and ideals which he embraced." Ben Cameron may have been disappointed, but was probably not surprised, that only two Fifth Circuit Court judges attended his father's funeral.[30]

During the summer, the College Board rewarded Ben Cameron's intelligence, hard work, and loyalty by promoting him to vice president, a position that required him to shuttle regularly between Sewanee and New York. Cameron also had taken on a consulting assignment with the Ford Foundation, joining former College Board president Frank Bowles there. Until the College Board hired someone to replace him as director of the Southern Regional Office, Cameron retained the responsibilities of that job as well, bringing him to realize and to confide in Leslie Dunbar, a member of the Special Committee on Examining Center Policy, "I have simply been overextended."[31]

With the most difficult part of their task behind them, two areas of disagreement surfaced between Cameron and Gibson. The first had to do with returning to ETS the responsibilities of the operation of test centers in the hard core and other southern states. Prior to the College Board taking on the responsibility of desegregating centers in the South, all matters relating to the actual administration of test centers—determining where centers were needed, which facilities were satisfactory, which people were suitable to serve as supervisors, and if centers were being operated in keeping with established testing procedures—had rested with ETS. Because ETS had little experience with centers in the South and had no office located in that region, and because the College Board had established its own Southern Regional Office, ETS had temporarily relinquished those responsibilities to Cameron and his staff. With the center desegregation project nearly completed, ETS wanted to regain its control of test center operations.[32]

In November 1964, Harry Crane, director of operational services at ETS, met with his staff and developed several interim "rules" to clarify how the management of testing centers would be delegated. For example, the Southern Regional Office would be involved in setting up new centers only in the five hard core states. Crane also wrote that because so many different people in his office had dealt with various issues related to center desegregation, a situation that occasionally had caused confusion among his staff, he advised that all telephone calls and written communications about the issue be directed to his assistant, Maymie Yarbrough. Finally, Crane, aware of Cameron's promotion, asked Gibson if ETS should continue to routinely copy Cameron on letters written to Gibson.[33] Gibson telephoned Crane to discuss the new rules and communication channels. Disagreeing only with Crane's decision to give Yarbrough all responsibilities for anything having to do with centers in the five hard core states, Gibson persuaded Crane that for matters not related to desegregation it would be more efficient for Gibson to continue to communicate with Justine Taylor, who had been his primary contact.[34]

A copy of Crane's letter to Gibson didn't reach Cameron until late November. Cameron responded to Crane at once in a letter marked "Confidential," explaining that he would share the letter with Robert Stoltz, his successor as director of the Southern Regional Office and Gibson's new supervisor, but "not directly" with Gibson. Cameron wanted the implementation of Crane's new rules left up to Stoltz and Crane alone. According to Cameron, Gibson had "become so thoroughly involved with all matters having to do with testing centers, both in the hard core states and elsewhere, that disengagement [on the part of Gibson] will be difficult."[35]

Cameron even further disengaged the Southern Regional Office staff from the day-to-day operations of test centers in the non-hard core states, stating that Crane need not send to Gibson copies of further "dealings" with those centers. Cameron admitted that Gibson disagreed with him on this point, holding that the Southern Regional Office should be advised of test center problems of any kind occurring in the region. Cameron, on the other side, took the position that unless the College Board and ETS wished to change their overriding test center policy, which applied to centers worldwide, problems related to issues other than desegregation were problems for ETS to correct, not the College Board or its Southern Regional Office. Cameron then asked Crane to continue to copy him on correspondence having to do with testing policy only, leaving other center matters to his successor, Stoltz. Cameron did not indicate to Crane that he was copying Stoltz in his letter, but he did send the new director a copy. At the bottom of the letter, Cameron added a note to Stoltz that reveals the extent of his and Gibson's disagreement: "There is, of course, nothing confidential in here [referring to the fact that he had penned "Confidential" across the top of the memo]. But I want to avoid getting into more arguments with Ben over this matter, and therefore wanted to restrict direct knowledge of this letter to you."[36]

In the meantime, Cameron and Gibson disagreed on another issue—publicity, which was central to Gibson's philosophy about his relationships with school, college, and military base representatives who had supported desegregating the College Board test centers. Gibson was adamant that their efforts remain quiet; Cameron was willing to be more flexible at this point. In a memo, Gibson inquired if Cameron had seen an article titled "Information for Applicants to Colleges in the United Negro College Fund" in a booklet just published by the United Negro College Fund (UNCF). It included a paragraph stating that the College

Board tested "all candidates for examination on an equal basis." Gibson understood that the College Board, to which he attributed the article, had not planned to "sanction any publicity, direct or indirect, about the desegregated status of test centers." He feared "complications" if the statement about testing all candidates on an equal basis were to draw a large number of black candidates to centers in white high schools in the hard core states. Acting in his capacity as an official agent of the College Board, Gibson unfailingly had promised school and college officials and military facility personnel that there would be "no publicity." Indeed, for some time, Gibson had feared that ETS might be eager to publicize news of the progress being made toward test center desegregation. Crediting the absence of any publicity to Cameron's influence, Gibson asked him to do what he could to prevent any future publicity that could further compromise Gibson's "pledge of no publicity." Of course, it was too late to do anything about the UNCF booklet.[37]

Cameron replied, with uncharacteristic sarcasm, that while he had not *read* the UNCF booklet, he had in fact *written* the section in question. He called Gibson's attention to the fact that similar wording also had been published in the College Board's annual report. Cameron, openly acknowledging their "disagreement," explained that it was a result of their different interpretations of the term "publicity." While the College Board and ETS would continue to refrain from any "general" newspaper articles, they were "obligated" to inform "the public concerned—specifically, our membership, and Negro candidates, of the accessibility of testing centers." As both men knew, making a public announcement about the successful desegregation of testing centers had been considered, but Cameron reminded Gibson that the College Board had "properly discarded" that idea. Cameron concluded, "The most we can assure superintendents is that we will make no general release for newspapers." There is no record of a response from Gibson, but he must have been dismayed by the discrepancy between his and Cameron's definitions of "no publicity."[38]

In early December 1964, Gibson wrote to Crane saying that he wanted to discuss with Cameron and his replacement, Robert Stoltz, the points Crane had raised in his letter about test center management in the southern region and the channels of communication between the Southern

Regional Office and ETS. Gibson conceded that it made sense for all matters pertaining to desegregation to be routed through Maymie Yarbrough, but pointed out that her lack of familiarity with southern centers in general would necessitate his own continued reliance on Justine Taylor for information he might need in order to make decisions about relocating centers, such as seating capacity, when desegregation was involved. Also, Gibson was concerned that Yarbrough, left solely to her own judgment, might inadvertently undo some of the good will he had worked so hard to establish. He advised Crane that it would be wise for Yarbrough to review each of Gibson's comprehensive reports on centers in a given area before making any requests for changes at a center within that area. Gibson also referred Crane to his test center history spreadsheet for use by ETS as a "ready reference on the progress of desegregation" at specific centers. Gibson's business-like but cordial letter indicated that he was finally prepared to relinquish his involvement with non-desegregation matters at test centers, but he informed Crane that his involvement with centers would actually expand in terms of the responsibility that Cameron had given him: reviewing any violations or suspected violations of the College Board desegregation policy "in any state in the union." How he would address a violation would be "worked out" between Cameron and himself.[39]

While Gibson composed his letter to Crane, agreeing to his reduced level of responsibility with regard to test centers, Cameron prepared for the December 10, 1964, meeting of College Board trustees in San Juan, Puerto Rico. Only four years after ETS president Henry Chauncey had announced that the College Board and ETS must desegregate College Board test centers, Cameron reported to the trustees that "all centers, not only those from which complaints had originally been received, were now desegregated." Each center had agreed to test all students without regard to race. Cameron then noted the speed with which this matter had been accomplished. Next, Cameron announced that the routine "maintenance" of testing centers was being returned to ETS, "although the establishment of new centers in the hard core states would continue for the time being under the direction of Ben Gibson." Very little fanfare accompanied Cameron's announcement of the successful completion of such a monumental task, although the minutes recorded that College Board president Richard Pearson had "called attention to" the work done by the Southern Regional Office and ETS.[40]

Listening attentively to Cameron's report was a new College Board trustee, Stephen J. Wright, president of Fisk University and member of Cameron's special committee. In his new role, Wright made two requests. First, emphasizing that most of the work to desegregate test centers had taken place prior to the passage of the 1964 Civil Rights Act, Wright asked that the College Board compose a follow-up report on the test center desegregation situation once that legislation had been in place for a year. Second, Wright asked that the College Board and ETS "maintain a firm position based on principles" with regard to advancing "the cause of equal opportunity and access for all." Many years later, when asked to reflect on his work with the College Board, Wright recalled and applauded the unique and significant position that the College Board had held: "It was one of the few organizations that had contacts and relationships with both higher education and secondary schools." Wright stated emphatically that the College Board "took seriously the opportunity to assist in the admission of black students to institutions of higher education all over the country."[41]

Fortunately for the College Board, the desegregation of test centers had not exacted a high price in terms of the numbers of southern institutions requiring College Board examinations. On the contrary, state colleges in North Carolina and the predominantly black state colleges of South Carolina and Virginia, along with the thirty colleges participating in the UNCF, had adopted the requirement during the previous four years. Although he modestly claimed that he had used only his "little influence" with that organization, Stephen Wright was responsible for the adoption of the College Board examinations by the UNCF.[42]

Competition from ACT was apparently not a concern for Cameron at the trustees' meeting, as he did not mention the rival organization in his presentation. While in 1960 College Board and ETS officials might have predicted that ACT would gain substantially from repercussions related to test center desegregation, that was not the case. ACT apparently had avoided the issue of test center accessibility altogether, testing students almost exclusively at colleges and universities, most of which remained segregated or which were only technically integrated. During the preceding few years, ACT had made only minor inroads in the five hard core states. The only states of these five where significant numbers of institutions required ACT examinations were Alabama and Mississippi. In Alabama, only three colleges required the SAT for admission: Birmingham-Southern College, St. Bernard College, and an additional institution that is not named in reports.[43] Gibson's correspondence and conversations with Birmingham-Southern officials provide an example of competition between the College Board and ACT. Birmingham-Southern, a small, private college that would become Samford University in 1965, was moving toward desegregating its student body. Its rival school, Howard College, also located in Birmingham, was not. In fact, Birmingham-Southern's president Howard Phillips wrote to Gibson that Howard's trustees publicly took "great pride" in the college's segregated status, openly bragging that it had refused to sign a compliance agreement under Title VI of the Civil Rights Act.[44]

ACT courted President Phillips, but he preferred the College Board and the SAT for Birmingham-Southern. His position was not universally supported, and he explained to Gibson in a letter that "tremendous pressures have been exerted on this institution to . . . participate in the program [ACT] most widely used in the State of Alabama . . . our participation in this program [SAT] not only serves as a deterrent in certain areas to recruitment, but it is used as a propaganda tool against us." Phillips elaborated that because ACT operated more testing centers in Alabama than the College Board did, students found the ACT more convenient, a situation that was "fanned into flames" by ACT representatives, according to Gibson. Phillips also shared that Birmingham-Southern's membership in the College Board actually had been used against the college "by people who referred to the College Board as an eastern snob outfit [Gibson's interpretation]," an idea planted by ACT representatives and one willingly taken up by southerners prepared to reject anything "Yankee." Even some of Phillips's faculty members wanted him to drop the SAT. But Phillips believed the College Board had a superior product in the SAT, as well as in its other services and materials, and remained loyal to that organization even when his own registrar became an ACT consultant.[45]

In Georgia, still the largest state by far in terms of numbers of candidates, not one institution required the ACT for admission in the 1963–64 academic year. Similarly, in Louisiana and South Carolina only one college in each state asked applicants to provide ACT scores for admission. By any measure, desegregating the test centers had not "killed" the SAT in the South, as Henry Chauncey had predicted in March 1961.[46] Desegregating the test centers had, as the College Board and ETS intended, facilitated a significant increase in the number of black candidates wanting to be tested. Cameron reported to the trustees that between 1961 and 1964 the number of black candidates in Georgia had risen by nearly 39 percent. In South Carolina and Mississippi the number of black candidates had tripled, "despite the fact that almost all testing was performed in white institutions."[47]

In Georgia, eliminating entirely the dual center system, wherein desegregated centers operated at both white and black schools in the same school district, remained a challenge, and Cameron reviewed for the trustees its history and status. He admitted that the existence of the dual center system was probably encouraging de facto segregation. In other words, black candidates typically selected a center at a black school, and white candidates a white school, even though each center was officially desegregated and had agreed to accept candidates of either race. The Southern Regional Office staff and ETS would close centers in black schools where they were no longer needed to provide adequate capacity, but Cameron emphasized that he would have to leave a few dual centers open for a time, not for racial reasons, but only in order to assure the seating capacity needed to test all candidates in or near their home communities.[48]

Henry Chauncey made one comment in response to Cameron's report. Noting that "voluntary" de facto segregation still existed, he cautioned that "pushing" the situation in Georgia much farther immediately "would have the primary effect of harming the black candidates." As president of ETS, Chauncey had stayed informed about center desegregation for all ETS clients.[49] Following the meeting, he wrote to Richard Pearson that the College Board and ETS had made "remarkable progress in the past three years" and that he was "confident that we shall soon see an end to what is a complicated and frustrating issue." Chauncey enclosed a new ETS policy on test centers that stipulated that it expected all dual centers to be eliminated by September 1, 1966. "Although capacity, location, and general suitability of facilities will be taken into account," the policy stated, "the intent is clearly to eliminate all centers which exist primarily for racial reasons."[50]

With the December meeting of the College Board behind him, Cameron began wrapping up the business of the Special Committee on Examining Center Policy. He had tried to assemble the committee during the spring of 1964, prior to his being promoted, but it was not a convenient time for many committee members. His schedule during the rest of the year had pushed the meeting farther into the future than he would have liked, so it was imperative that he and Ben Gibson meet with the group as soon as possible, not only to inform them officially of the progress that had been made in desegregating the centers, but also in order to ask them to address a related matter.[51]

In early January 1965, Leslie Dunbar, executive director of the Southern Regional Council and a member of the special committee, wrote to Cameron. Dunbar wanted to "raise a speculative and tentative sort of question with you." Referring to passage of the Civil Rights Act of 1964, Dunbar noted that there had been "two years of change and progress" since the committee had met in 1962, bringing "a great many American institutions to accept higher standards of racial equity." In light of those higher standards, he wondered if the committee might expand its reach and take a further step beyond its 1962 recommendations. "To be both frank and specific," he confided to Cameron, "I am worried about Westminster Schools here in Atlanta, which continues to adhere to a racially exclusive admission policy." Westminster Schools was a member of the College Board and a testing center, and its headmaster, William Pressly, was a member of the special committee. Dunbar continued: "I seriously question whether now, in the light of all that has happened since 1962, CEEB [the College Board] should continue to utilize and benefit from the facilities of a segregated school."[52] Cameron replied immediately, assuring Dunbar that the committee would meet during the next few months. Cameron reported that "during the current testing year every College Board center will accept every candidate without discrimination." Referring to the troublesome dual testing center system in Georgia, Cameron conceded that "the slate is not quite as clean as we would like for it to be" and explained that he anticipated that it would "probably be another year before we can do away with all such centers."[53]

Cameron then addressed Dunbar's question about continuing desegregated centers in segregated schools, which he believed "resolved itself" into three components. "One is philosophical, one is practical, and one has to do with the Westminster Schools." From a philosophical point of view, Cameron wrote that if the College Board refused to deal with schools that remained segregated, it was putting itself "into a position of accrediting" schools. From a practical view, Cameron believed that insisting that institutions that served as testing centers be desegregated themselves might raise difficulties in many areas of the South; however, he conceded that those difficulties "probably would not be insurmountable." Addressing the specific situation of Westminster Schools, Cameron told Dunbar that Pressly, the school's headmaster, who had worked closely with Cameron on a series of workshops for underprivileged children, was optimistic about the eventual desegregation of his school. Pressley had told Cameron that within a year or two he would be able to persuade his board to desegregate. Cameron was "convinced that Bill Pressly is sincere in his desire to accomplish integration" and would be successful "relatively soon." In fact, Pressly's school did admit its first black students during the next academic year, 1966–67. Cameron acknowledged that Dunbar's question was a difficult one, and that it was "an entirely legitimate subject for discussion by the Committee."[54]

Cameron and Gibson were able to assemble most of the committee members for a June 17, 1965, meeting in Atlanta. Those present were Arthur Howe, chairman of the committee; Leslie Dunbar; William Pressly; and Stephen Wright. Cameron and Gibson represented the College Board, and Ned Terral attended on behalf of ETS. Again, J. Alton Burdine and Ralph McGill were unable to attend.

After approving the minutes from its first meeting in 1962, the committee heard Cameron's report. All test centers in all southern states were operating in compliance with the trustees' policy, and the goal of full compliance had been reached one year earlier than expected. In view of this success and in view of the considerable impact that the 1964 Civil Rights Act was having on school system integration throughout the South, Cameron supported returning all responsibilities for establishing and maintaining test centers to ETS, a change that was already under way.[55]

Stephen Wright then directed the committee's attention to a paragraph in Cameron's report that described the strategy that Cameron and Gibson had employed in their negotiations with school officials, enjoying especially Cameron's remark that sometimes "two hours of listenin' and talkin'" had been necessary for success. Wright, himself a civil rights movement veteran, praised the strategy, stating that "the content and spirit of the paragraph are worthy of a detailed exposition because of the possible significance which the approaches and methods used in the negotiations might have for others involved in similar undertakings." In other words, Wright believed that the strategy of "quiet persuasion" had been crucial to the success of the project and a worthy model for similar efforts.[56]

The committee still had work to do before it adjourned. After taking care of some housekeeping regarding staff reports, it heard a report from Terral on new official procedures ETS had developed for assuring that all test centers would be operated in a nondiscriminatory manner. The procedures included informing candidates that they would be tested without discrimination, informing center supervisors that lunch facilities must be available to all candidates regardless of race, and requiring center supervisors to sign a statement that they would operate test centers without discrimination. The committee then turned its attention to the problematic question of continuing eligibility for College Board membership for institutions that continued to be segregated. While acknowledging that this question was outside its scope, the committee believed the question was significant and adopted a resolution asking the College Board to "review its official relationships with any institution which remains segregated."[57]

In further business, the committee addressed the status of dual testing centers in Georgia, noting that "all centers, whether in predominantly black or predominantly white institutions, have agreed to test all candidates, and that most centers have tested candidates of the other race." The committee agreed that for the time being they could not do much more in eliminating the dual system, due to the ever-increasing demand for more capacity. The committee members requested that the staffs of the College Board and ETS "eliminate *de facto* segregation as rapidly as possible by closing one [center] of a dual-center arrangement wherever both centers are not needed."[58]

Next, the committee reviewed the original desegregation policy adopted by the College Board trustees in 1962 and agreed that it was still sound. They found the implementation resolution to be no longer necessary since the desegregation of centers was complete for all practical purposes. Finally, the committee resolved "That, inasmuch as its purposes have been accomplished, the Special Committee on Examining Center Policy request the Trustees of the College Entrance Examination Board to discharge it." Their task complete and their structure no longer required, the committee adjourned, unaware that this was not to be the end of the committee's involvement in desegregation issues and the College Board.[59]

In July 1965, Arthur Howe, chair of the committee, wrote Richard Pearson an "overdue" letter, reporting on the committee's recent meeting. Howe warmly praised both Cameron and Gibson, reporting "that the story of what Ben Gibson and Ben Cameron have achieved is a most inspiring one. Though it would be inappropriate to publicize the matter now, I hope that a careful record will be preserved for the future. Certainly, these two men deserve credit for a remarkable achievement." Howe informed Pearson that the committee had asked that it be "discharged on the grounds that the objectives initially assigned it have been achieved." But in Howe's mind, one matter still remained. He "felt strongly" about Leslie Dunbar's proposal that "all institutions which could not demonstrate compliance with the national move toward integration should be barred as testing centers." This was "all a bit delicate" in light of the situation at Westminster Schools and the fact that Bill Pressly was a member of the committee. Howe confessed that he had been relieved that the committee had referred the matter to the trustees of the College Board instead of debating the issue among themselves and making its own recommendation.[60]

The important matter of the College Board's relationship with educational institutions that remained segregated was one that the College Board debated over a period of many months and at various levels of the organization, including with individual members of the disbanded Special Committee on Examining Center Policy. It was not until 1966 that the trustees took the landmark step of barring the membership applications of segregated schools and colleges and approved the following policy:

> *Whereas,* The College Entrance Examination Board was organized to serve educational organizations in the responsible administration of the transition of students from secondary schools to colleges and other institutions of higher learning; and
>
> *Whereas,* The exclusion of qualified students from educational institutions by reason of their race or color is inimical to the educational purposes of the Board;
>
> NOW THEREFORE BE IT RESOLVED: by the members of the College Entrance Examination Board, in meeting assembled, that: *The Board of Trustees shall not recommend for membership in the College Entrance Examination Board any institution which practices racial segregation* [emphasis added].[61]

The policy was modified in 1967 to include wording that also eliminated consideration for membership those institutions that practiced discrimination on the basis of "religion or creed, or national origin." An exception would be made for "members of various religious faiths to establish and maintain educational institutions exclusively or primarily for students of their own faith."[62]

The resolution fell short of expelling from membership those segregated institutions that were already members, but by this time nearly all current member schools and colleges had integrated. Ben Gibson and others at the College Board maintained a close watch on the progress of desegregation throughout the South. By the spring of 1966, only six member colleges in the five hard core states, most of them very small, were categorized by the U.S. Office of Education as not appearing on the published register of institutions that had signed an "Assurance of Compliance" agreement, an indication that they remained segregated. One of those six member colleges was private LaGrange College, located in LaGrange, Georgia, and Cameron and Gibson continued to watch events unfold there. In a memo to the staff executive committee, Cameron wrote: "The Board of Trustees of LaGrange College in Georgia is adamant in maintaining segregation, and anticipates enough support from the Callaway family to offset any possible loss in federal court," meaning that the Callaways would replace any lost federal funding. Despite those circumstances, the administrators at the college had continued to allow a desegregated test center to operate there. LaGrange College would not admit its first black student until 1968.[63]

With regard to secondary schools in the five hard core states, it appeared that by April 1966, none of the school districts considered by the U.S. Office of Education to be in a state of noncompliance operated a testing center. Cameron and Gibson were frustrated in their efforts to keep up with the federal compliance status of schools. As desegregation litigation continued throughout the region, its outcomes continually changed the status of school districts. The two men found the lists of public secondary schools in and out of compliance, published by the federal government, "woefully incomplete." According to Cameron, the federal government had so far ignored entirely the issue of private secondary schools. Presumably, Cameron and Gibson relied on personal contacts to track the progress of desegregation in schools of interest to them.[64] Gibson, charged with the task of reviewing reported or suspected violations of the College Board's policy on desegregation, from time to time was alerted to possible racial discrimination at test centers. By the summer of 1965, he had investigated four such incidents. The outcomes were encouraging, with Gibson finding only one case of actual racial discrimination in a high school in Arkansas.[65]

If Cameron and Gibson's relationship had become strained during the stressful months of 1964, it appears to have mended over the months that followed. Although Gibson had begun reporting to Cameron's replacement Robert Stoltz, he maintained a close professional and personal association with Cameron, occasionally sending him humorous memos acknowledging milestones in their quiet campaign to desegregate test centers. In 1967, when Gibson was finally able to close the Columbus Air Force Base center, in Columbus, Mississippi, the last military base used as a test center, and relocate it to Mississippi State University in Starkville, he wrote Cameron this upbeat celebratory memorandum:

> Well, it seems somehow fitting that the long odyssey commissioned at the Trustees' Meeting, December 8, 1960, Palo Alto, California, and fired up over fried chicken (southern, suh!) and liver at the Pig-N-Whistle in Atlanta, should terminate in the sovereign state of Mississippi in the spring of 1967.[66]

College Board staff members in New York approached Gibson in early 1967 about writing an article on the desegregation of test centers for a College Board publication. Gibson gave the request thoughtful consideration but ultimately refused. His reason had to do with continuing to protect the identities of those school and college officials who had cooperated with the College Board. Gibson strongly believed that many of these people had assumed considerable risk, and he and Cameron had protected them with a "breathless stillness which we have never stirred." In a memo to Cameron, Gibson wrote that the conditions that had made avoiding publicity "fruitful" still existed in some areas. Desegregation was, even now, "contested, slowed down, tampered with." If the people who had supported their efforts were exposed, Gibson feared that they would "be penalized as greatly as possible."[67]

Gibson agreed that "the moral motivation of the Board" and the voluntary assistance by school officials were well worth an article and were worth "more than a general treatment." If an article were written within the next few years, the author would have to protect the identities of institutions and their officials. In Gibson's opinion, that kind of article, one that could not name the players in the piece, "would be a meaningless one." Should the College Board decide that an article was needed relatively soon, "before 1969," he suggested that they "ought to turn to a poet, gifted in the art of saying nothing obscurely."[68]

Cameron, who once modestly described his role in test center desegregation as "just flying by the seat of your pants and seeing what you could do," was also pressed to write an article, but, as he admitted years later, he "hid" behind Gibson, agreeing that if Ben Gibson wrote about their work from his perspective, only then would Ben Cameron add his views. Neither complied.[69]

Epilogue

To respond [to the needs of minority youth] in ways that are consistent
with the intent of the 1954 Supreme Court decision.
—College Board goal, 1975

True equality of access [to postsecondary education] can be achieved
only by the integration of social and cultural differences among the
majority and minority alike.
—George Hanford, College Board president, 1975

In 1975, ten years after the conclusion of the test center desegregation
project, the College Board celebrated its seventy-fifth birthday. As an important part of that event, the organization reviewed its role and mission,
and a critical component of that review included the College Board's work
to help minority youth. Highlighted in the extensive report were histories
of College Board demonstration guidance projects, scholarship programs,
efforts to promote the proper use of the SAT in admissions, and test
center desegregation, all begun between 1956 and 1960, and, with the
exception of test center desegregation, all continuing in some form into
the mid-1970s. The report noted that while minority students were certainly being tested under desegregated conditions, on occasion they still
experienced racial discrimination related to both registering and sitting
for the SAT.[1]

By 1970, Ben Gibson apparently was no longer solely responsible for handling test center complaints of this kind; instead, ETS personnel were now involved. Unfortunately, as school desegregation continued to spread, white southerners continued to actively oppose the presence of black students in their schools. The practice of this opposition extended to some white teachers and guidance counselors, and racial incidents related to the SAT continued. In late 1970, in an effort to understand the problem better, ETS staff member Garrison Hedrick surveyed sixteen black high school guidance counselors from around the country, but primarily from the South, about the treatment of black students wishing to take the SAT. Responses varied, but the counselors were "unanimous" on four points, summarized by Hedrick:

1. There is a definite *communication gap* existing between minority students and high school counselors, especially when the counselor is not a member of the student's minority group;

2. Minority students too often have *difficulty obtaining test information* and registration materials from their counselors (some comments indicate that the person meant that counselors do not publicize the SAT to minority students, especially those in non-academic programs, or encourage them to come to the guidance office for SAT registration materials);

3. Non-minority counselors often tell minority students that the *test (SAT)*, is not something they should bother about;

4. *Test centers* are not located in areas which are convenient to or comfortable for minority students.

Samuel Johnson, one of the surveyed black counselors and also director of the National Scholarship Service and Fund for Negro Students in Atlanta, was "very vocal" about his complaints and provided Hedrick detailed information. Not surprisingly, Mississippi centers were the source of the majority of complaints Johnson cited. After being supplied with a "code" phrase by Johnson—"Mr. J. told me to speak with you"—Hedrick then telephoned four black Mississippi guidance counselors suggested by Johnson. Below are their candid comments as Hedrick transcribed them.

The white counselors in my school refused to tell the minority students about the fee waiver program. [The College Board and ETS waived the testing fee for needy students.] Many of my minority students don't attempt to go to college because they are told the test is not for them.

Two of my former students who took the SAT last year were refused an answer to their questions during an SAT administration.

Last year I took a group of my students to Jackson, Mississippi to take the SAT and they were treated rudely at the test center (St. Joseph H.S.) and were so frightened by the hostile environment they did poorly on the test. The next administration of the SAT (Jan. 70) I took my students to Greenwood, Mississippi where Mr. Raines was a proctor at the test center and my students seeing him present were much more at ease, were not treated rudely, and thus did much better on their exams.

My students tell us that the blacks and whites sit on separate sides of the test room (St. Francis H.S.) and the supervisor will stand on the white side and give the test instructions—black students are ignored when they ask questions during a test administration. Most of my students do not want to register to take the SAT or ACT because they are aware of the way other blacks have been treated at test centers.

White counselors are refusing to give information to black students. Black students are told to sit on one side of the test room. Counselors are telling the students they won't do well on the test when they take it.

A further complaint may have left ETS's New Jersey-based Hedrick perplexed. According to Samuel Johnson, "most black students cannot understand the Southern-white test supervisor because of the supervisor's drawl . . . black people—even those who speak 'flat' English—do not have a drawl." Hedrick probably then questioned if the "communication gap" described by his survey respondents was as basic as a dialect barrier. One wonders how widespread and harmful to black students' education this communication problem was.

Hedrick concluded that "something is rotten in Denmark" and that the telephone interviews supported what he had learned through his earlier survey. He summarized all of the complaints from the black counselors into two main concerns—minority students' public access to SAT information and their "freedom from fear" during testing—and then recommended that ETS and the College Board become "more active in alleviating the hostile environments that some test candidates have encountered." Succeeding would require ETS providing more direct test observation, the appointment of more minority test center supervisors, and more test centers in areas where the black students lived.[2]

Subsequently, the College Board did call for more sensitivity to the problems of minority test candidates, and ETS established the Committee on Hostile Test Center Environment. That group soon developed specific and detailed guidelines for the testing of minority students. By 1975, ETS had implemented several changes in its test administration practices in a serious attempt to minimize racial discrimination. It had opened centers in minority communities, instructed center supervisors about equal treatment of test candidates, assessed the "climates" at test centers "with respect to minority students," and recruited test supervisors who would maintain equitable testing conditions. In this context, the work of Ben Cameron, Ben Gibson, and others to desegregate test centers in the five hard core states is shown to have been only a beginning—part of a much broader effort by the College Board and ETS to provide equitable testing conditions for all candidates in support of widening access to higher education.[3]

The fact that many minority test candidates preferred to take College Board tests in settings in which they were not in the minority would not have surprised Cameron and Gibson. University System of Georgia testing specialist John Hills had spoken on behalf of black high school students in Americus, Georgia, when, in making a case to Cameron for temporarily preserving the dual test center system, he reminded Cameron that it would be "inhuman" to require the students to take the College Board exams at white Georgia Southwestern College instead of at their own, still black, segregated school.[4]

In retrospect, would it have been more beneficial to southern black students to have created dual test center systems throughout the hard core South and simply to have waited for school desegregation to unfold? This question has no viable answer, but, in addition to meeting its goals of testing all candidates and testing them under standard conditions, the campaign of quiet persuasion may have generated other positive consequences. Perhaps the fact that the College Board and ETS were committed to center desegregation empowered and inspired white and black school and college officials to work toward desegregation in their institutions and communities. Perhaps the fact that two respected national organizations were attending to their students' difficulties gave hope to black principals, guidance counselors, and teachers. Perhaps taking the SAT together on a Saturday morning was the first integrated event in the lives of both black and white students, and they gained something important from that experience.

Those lesser possible outcomes aside, the College Board and ETS could not wait for school desegregation. For them, that was not an option. Their leaders believed segregation was both morally wrong and unlawful. Significantly, they understood that the consensus among black people and a growing number of whites was that from the beginning "separate but equal" facilities had yielded only poor schools for their children, and College Board and ETS leaders knew they were accountable to black students as well as white. They hoped for success in removing one barrier to higher education, and they worked diligently toward that success.

In 1975, the College Board described its center desegregation project as a part of its goal "to respond [to the needs of minority youth] in ways that are consistent with the intent of the 1954 Supreme Court decision." On the occasion of its seventy-fifth birthday, leaders of the College Board continued to believe that "True equality of access [to postsecondary education] can be achieved only by the integration of social and cultural differences among the majority and minorities alike." Recognizing that for some "deep-rooted cultural, educational, and economic disadvantages" represented "formidable" barriers to college, the College Board hoped to continue to lower those barriers and acknowledged that its work in that area had only begun.[5]

As to what later occurred in the lives of those who worked intimately with test center desegregation, some events are known. Stephen J. Wright headed the United Negro College Fund (UNCF) from 1966 until 1970 when he became the first minority vice president of the College Board. He also served as its acting president for a brief time in 1973. In 1976, he became a senior advisor to the College Board, continuing his work on programs to promote college attendance by minority youth. Wright served on dozens of boards and task forces, most related to education. One variation was his service, from 1966 to 1969, on the Arms Control and Disarmament Advisory Committee, and it may be that his friend James Evans was instrumental in that appointment. Wright, an avid scholar, continued his practice of reading one thousand pages a day until the time of his death, in 1996, at the age of 85.[6]

James C. Evans retired from his duties at the Pentagon at some point in the mid-1960s. In 1967, a letter of thanks from the College Board commemorating the closing of the last military base test center was forwarded to a successor. Evans continued to teach electrical engineering classes at Howard University until 1970 and died in 1988 at the age of 87.[7]

Howard F. Moseley left Savannah High School in 1965 to join the faculty of Georgia Southern College in Statesboro as an associate professor of education only a few months after the college admitted its first black student. In 1974, he was appointed head of the Department of School Service Personnel Preparation in the college's School of Education, where he currently holds emeritus status.[8]

Ben Gibson retired from the College Board on July 1, 1979, at the age of 68. The College Board honored him with a gift certificate for gardening supplies and a gold watch. Juxtaposing the two gifts, Gibson quipped in a letter to daughter Jean, "Guess what? Bib overalls are the only garment still made with a watch pocket." Retirement brought both "gladness and sadness" to Gibson, who regretted "being separated from good friends with whom I have worked so closely." Later that year, Gibson enjoyed hiking the Canadian Rockies with his son while making plans for retirement projects—gardening, painting, writing, and Japanese flower arranging. Sadly, upon his return from Canada, he immediately fell ill and passed away several weeks later, in January 1980.[9]

Ben Cameron remained in his position as vice president of the College Board until 1970 and continued to act as a consultant for the organization until 1974. His departure from Sewanee, Tennessee, allowed the College Board to act on its plan to relocate the Southern Regional Office to a more accessible site. Following a great deal of research and discussion, the trustees selected Atlanta as the new location and moved the office to that city in 1970. In 1974, Cameron became a senior associate with the Research Triangle Institute in North Carolina, where he developed research projects in higher education and equal educational opportunity. He later retired to Awendaw, South Carolina, where a College Board staff member interviewed him in 1989. Cameron told the interviewer that at some point he had become "very disillusioned" with all institutions, not just the College Board, for reasons he did not explain. Yet he also stated during the same interview that he "never regretted" having gone to work for the College Board. Ben Cameron died in 1999 at age 78.[10]

Notes

INTRODUCTION

1. George H. Hanford, *Minority Programs and Activities of the College Entrance Examination Board* (New York: College Entrance Examination Board, 1975), 1–4.

2. Peter Wallenstein, "Black Southerners and Non-Black Universities: Desegregating Higher Education, 1935–1967," *History of Higher Education Annual* (1999): 123.

3. "Oral History Interview with Ben Cameron," New York, College Entrance Examination Board Archives, 1989, 1–4, 23. Hereafter referred to as Cameron interview. Hereafter referred to as College Board Archives.

4. Numan V. Bartley, *The Rise of Massive Resistance: Race and Politics in the South During the 1950's* (Baton Rouge: Louisiana State University Press, 1969), 235–36.

5. Ben Gibson and Ben Cameron, "Georgia Testing Centers," Iron Mountain, N.Y., College Board Archives, Box 1645, Southern Regional Office. Hereafter referred to as Iron Mountain Box 1.

6. Doris V. Foster to Frank D. Ashburn, July 30, 1961, Iron Mountain, N.Y., College Board Archives, Box 1588, "Desegregation of Southern Testing Centers." Hereafter referred to as Iron Mountain Box 2 1.

7. Ibid.

8. Reed Sarratt, *The Ordeal of Desegregation: The First Decade* (New York: Harper & Row, 1966), 359.

9. Ben Gibson to Ben Cameron (memorandum), February 1, 1964, Iron Mountain Box 1.

CHAPTER ONE

1. Gary D. Saretzky, "Desegregation of LSAT Test Centers: An Historical Minute," Princeton, N.J., Educational Testing Service Archives, microfilm, Box 7, Folder 56, December 20, 1973, 1. Hereafter referred to as ETS Archives, microfilm.

2. "Law School Admission Test Papers, 1945–1973," Educational Testing Services Archives, 2. Hereafter referred to as ETS Archives.

3. Ibid., 2.

4. Ibid., 2–3.

5. Ibid., 3.

6. "LSAT Per Candidate Income and Expenses, 1945–1965," ETS Archives, microfilm, 1.

7. Robert A. Pratt, *We Shall Not Be Moved: The Desegregation of the University of Georgia* (Athens: University of Georgia Press, 2002), ix.

8. James T. Patterson, *Brown v. Board of Education: A Civil Rights Milestone and Its Troubled Legacy* (New York: Oxford University Press, 2001), 15.

9. Edward J. Littlejohn and Leonard S. Rubinowitz, "Black Enrollment in Law Schools: Forward to the Past," *Thurgood Marshall Law Review* (1986): 415–19.

10. Bhishma Kumar Agnihotri, "Negro Legal Education and 'Black' Law Schools," *Loyola Law Review* 17, no. 2 (1971): 248.

11. Patterson, *Brown v. Board of Education*, 12; Pratt, *We Shall Not Be Moved*, 4.

12. Patterson, *Brown v. Board of Education*, 14–15.

13. Robert A. Leflar, "Legal Education: Desegregation in Law Schools," *American Bar Association Journal* 43 (February 1957): 145–49.

14. Patterson, *Brown v. Board of Education*, 21–23, 38–39.

15. Numan V. Bartley, *The New South, 1945–1980: The Story of the South's Modernization* (Baton Rouge: Louisiana State University Press, 1995), 158–60.

16. Leflar, "Legal Education," 145–49. The private law schools admitting black students were the University of Louisville (Kentucky), St. Louis University (Missouri), the University of Kansas City (Missouri), Washington University (Missouri), St. Mary's University (Texas), American University (District of Columbia), Catholic University (District of Columbia), and Georgetown University (District of Columbia).

17. Adam Fairclough, *Race & Democracy: The Civil Rights Struggle in Louisiana, 1916–1972* (Athens: University of Georgia Press, 1995), 155.

18. Ibid., 149–50, 156–61.

19. W. O. Powell to Gentlemen, August 11, 1953, ETS Archives; Ben Cameron, "Negotiations for Compliance with Trustees' Center Policy, 1961–65," College Board Archives, 2.

20. Josephine B. Hammond to W. O. Powell, August 17, 1953, ETS Archives.

21. Hammond to Tandy W. McElwee, August 17, 1953, ETS Archives.

22. McElwee to Hammond, August 21, 1953, ETS Archives.

23. Hammond to McElwee, August 25, 1953, ETS Archives.

24. "LSAT Per Candidate Income and Expenses, 1945–1965," ETS Archives, 1.

25. "Summary," January 15, 1962, ETS Archives.

26. Southern Education Reporting Service Report, "Degree of Desegregation in Southern School Districts," September 1960, photocopy, ETS Archives; "765 School Districts Desegregated," *Southern School News* 7, no. 3 (September 1960): 1, 8.

27. Paul G. Haskell to Henry Chauncey (memorandum), October 28, 1960, ETS Archives, microfilm.

28. Clarence Clyde Ferguson Jr., "Opinion of Counsel," September 23, 1960, ETS Archives, microfilm, 14–15.

29. Ethel Kaveney to John A. Winterbottom (memorandum), August 12, 1960, ETS Archives.

30. George H. Deer and Amelia Hatcher to Harold L. Crane Jr., August 9, 1960, ETS Archives.

31. Ethel Kaveney to John A. Winterbottom (memorandum), August 12, 1960, ETS Archives.

32. Fairclough, *Race & Democracy,* 265–72; Jevallier Jefferson, "The Southern University 16: A Tribute to 16 African-American College Students Whose Sacrifices Improved the Lives of All of Us," The Black Collegian Online, First Semester 2004, www.black-collegian.com/issues/1stsem04/southern16_2004.

33. Fairclough, *Race & Democracy,* 265–72; Jefferson, "Southern University 16."

34. *The New York Times,* March 30, 1960, 25.

35. Clarence Clyde Ferguson Jr., "Opinion of Counsel," September 23, 1960, ETS Archives, microfilm, 14–15.

36. Bartley, *New South, 1945–1980, 299.*

37. Kaveney to Deer and Hatcher, August 15, 1960, ETS Archives, microfilm.

38. Winterbottom to "The Record" (memorandum), August 24, 1960, ETS Archives, 1–2.

39. Donald T. Moss, interview by author, 2005.

40. Winterbottom to "The Record" (memorandum), August 24, 1960, ETS Archives, 1–2.

41. *California Voice,* "Jim Crow Aptitude Test Draws Protest," August 19, 1960, ETS Archives, microfilm.

42. Roy Wilkins, *Standing Fast: The Autobiography of Roy Wilkins* (New York: Viking Press, 1982), 219, 267, 272; Jonas Gilbert, *Freedom's Sword: The NAACP and the Struggle Against Racism in America* (New York: Routledge, 2005), 161–62, 177, 307–8.

43. Winterbottom to William W. Turnbull (memorandum), September 19, 1960, ETS Archives, 1.

44. Ibid., 2–3.

45. Ibid., 3.

46. Malcolm D. Talbott, Newark, N.J., to Winterbottom, September 16, 1960, ETS Archives, microfilm.

47. Clarence Clyde Ferguson Jr., "Opinion of Counsel," September 23, 1960, ETS Archives, microfilm, 1–20.

48. Ferguson, to Gentlemen, Educational Testing Service, September 23, 1960, ETS Archives, 1.

49. Winterbottom to Turnbull (memorandum), September 27, 1960, ETS Archives, microfilm, 1–3.

50. A. L. Benson to Winterbottom (memorandum), October 17, 1960, ETS Archives, microfilm.

51. Ferguson, to Gentlemen, Educational Testing Service, September 23, 1960, ETS Archives, 1.

52. Harold L. Crane Jr. to "The Record" (memorandum), October 11, 1960, ETS Archives, microfilm; Joseph E. Terral to Winterbottom (memorandum), October 28, 1960, ETS Archives, microfilm; Winterbottom to Melvin G. Shimm, October 31, 1960, ETS Archives, microfilm; William B. Bretnall to Terral (memorandum), October 31, 1960, ETS Archives, microfilm.

53. Winterbottom to "The File" (memorandum), November 1, 1960, ETS Archives, microfilm; Winterbottom to "The File" (memorandum), November 3, 1960, ETS Archives, microfilm; Ray Forrester to Winterbottom, November 1, 1960, ETS Archives, microfilm; "Educational Testing Service Observer's Report," November 12, 1960, ETS Archives, microfilm, 4.

54. Carol McDonough to Winterbottom (memorandum), November 23, 1960, ETS Archives, microfilm.

55. Elmer Day to Crane and Winterbottom (memorandum), November 15, 1960, ETS Archives, microfilm.

56. ETS Minutes of the Executive Committee, November 3, 1960, ETS Archives, 19.

57. Ibid., 20.

58. Ibid., 20–21.

59. Winterbottom to Terral and Robert L. Ebel (memorandum), October 18, 1960, ETS Archives, microfilm; Diane Lucas to Mrs. Van Doren (memorandum), October 13, 1960, ETS Archives, microfilm.

60. Jack B. Tate to Winterbottom, October 31, 1960, ETS Archives, microfilm; Winterbottom to Tate, November 3, 1960, ETS Archives, microfilm.

61. ETS Minutes of the Board of Trustees, November 29, 1960, ETS Archives, 6–8.

62. Winterbottom to Talbott (memorandum), December 2, 1960, ETS Archives, 1–8.

63. Winterbottom to "The File" (memorandum), January 4, 1961, ETS Archives, 1.

64. Winterbottom, "DRAFT: Covering letter for Segregation Questionnaire," December 27, 1960, ETS Archives, microfilm, 1–2.

65. H. L. Crane to "The Record" (memorandum), July 26, 1961, ETS Archives, 1.

66. Murray S. Work to Crane, February 23, 1961, ETS Archives, microfilm.

67. Ibid.

68. Ibid.

69. Patterson, *Brown v. Board of Education,* 107–9; Bartley, *New South, 1945–1980,* 251–53; Fairclough, *Race & Democracy,* 234–60.

70. Fairclough, *Race & Democracy,* 262–64.

71. Winterbottom, "DRAFT: Questionnaire," December 27, 1960, ETS Archives, microfilm.

72. Gary D. Saretzky, "Desegregation of LSAT Test Centers: An Historical Minute," Princeton, N.J., Educational Testing Service Archives, microfilm, Box 7, Folder 56, December 20, 1973.

73. "A summary of first-hand contacts made at the 28 LSAT 1961–1962 Bulletin of information centers, January 15, 1962," ETS Archives, 1–4.

74. Winterbottom to Ben Johnson, January 12, 1962, ETS Archives, microfilm.

75. Gary D. Saretzky, "Desegregation of LSAT Test Centers: An Historical Minute," Princeton, N.J., Educational Testing Service Archives, microfilm, Box 7, Folder 56, December 20, 1973.

76. L. Layton Wolfram to Winterbottom (memorandum), April 13, 1962, ETS Archives, 2.

77. Wolfram to Crane, Terral, Winterbottom, Cameron (memorandum), February 6, 1963, ETS Archives, microfilm; Clyde W. Hall, *One Hundred Years of Educating at Savannah State College, 1890–1990* (East Peoria, Ill.: Versa Press, 1991), 159.

78. Wolfram to Crane, Terral, Winterbottom, Cameron (memorandum), February 6, 1963, ETS Archives, microfilm.

79. Winterbottom to Crane, Terral (memorandum), February 11, 1963, ETS Archives, microfilm.

80. Ibid.

81. ETS "Desegregation at Testing Centers," May 1961, ETS Archives.

CHAPTER TWO

1. College Entrance Examination Board of Trustees Meeting, December 8–9, 1966, Agenda Attachment, New York, College Entrance Examination Board Archives, 9. Hereafter referred to as College Board Archives.

2. Ben Cameron Vita, College Board Archives.

3. Harvey E. Couch, *A History of the Fifth Circuit, 1891–1981* (published under the auspices of the Bicentennial Committee of the Judicial Conference of the United States), 91.

4. College Entrance Examination Board Summary Report of the Board of Trustees, December 10, 1959, College Board Archives, 5–6.

5. George H. Hanford, *Life with the SAT: Assessing Our Young People and Our Times* (New York: College Entrance Examination Board, 1991), 79. Ibid, 1, 2.

6. Ben Cameron, "Report on the Southern Regional Office, December 8, 1960," College Board Archives, 1–3.

7. Ibid., 3.

8. Ben Cameron, "Report on the Southern Regional Office, December 10, 1959," College Board Archives, 2; "Oral History Interview with Stephen Wright," College Board Archives, 4.

9. Ben Cameron, "Conference on Testing Negro Candidates in College Board Centers in Georgia," College Board Archives, 1.

10. Ibid., 1, 2.

11. Ibid., 2.

12. Ibid.

13. Ibid., 3.

14. Ben Cameron, "Conference on Testing Negro Candidates in College Board Centers in Georgia," College Board Archives, 1.

15. College Entrance Examination Board of Trustees Meeting, December 8–9, 1966, Agenda Attachment, New York: College Entrance Examination Board Archives,, 13.

16. Ben Cameron, "Report on the Southern Regional Office, December 8, 1960," College Board Archives, 1.

17. Ben Cameron, "Confidential Background Material for the Committee on Examining Center Policy," College Board Archives, 11.

18. Ibid. "Oral History Interview with Ben Cameron," College Board Archives, 3. Hereafter referred to as Cameron interview.

19. College Entrance Examination Board Summary Report of the Board of Trustees, December 10, 1959, College Board Archives, 1.

20. Ben Cameron, "Report on the Southern Regional Office, December 8, 1960," College Board Archives, 3.

21. Ibid., attachment, College Entrance Examination Board of Trustees, 1960–61.

22. Ibid., 3–5.

23. College Entrance Examination Board Summary Report of the Board of Trustees Meeting, December 8, 1960, College Board Archives. 1.

24. Educational Testing Service, *Annual Report to Board of Trustees,* 1960–61, ETS Archives.

25. Nicholas Lemann, *The Big Test: The Secret History of the American Meritocracy* (New York: Farrar, Straus and Giroux, 1999), 16–19.

26. College Entrance Examination Board Summary Report of the Board of Trustees Meeting, December 8, 1960, College Board Archives, 2.

27. Ibid.

28. Cameron interview, 4.

29. College Entrance Examination Board of Trustees, Minutes of Meeting of December 8, 1960, 4.

30. Ibid.

31. Richard Pearson to Henry S. Dyer, December 28, 1960, College Board Archives.

32. Ben Cameron to William Bretnall, transcript attachment, January 17, 1961, College Board Archives, 58–68.

33. Ibid., 68.

34. Ibid.

35. Ben Cameron to Richard Pearson, January 20, 1961, College Board Archives.

36. Cameron interview, 8; Stephen J. Wright Vita, College Board Archives, 1–2; obituary of Stephen Wright, *The New York Times,* April 19, 1996, Late Edition, Final.

37. Kevin M. Kruse, *White Flight: Atlanta and the Making of Modern Conservatism* (Princeton: Princeton University Press, 2005), 39, 180.

38. Richard Pearson to Trustees (memorandum), March 6, 1961, College Board Archives.

39. Joseph E. Terral, "Report on Segregation-Desegregation at ETS Testing Centers in the Southern and Border States," College Board Archives, 1.

40. Ibid., 5; Patrick J. Gilpin, "Charles S. Johnson and the Southern Educational Reporting Service," *Journal of Negro History* 63, no. 3 (July 1978): 197–208; Gene Roberts and Hank Klibanoff, *The Race Beat: The Press, the Civil Rights Struggle, and the Awakening of a Nation* (New York: Vintage Books, 2007), 57.

41. Joseph E. Terral, "Report on Segregation-Desegregation at ETS Testing Centers in the Southern and Border States," College Board Archives, 5, 8.

42. Ibid., 9.

43. Ibid., 2.

44. Ibid.

45. Ibid., 6.

46. Ibid.

47. Ibid., 9

48. Ben Cameron, "Racial Segregation in College Board Test Centers," Table 1, College Board Archives; Educational Testing Services "Annual Report, 1959–60," College Board Archives.

49. Ben Cameron, "Racial Segregation in College Board Test Centers," College Board Archives, 1, 3, 4.

50. Ibid., 3.

51. Ibid., 4, 5.

52. Ibid., 5.

53. Southern Education Reporting Service, "Status of School Segregation-Desegregation in the Southern and Border States," photocopy, ETS Archives, November 1960; Bartley, *Rise of Massive Resistance*, 126–28.

54. Bartley, *Rise of Massive Resistance*, 126–28.

55. Southern Education Reporting Service, "Status of School Segregation-Desegregation in the Southern and Border States," photocopy, ETS Archives, November 1960.

56. Ibid.

57. Pratt, *We Shall Not Be Moved*, 42.

58. Bartley, *Rise of Massive Resistance,* 116–17; "The Southern Manifesto" from *Congressional Record,* 84th Congress, Second Session, vol. 102, part 4 (March 12, 1956), Washington, D.C., Governmental Printing Office, 1956.

59. Bartley, *Rise of Massive Resistance,* 82–83.

60. Patterson, *Brown v. Board of Education,* 96–99; Bartley, *Rise of Massive Resistance,* 83–106.

61. Patterson, *Brown v. Board of Education,* 22.

62. Ibid., xix–xviii.

63. Ben Cameron, "Racial Segregation in College Board Test Centers," College Board Archives, 5.

64. Ibid., 5, 6.

65. Ibid., 6.

66. Jerry S. Davis, interview by author, February 4, 2005.

67. Ben Cameron, "Racial Segregation in College Board Test Centers," College Board Archives, 6.

68. Ibid., 7.

69. Ibid.

70. College Entrance Examination Board of Trustees, Minutes of Meeting of March 15–16, 1961, College Board Archives, 10.

71. Cameron interview, 4.

72. Ben Cameron, "Racial Segregation in College Board Test Centers," College Board Archives, 10, 11.

CHAPTER THREE

1. J. H. Wells to Justine Taylor, March 30, 1961, Iron Mountain, N.Y., College Board Archives, Box 1645, "Southern Regional Office. Hereafter referred to as Iron Mountain Box 1. D. W. Bramlett to Justine Taylor, March 18, 1961, Iron Mountain Box 1; Taylor to Wells, April 5, 1961, Iron Mountain Box 1; Taylor to Bramlett, March 27, 1961, Iron Mountain Box 1.

2. Ben Cameron to Harold Crane, April 14, 1961, New York, College Entrance Examination Board Archives. Hereafter referred to as College Board Archives.

3. Ibid, attached note.

4. Edward W. Noyes to Ben Cameron, April 13, 1961, College Board Archives, 1, 2.

5. Ben Cameron to Harold Crane, April 27, 1961, College Board Archives.

6. Ibid. Ben Cameron to John Hills, April 27, 1961, College Board Archives.

7. Ben Cameron to Harold Crane, April 27, 1961, College Board Archives.

8. Harold L. Crane to "The Record," July 26, 1961, College Board Archives, 1.

9. Ibid.

10. Ibid., 2.

11. Ibid., 1, 2.

12. Ibid., 2.

13. ETS Confidential Report, "Special College Board Desegregation Procedures," July 26, 1961, College Board Archives, 1.

14. Ibid., 2.

15. Ibid., 1, 2, 3.

16. Letter from Ben Cameron to Harold Crane, August 3, 1961, College Board Archives, 1.

17. Joseph E. Terral to Ben Cameron, July 10, 1961, College Board Archives.

18. Ben Cameron to J. E. Terral, September 8, 1961, College Board Archives, 1.

19. Ben Cameron to J. E. Terral, August 17, 1961, College Board Archives.

20. Ibid.

21. Bartley, *New South, 1945–1980*, 151.

22. Patterson, *Brown v. Board of Education*, 11.

23. Stephen G. N. Tuck, *Beyond Atlanta: The Struggle for Racial Equality in Georgia, 1940–1980* (Athens: University of Georgia Press, 2001), 77.

24. Jerry S. Davis and Kingston Johns, conversation with author, February 4, 2005; Davis interview with author, March 5, 2007. (Davis and Johns worked for the Southern Regional Office in the late 1960s and 1970s.)

25. Ben Gibson's journal, undated entry, 187.

26. Ibid., July 17, 1946, 113.

27. Ibid., July 26, 27, 1946, 118–20.

28. Ben Cameron to Ben Gibson, November 29, 1961, College Board Archives, 2.

29. Ibid., 3, 4.

30. Ibid., 4.

31. Ibid.

32. Ben Cameron, "Report to the Trustees, December, 1961," College Board Archives, 1.

33. Ibid., 9.

34. Ibid.

35. College Entrance Examination Board of Trustees, Minutes of Meeting of March 14, 1961, College Board Archives, 2.

36. Cameron, "Report to the Trustees, December, 1961," College Board Archives, 7; Darrell R. Morris, Report on Centenary College of Louisiana, January 23, 1962.

37. Cameron, "Report to the Trustees, December, 1961," College Board Archives, 3, 5.

38. Ben Cameron to Richard Pearson, January 31, 1962, College Board Archives, 1, 2.

39. Ibid.

40. Richard Pearson to Ben Cameron, February 16, 1962, College Board Archives, 1, 2.

41. College Entrance Examination Board of Trustees, Minutes of Meeting of March 14–15, 1962.

42. J. E. Terral to Ben Cameron, March 23, 1962, College Board Archives.

43. Ibid.

44. Ben Cameron to Helen Gise, April 12, 1962, New York: College Board Archives, Microfilm Reel 93. Hereafter referred to as College Board Archives, microfilm.

45. Edward S. Noyes to Frank D. Ashburn, April 17, 1962, College Board Archives, microfilm.

46. Edward S. Noyes to J. Alton Burdine, April 24, 1962, College Board Archives, microfilm.

47. Jerome Karabel, *The Chosen: The Hidden History of Admission and Exclusion at Harvard, Yale, and Princeton* (Boston: Houghton Mifflin, 2005), 321, 325, 327, 381.

48. Bartley, *Rise of Massive Resistance*, 138.

49. Texas State Historical Association, "Burdine, John Alton," www.tshaonline.org/handbook/online/articles/fbu25.

50. Wallenstein, "Black Southerners and Non-Black Universities," 140.

51. Sarratt, *Ordeal of Desegregation*, 306–10.

52. Leslie W. Dunbar, "The Southern Regional Council," *Annals of the American Academy of Political and Social Science* 357, no. 1(January 1965): 108–12; Civil Rights Digital Library, University of Georgia Libraries, Digital Library of Georgia, "Oral History Interview with Leslie W. Dunbar," December 18, 1978. www.docsouth.unc.edu/sohp/G-0075/excerpts/excerpt_2531.html; Leslie W. Dunbar, "The Changing Mind of the South: The Exposed Nerve," *Journal of Politics* 26, no. 1 (February 1964): 7.

53. Morton Sosna, *In Search of the Silent South: Southern Liberals and the Race Issue* (New York: Columbia University Press, 1977), viii; Ralph McGill, *The South and the Southerner* (Boston: Little, Brown, 1963), 218.

54. John Egerton, *Speak Now Against the Day: The Generation Before the Civil Rights Movement in the South* (New York: Alfred A. Knopf, 1994), 625–26.

55. Sarratt, *Ordeal of Segregation*, 258.

56. William L. Pressly, *The Formative Years at Atlanta's Westminster Schools* (Atlanta: McGuire Publications, 1991), 137–51.

57. John L. Lewis with Michael D'Orso, *Walking in the Wind: A Memoir of the Movement* (New York: Simon and Schuster, 1998), 109.

58. Stephen J. Wright, "The Southern Negro," in *The New Negro*, ed. Mathew H. Ahmann (New York: Biblo and Tannen, 1969), 8–9.

59. Ibid., 19.

60. "Oral History Interview with Stephen Wright," New York, College Entrance Examination Board Archives, 4–5. Hereafter referred to as College Board Archives.

61. Southern Education Reporting Service, *Statistical Summary of school segregation-desegregation in the Southern and border states, 1964–65*; Ben Cameron, "Background Material for the Committee on Examining Center Policy," September 20, 1962, College Board Archives, 5, 6, 7.

62. Ben Cameron, "Background Material for the Committee on Examining Center Policy," September 20, 1962, College Board Archives ; Sarratt, *Ordeal of Desegregation*, 7.

63. Bartley, *New South, 1945–1980*, 307.

64. Ibid., 335.

65. Ben Cameron, "Background Material for the Committee on Examining Center Policy," September 20, 1962, College Board Archives, 7, 8, 9.

66 Ibid., 8, 9; Glenn T. Eskew, *But for Birmingham: The Local and National Movements in the Civil Rights Struggle* (Chapel Hill: University of North Carolina Press, 1997), 264.

67. Ben Cameron, "Background Material for the Committee on Examining Center Policy," September 20, 1962, College Board Archives, 8.

68. Ibid., 7.

69. Ibid., 10.

70. Ibid., 9.

71. Joseph Crespino, *In Search of Another Country: Mississippi and the Conservative Counterrevolution* (Princeton: Princeton University Press, 2007), 4–5.

72. Ben Cameron, "Background Material for the Committee on Examining Center Policy," September 20, 1962, College Board Archives, 10, 11, 12.

73. Ibid., 12, 13.

74. Ibid., 15, 16.

75. Ibid., 16.

76. Committee on Examining Center Policy Minutes, October 1, 1962, College Board Archives, 2.

77. College Entrance Examination Board of Trustees Meeting Minutes, March 15–16, 1961, College Board Archives, 10.

78. Committee Minutes, October 1, 1962, College Board Archives, 2.

79. Ibid., 4.

80. Ibid., 3.

81. Ibid., 4, 5, 6.

82. Ibid., 7.

83. Ibid., 7, 8.

84. Ibid., 5.

85. Ibid., 8.

86. Ben Cameron to Richard Pearson, November 14, 1962, College Board Archives.

CHAPTER FOUR

1. "Oral History Interview with Stephen Wright," New York, College Entrance Examination Board Archives, 2, 3; obituary of James C. Evans, *The New York Times*, April 23, 1988.

2. Ben Cameron to Richard Pearson, November 14, 1962, Iron Mountain, N.Y., College Board Archives, Box 1645, "Southern Regional Office." Hereafter referred to as Iron Mountain Box 1. James C. Evans to Stephen Wright, November 9, 1962, Iron Mountain Box 1, 1.

3. James C. Evans to Stephen Wright, November 9, 1962, Iron Mountain Box 1, 1, 2.

4. Alan L. Gropman, "The Air Force Integrates: Blacks in the Air Force from 1945 to 1964" (doctoral dissertation, Tufts University, 1975), 197, 325, 350; Lee Nichols, *Breakthrough on the Color Front* (New York: Random House, 1954), 78, 79.

5. Gropman, "Air Force Integrates," 348, 350.

6. Stephen Wright to Ben Cameron, November 10, 1962, Iron Mountain Box 1; Ben Cameron to Stephen Wright, November 14, 1962, Iron Mountain Box 1.

7. Jack Greenberg, *Crusaders in the Courts: How a Dedicated Band of Lawyers Fought for the Civil Rights Revolution* (New York: Basic Books, 1992), 321; Couch, *History of the Fifth Circuit, 1891–1981*, 91.

8. Couch, *History of the Fifth Circuit, 1891–1981*, 94.

9. "Oral History Interview with Ben Cameron," College Board Archives, 18. Hereafter referred to as Cameron interview.

10. Couch, *History of the Fifth Circuit, 1891–1981*, 91.

11. Cameron interview, 27.

12. Ibid., 20, 21; Jack Bass, *Unlikely Heroes: The Dramatic Story of the Southern Judges of the Fifth Circuit Who Translated the Supreme Court's Brown Decision into a Revolution for Equality* (New York: Simon and Schuster, 1981), 232.

13. Cameron to Pearson, November 14, 1962, notes written on document.

14. "College Entrance Examination Board Resolution Adopted by the Board of Trustees, December 13–14, 1962," College Board Archives.

15. Ben Cameron, "Report to the Trustees, December, 1962," College Board Archives, 6, 7.

16. Ibid., 7, 8.

17. Ben Gibson to Ben Cameron (memorandum), January 8, 1963, College Board Archives, 2.

18. Ben Cameron to James Evans, January 10, 1963, Iron Mountain Box 1.

19. Richard Pearson to Frank Bowels and George Hanford (memorandum), January 17, 1963, Iron Mountain Box 1.

20. James Evans to Stephen Wright, January 18, 1963, Iron Mountain Box 1, 1, 2.

21. Frank H. Bowles to Norman S. Paul, January 22, 1963, Iron Mountain Box 1.

22. Ibid., Attachment II.

23. Ibid., Attachment IV.

24. Ben Cameron to Stephen S. Jackson (and attachments), January 30, 1963, Iron Mountain Box 1.

25. Norman Paul to Under Secretaries of the Army, Navy, and Air Force (memorandum), February 19, 1963, Iron Mountain Box 1; Stephen Jackson to Frank Bowles, March 1, 1963, Iron Mountain Box 1.

26. Ben Cameron to Commanding Officers, March 11, 1963, Iron Mountain Box 1; Justine Taylor to Ben Cameron, February 22, 1963, Iron Mountain Box 1.

27. Layton Wolfram to Ben Cameron, March 13, 1963, Iron Mountain Box 1; James Buford to Ben Cameron, March 19, 1963, Iron Mountain Box 1; Fairclough, *Race & Democracy*, 285–86; *Southern School News* 11, no. 12 (June 1965): 14; Southern Education Reporting Service, *Statistical summary of school segregation-desegregation in the Southern and border States, 1966–67*, 17.

28. Bartley, *New South, 1945–1980*201–2; Jason Morgan Ward, *Defending White Democracy: The Making of a Segregationist Movement and the Remaking of Racial Politics, 1936–1965* (Chapel Hill: University of North Carolina Press, 2011), 151.

29. James Buford to Ben Cameron (memorandum, Centenary College), March 19, 1963, Iron Mountain Box 1.

30. James Buford to Ben Cameron (memorandum, C. E. Byrd High School), March 19, 1963, Iron Mountain Box 1.

31. Ben Gibson to Ben Cameron (memorandum, Hunter AFB), March 18, 1963, Iron Mountain Box 1; Ben Gibson to Ben Cameron (memorandum, Fort Stewart), March 18, 1963, Iron Mountain Box 1; Richard M. Dalfiume, *Desegregation of the U.S. Armed Forces:*

Fighting on Two Fronts, 1939–1953 (Columbia: University of Missouri Press, 1969), 220–21; Ben Gibson to Ben Cameron (memorandum), March 18, 1963, Iron Mountain Box 1; Morris J. MacGregor Jr., *Integration of the Armed Forces, 1940–1965*, chapter 20, www.history .army.mil/books/integration/IAF-FM.htm.

32. Dalfiume, *Desegregation of the U.S. Armed Forces*, 222; Sarratt, *Ordeal of Desegregation*, 66–67.

33. Ben Gibson to Ben Cameron (memorandum), September 22, 1961, Iron Mountain Box 1.

34. Ibid.; Ben Cameron, Negotiations for Compliance with Trustees' Center Policy, 1961–65, College Board Archives, 2.

35. Ben Gibson to Ben Cameron (memorandum), November 22, 1961, Iron Mountain Box 1, 2.

36. Ben Cameron to Layton Wolfram, September 18, 1961, College Board Archives; Ben Gibson to Ben Cameron (memorandum), September 22, 1961, Iron Mountain Box 1.

37. Ben Gibson to Ben Cameron, March 25, 1963, Iron Mountain Box 1.

38. Wilkins, *Standing Fast*, 285.

39. Bartley, *New South, 1945–1980*, 324–28.

40. Ben Gibson to Ben Cameron (memorandum, Albany report), March 25, 1963, Iron Mountain Box 1, 2.

41. Ibid.

42. *Atlanta Constitution*, "Suit Asks Integration in Dougherty," April 8, 1962, photocopy, Iron Mountain Box 1.

43. Ben Gibson to Ben Cameron (memorandum, Albany report), April 10, 1963, Iron Mountain Box 1; Ben Gibson to Ben Cameron (memorandum, Fort Benning report), March 25, 1963, Iron Mountain Box 1.

44. Ben Gibson to Ben Cameron (memorandum, Maxwell Air Force Base report), January 9, 1963, Iron Mountain Box 1, 1, 3, 4.

45. Ben Gibson to Ben Cameron (memorandum, Maxwell Air Force Base report), March 25, 1963, Iron Mountain Box 1; *Southern School News* 10, no. 3 (September 1963): 1.

46. Ben Gibson to Lt. Colonel Carl H. Hanson, May 21, 1963, Iron Mountain Box 1; Ben Cameron to Lt. Colonel Howard Moore, May 21, 1963, Iron Mountain Box 1.

47. Ben Gibson to Ben Cameron (memorandum), March 27, 1963, Iron Mountain Box 1.

48. Ben Gibson to Ben Cameron (memorandum, Robins and Hunter Air Force Base reports), April 8, 1963, Iron Mountain Box 1.

49. Ben Cameron to base commanders, April 11, 1963, Iron Mountain Box 1.

50. *Air Force Times*, "Services to Offer Facilities for College Tests in South," April 10, 1963, photocopy, Iron Mountain Box 1; Ben Cameron to James Evans, October 16, 1963, Iron Mountain Box 1.

51. Ben Gibson to Ben Cameron (memorandum), April 19, 1963, Iron Mountain Box 1.

52. Ben Gibson to Ben Cameron (memorandum, Keesler, Columbus, Greenville Air Force Base report), April 19, 1963, Iron Mountain Box 1; Sarratt, *Ordeal of Desegregation*, 359.

53. Ben Gibson to Ben Cameron (memorandum), April 18, 1963, Iron Mountain Box 1.

54. Ben Cameron (telephone memorandum), May 6, 1963, Iron Mountain, N.Y., College Board Archives, Box 1588, "Desegregation of Southern Test Centers." Hereafter referred to as Iron Mountain Box 2.

55. Cameron interview, 16, 17.

56. Ibid., 12, 13; M. Ron Cox Jr., "Integration with [Relative] Dignity: The Desegregation of Clemson College and George McMillan's Article at Forty," in *Toward the Meeting of the Waters: Currents in the Civil Rights Movement of South Carolina during the Twentieth Century*, ed. Winfred B. Moore Jr. and Orville Vernon Burton (Columbia: University of South Carolina Press, 2008), 275–76.

57. Cameron interview, 12, 13.

58. L. Currie McArthur, "Statement on Sumter High School Examining Center for the College Entrance Examinations, June 13, 1963," Iron Mountain Box 1; Harold Crane to school principals, October 8, 1963, Iron Mountain Box 2.

59. Cameron interview, 13, 14.

60. Ben Cameron to Robert C. Edwards, April 2, 1963, Iron Mountain Box 2; Ben Cameron to Robert C. Edwards, April 13, 1963, Iron Mountain Box 2.

61. Ben Cameron, Beaufort, South Carolina file, May 1963 correspondence, Iron Mountain Box 2.

62. Ben Cameron, "Summary of South Carolina Centers, May 15, 1963," Iron Mountain Box 2.

63. Ben Cameron to James Evans, October 16, 1963, Iron Mountain Box 1; Harold Crane to school principals, October 8, 1963, Iron Mountain Box 1; Margaret Van Doren to Marjorie Wheat (letter), January 27, 1964, ETS Archives.

64. Ben Gibson to Ben Cameron (memorandum, Redstone Arsenal report), August 2, 1963, Iron Mountain Box 1, 1, 2.

65. *Southern School News* 10, no. 3 (September 1963): 12.

66. George H. Hanford to Ben Gibson, July 16, 1963, Iron Mountain Box 1; Charles M. Holloway to Messrs. Pearson, Noyes, Hanford, Mrs. Gise (memorandum), July 8, 1963, Iron Mountain Box 1; Ben Cameron to Frank Bowles, October 4, 1963, Iron Mountain Box 1.

CHAPTER FIVE

1. George H. Hanford to Ben Gibson, July 16, 1963, Iron Mountain, N.Y., College Entrance Examination Board Archives, Box 1645, "Southern Regional Office." Hereafter referred to as Iron Mountain Box 1.

2. Ben Cameron to George Hanford, July 23, 1963, Iron Mountain Box 1.

3. Ibid.

4. Ben Gibson to Ben Cameron, July 15, 1963, Iron Mountain Box 1.

5. Frank Bowles to Richard Pearson, February 15, 1963, Iron Mountain Box 1; Richard Pearson to Ben Cameron, March 11, 1963, Iron Mountain Box 1; Ben Cameron to Richard Pearson, March 25, 1963, Iron Mountain Box 1.

6. Ben Cameron to Richard Pearson, March 25, 1963, Iron Mountain Box 1.

7. Ben Cameron to Frank Bowles, October 4, 1963, Iron Mountain Box 1.

8. Frank Bowles to Howard Callaway, October 9, 1963, Iron Mountain Box 1, 1, 2; Kruse, *White Flight,* 231.

9. Ben Cameron (memorandum "for the files"), October 22, 1963, Iron Mountain Box 1.

10. Ibid.; Ben Cameron to Harmon Caldwell, October 22, 1963, Iron Mountain Box 1; Ben Cameron, "Negotiations for Compliance with Trustees' Center Policy, 1961–65," New York, College Entrance Examination Board Archives. Hereafter referred to as College Board Archives.

11. ETS "Cancelled Centers–Trustees' Policy, October 17, 1963," Iron Mountain Box 1.

12. Ibid.

13. Ben Gibson, Georgia map, untitled, Iron Mountain Box 1; Ben Gibson, center spreadsheets, untitled, Iron Mountain Box 1.

14. Ben Gibson to George Hanford, November 5, 1963, Iron Mountain Box 1.

15. Ben Cameron to Arthur Howe, October 4, 1963, New York, College Entrance Examination Board Archives, Microfilm Reel 93.

16. Ben Gibson to Ben Cameron (memorandum, Savannah High School report), October 1, 1963, Iron Mountain Box 1, 1.

17. Tuck, *Beyond Atlanta,*, 207–8; Marion Orr and Hanes Walton Jr., "Life on the Leading Edge of Democratic Reform: Student Perspectives on School Desegregation," *PS: Political Science and Politics* (April 2004).

18. Ben Gibson to Ben Cameron (memorandum, Savannah High School report), October 1, 1963, Iron Mountain Box 1, 1, 2.

19. Ibid., 2.

20. Ibid.

21. Ben Gibson to Ben Cameron (memorandum, Beach High School report), October 1, 1963, Iron Mountain Box 1.

22. Ben Gibson to Ben Cameron (memorandum, Thord Marshall, Chatham County schools report), October 1, 1963, Iron Mountain Box 1.

23. Ben Gibson to Ben Cameron (memorandum, Groves High School report), October 1, 1963, Iron Mountain Box 1; Orr and Hanes, "Life on the Leading Edge."

24. Ben Gibson to Ben Cameron (memorandum, Jenkins High School report), October 1, 1963, Iron Mountain Box 1; Ben Gibson to Ben Cameron (memorandum, Benedictine Military School report), October 1, 1963.

25. Ben Gibson to Ben Cameron (memorandum, Armstrong College report), October 1, 1963, Iron Mountain Box 1; James Buford to Ben Cameron (memorandum, Armstrong College report), January 23, 1963, Iron Mountain Box 1.

26. Ben Gibson to Ben Cameron (memorandum, Savannah State College report), October 1, 1963, Iron Mountain Box 1, 1, 2.

27. Ben Gibson to Ben Cameron (memorandum, St. Vincent's Academy report), April 9, 1963, Iron Mountain Box 1, 1, 2, 3; Ben Gibson to Ben Cameron (memorandum, St. Vincent's report), October 1, 1963, Iron Mountain Box 1.

28. Ben Gibson to Ben Cameron (memorandum, St. Vincent's Academy report), April 9, 1963, Iron Mountain, Box 1, 2, 3.

29. Ben Gibson to Ben Cameron (memorandum, St. Vincent's Academy report), October 1, 1963, Iron Mountain Box 1, 2, 3; *Southern School News* 10, no. 3 (September 1963): 8.

30. Ben Gibson to Ben Cameron (memorandum, Bainbridge High School report), October 1, 1963, Iron Mountain Box 1.

31. Ben Gibson to Ben Cameron (memorandum, Albany High School report), October 1, 1963, Iron Mountain Box 1.

32. "Oral History Interview with Ben Cameron," College Board Archives, 16, 17. Hereafter referred to as Cameron interview.

33. Ibid., 19, 20.

34. Bass, *Unlikely Heroes*, 231–33.

35. Cameron interview, 21–22.

36. ETS "Cancelled Centers–Trustees' Policy, October 17, 1963," Iron Mountain Box 1.

37. Ben Gibson, "Mississippi, Recommendations on Testing Centers," Iron Mountain, N.Y., College Board Archives, Box 1588, "Desegregation of Southern Test Centers." Hereafter referred to as Iron Mountain Box 2.

38. Maria R. Lowe and J. Clint Morris, "Civil Rights Advocates in the Academy: White Pro-integrationist Faculty at Millsaps College," *Journal of Mississippi History* 69, no. 2 (2007): 121–37.

39. Ben Cameron (memorandum, handwritten), May 6, 1963, Iron Mountain Box 2; H. E. Finger Jr. to Ben F. Cameron Jr., May 15, 1963, Iron Mountain Box 2.

40. W. M. Dalehite to Margaret Van Doren, November 20, 1962, Iron Mountain Box 2.

41. Ben Cameron, notes written on November 15, 1961, memorandum from L. Layton Wolfram, November 20, 1961, Iron Mountain Box 2; Ben Cameron to Mrs. William V. Taylor, December 5, 1962, Iron Mountain Box 2.

42. Ben Gibson to W. M. Dalehite, August 6, 1963, Iron Mountain Box 2; W. M. Dalehite to Ben Gibson, August 9, 1963, Iron Mountain Box 2.

43. Harold Crane to W. M. Dalehite, September 3, 1963, Iron Mountain Box 2; W. M. Dalehite to Harold Crane, September 10, 1963, Iron Mountain Box 2; Ben Gibson to Ben Cameron (memorandum, Central High School report), September 13, 1963, Iron Mountain Box 2, 1, 2.

44. Ben Gibson to Ben Cameron (memorandum, Central High School report), September 13, 1963, Iron Mountain Box 2, 1, 2.

45. Ben Gibson to Ben Cameron (memorandum, Murrah High School report), September 13, 1963, Iron Mountain Box 2, 1, 2.

46. Marjorie Wheat (telephone memorandum), September 25, 1963, Iron Mountain Box 2.

47. Ben Cameron (telephone memorandum), September 25, 1963, Iron Mountain Box 2; Ben Cameron (telephone memorandum), September 26, 1963, Iron Mountain Box 2.

48. Ben Gibson to Ben Cameron (memorandum), October 18, 1963, Iron Mountain Box 2, 1.

49. Ibid., 2, 3.

50. Ben Gibson to Ben Cameron (memorandum), October 17, 1963, Iron Mountain Box 2.

51. Ibid.

52. Ibid., 1, 2.

53. Ibid., 2.

54. Ibid., 2, 3; Sarratt, Ordeal of Segregation, 252.

55. Ben Gibson to Ben Cameron (memorandum), October 17, 1963, Iron Mountain Box 2, 4.

56. Sarratt, Ordeal of Segregation, 265–67. Crespino, In Search of Another Country, 70–72.

57. Ben Gibson to Ben Cameron (memorandum, Bishop Allin report), October 17, 1963, Iron Mountain Box 2; Ben Gibson to Ben Cameron (memorandum, Bishop Jerow [sic] report), October 18, 1963, Iron Mountain Box 2; Michael V. Namaroto, The Catholic Church in Mississippi, 1911–1984: A History (Westport, Conn.: Greenwood Press, 1998), 89–91.

58. Ben Gibson to Ben Cameron (memorandum, Bishop Jerow [sic] report), October 18, 1963, Iron Mountain Box 2.

59. Ibid.

60. Cameron interview, 15.

61. Ben Cameron to James C. Evans (two letters), October 16, 1963, Iron Mountain Box 2.

62. Willard C. Stewart to Ben Cameron, November 29, 1963, Iron Mountain Box 2.

63. Ben Cameron (memorandum "for the files"), October 22, 1963, Iron Mountain Box 1; Ben Cameron to Julius Gholson, October 22, 1963, Iron Mountain Box 1.

64. Ben Cameron (memorandum "for the files"), October 22, 1963, Iron Mountain Box 1.

65. Ben Gibson to Ben Cameron (memorandum, Columbus report), October 29, 1963, Iron Mountain Box 1, 1; Ben Gibson to Ben Cameron (memorandum, Edison High School report), October 29, 1963, Iron Mountain Box 1.

66. Ben Gibson to Ben Cameron (memorandum, Valdosta State College report), October 29, 1963, Iron Mountain Box 1, 1, 3; James Buford "Center Report," January 7, 1962, Iron Mountain Box 1.

67. Ben Gibson to Ben Cameron (memorandum, Thomasville High School report), October 29, 1963, Iron Mountain Box 1.

68. Ben Gibson to Ben Cameron (memorandum, Pelham High School report), October 29, 1963, Iron Mountain Box 1; Ben Gibson to Ben Cameron (memorandum, Cook County Schools report), October 29, 1963, Iron Mountain Box 1, 1, 2.

69. Ben Gibson to Ben Cameron (memorandum, Moultrie Schools report), October 19, 1963, Iron Mountain Box 1; Ben Gibson (memorandum, Crisp County Schools report), October 29, 1963, Iron Mountain Box 1.

70. Ben Gibson to Ben Cameron (memorandum, LaGrange School System report), October 29, 1963, Iron Mountain Box 1.

71. Ben Gibson to Ben Cameron (memorandum, Columbus report), October 29, 1963, Iron Mountain Box 1, 1, 2.

72. Ben Cameron to Ben Gibson (memorandum, Georgia Southwestern College report), October 29, 1963, Iron Mountain Box 1; Ben Gibson to Ben Cameron (memorandum, Georgia Southwestern College report), May 15, 1963, Iron Mountain Box 1.

73. Ben Gibson, "Georgia 1964–65 Testing Centers," Iron Mountain Box 1.

74. Ben Gibson (telephone memorandum), August 31, 1964, Iron Mountain Box 1; Ben Gibson to Harold E. McNabb, August 31, 1964, Iron Mountain Box 1.

75. Ben Gibson to Ben Cameron (memorandum, Bibb County schools report), March 30, 1964, Iron Mountain Box 1.

76. Ben Gibson to Ben Cameron (memorandum, Edison High School report), May 25, 1964, Iron Mountain Box 1.

77. Ben Gibson to H. Titus Singletary, February 25, 1964, Iron Mountain Box 1; H. Titus Singletary to Ben Gibson, March 11, 1964, Iron Mountain Box 1.

78. Ben Gibson to Ben Cameron (memorandum, LaGrange schools report), March 16, 1964, Iron Mountain Box 1; Ben Gibson to Belah Lancaster, July 21, 1964, Iron Mountain Box 1; Ben Gibson (telephone memorandum), September 28, 1964, Iron Mountain Box 1.

79. Ben Gibson to Ben Cameron (memorandum, Muscogee-Columbus schools report), March 13, 1964, Iron Mountain Box 1.

80. William B. King to Ben Gibson, December 12, 1963, Iron Mountain Box 1; John R. Hills to Ben Gibson, December 12, 1963, Iron Mountain Box 1.

81. Ibid.; Ben Gibson to Ben Cameron (memorandum, Georgia Southwestern College report), October 29, 1963, Iron Mountain Box 1.

82. Ben Gibson to Ben Cameron (memorandum, Sumter Higher School report), February 13, 1964, Iron Mountain Box 1.

83. Ibid.

84. Ben Gibson to Ben Cameron (memorandum, Toombs County schools—Lyons High schools report), February 11, 1964, Iron Mountain Box 1.

85. Ibid., 2.

86. Ibid., 3.

87. Ben Gibson, "Georgia 1964–65 Testing Centers," attachment to letter to Justine Taylor, April 17, 1964.

88. John R. Hills to Ben Gibson, December 12, 1963, Iron Mountain Box 1.

CHAPTER SIX

1. Ben Gibson to Ben Cameron and Richard Pearson (memorandum), January 3, 1964, Iron Mountain, N.Y., College Board Archives, Box 1645, "Southern Regional Office." Hereafter referred to as Iron Mountain Box 1.

2. Ibid.; Centenary College Centennial Timeline: www.centenary.edu/centennial/
timeline.

3. Alfred B. Fitt to Richard Pearson, March 25, 1964, Iron Mountain Box 1, 1, 2.

4. Ibid.

5. Ben Cameron (memorandum "for the record"), April 13, 1964, Iron Mountain Box 1; "Oral History Interview with Ben Cameron," New York, College Entrance Examination Board Archives, 10–11. Hereafter referred to as Cameron interview. Hereafter referred to as College Board Archives.

6. Ben Cameron (memorandum "for the record"), April 13, 1964, Iron Mountain Box 1.

7. Ben Gibson to Ben Cameron (memorandum, Father Koury meeting report), March 4, 1963, Iron Mountain, N.Y., College Board Archives, Box 1588, "Southern Regional Office." Hereafter referred to as Iron Mountain Box 2.

8. Ben Gibson to Ben Cameron (memorandum, Bolick visit report), March 9, 1964, Iron Mountain Box 2.

9. Ibid.

10. Ben Gibson to Ben Cameron (memorandum, Levenway visit report), March 9, 1964, Iron Mountain Box 2.

11. Ben Cameron to Alfred B. Fitt, June 1, 1964, Iron Mountain Box 1.

12. Alfred B. Fitt to Roy K. Davenport, David Clinard, Benjamin Fridge, June 4, 1964, Iron Mountain Box 1; Ben Cameron to Alfred B. Fitt, August 24, 1964, Iron Mountain Box 1; James C. Evans to Ben Cameron, September 1, 1964, Iron Mountain Box 1.

13. James C. Evans to Ben Cameron, September 1, 1964, Iron Mountain Box 1.

14. Bartley, *New South, 1945–1980*, 339.

15. Patterson, *Brown v. Board of Education*, 123–31.

16. George Derek Musgrove, *Rumor, Repression, and Racial Politics: How the Harassment of Black Elected Officials Shaped Post-Civil Rights America* (Athens: University of Georgia Press, 2012), 17–19.

17. Dan B. Carr to H. L. Crane, August 17, 1964, Iron Mountain Box 1.

18. *Southern School News* 11, no. 3 (September 1964): 1.

19. Ben Gibson to Ben Cameron (memorandum), January 13, 1964, Iron Mountain Box 1.

20. Ibid.

21. Ibid., 2.

22. Ben Gibson, spreadsheet, untitled, Iron Mountain Box 1; Ben Gibson to George H. Hanford, October 7, 1964, Iron Mountain Box 1.

23. Ben Gibson, report on test centers by state, untitled, fall 1964, Alabama section, Iron Mountain Box 1; Ben Cameron, "Summary of Discussion of Examining Center Policy," December 10, 1964; Ben Cameron, "Confidential Background Material for the Committee on Examining Center Policy," Appendix V, September 20, 1962, College Board Archives.

24. Ibid., Georgia information.

25. Ibid., Louisiana information.

26. Ibid., Mississippi information.

27. Ibid., South Carolina information.

28. Sarratt, *Ordeal of Desegregation*, 359; Ben Cameron, "Confidential Background Material for the Committee on Examining Center Policy," College Board Archives.

29. Ben Cameron, "Confidential Background Material for the Committee on Examining Center Policy," College Board Archives.

30. Bass, *Unlikely Heroes*, 250.

31. Ben Cameron to Leslie W. Dunbar, January 4, 1965, Iron Mountain Box 1; Cameron interview, 23.

32. Harold L. Crane to Ben Gibson, November 10, 1964, Iron Mountain Box 1.

33. Ibid.

34. Ben Gibson to Harry Crane (telephone memorandum), November 25, 1964, Iron Mountain Box 1; Ben Gibson to Harold L. Crane, December 8, 1964, Iron Mountain Box 1.

35. Ben Cameron to Harold L. Crane, November 23, 1964, Iron Mountain Box 1.

36. Ibid., 2.

37. Ben Gibson to Ben Cameron (memorandum), October 14, 1964, Iron Mountain Box 1, 1.

38. Ben Cameron to Ben Gibson (memorandum), November 23, 1964, Iron Mountain Box 1.

39. Ben Gibson to Harold L. Crane, December 8, 1964, Iron Mountain Box 1, 2.

40. College Entrance Examination Board, Minutes of meeting of Board of Trustees, December 10–11, 1964, College Board Archives, 9.

41. Ibid., 10; "Oral History Interview with Stephen Wright," College Board Archives, 4. Hereafter referred to as Wright interview.

42. Wright interview, 2.

43. The American College Testing Program, "Student Information Bulletin," Iowa City, Iowa, American College Testing Program, Inc., 1963.

44. President Howard M. Phillips to Ben Gibson (letter), November 10, 1965; Ben Gibson (memorandum, Birmingham-Southern), May 18, 1984.

45. Ibid.

46. Cameron interview, 6.

47. Ben Cameron, "Summary of Discussion of Examining Center Policy," Iron Mountain Box 1, 4.

48. Ibid., 3.

49. Ibid., 4.

50. Henry Chauncey to Richard Pearson, March 29, 1965, Iron Mountain Box 1.

51. Ben Cameron to Leslie W. Dunbar, January 4, 1965, Iron Mountain Box 1.

52. Leslie W. Dunbar to Ben Cameron, December 31, 1964, Iron Mountain Box 1.

53. Ben Cameron to Leslie W. Dunbar, January 4, 1965, Iron Mountain Box 1, 1, 2.

54. Ibid., 2, 3.

55. Special Committee on Examining Center Policy, Minutes of Meeting, June 17, 1965, Iron Mountain Box 1, 1, 2.

56. Ibid., 2, 3.

57. Ibid., 3–6.

58. Ibid., 6, 7.

59. Ibid., 7.

60. Arthur Howe to Richard Pearson, July 8, 1965, Iron Mountain Box 1.

61. College Entrance Examination Board, "Annual Meeting Proceedings, 1966," College Board Archives, 33.

62. College Examination Board, "Board of Trustees Resolution/Action, September 27–28, 1967," College Board Archives.

63. Ben Gibson, member college report, untitled, Iron Mountain Box 1, 1; Ben Cameron to Staff Executive Committee (memorandum), April 5, 1966, Iron Mountain Box 1, 2.

64. Ben Cameron to Staff Executive Committee (memorandum), April 5, 1966, Iron Mountain Box 1, 2.

65. Ben Gibson, "Violations of the Trustees' Center Policy, Reported or Suspected," College Board Archives, 1.

66. Ben Gibson to Ben Cameron (memorandum), April 3, 1967.

67. Ben Gibson (telephone memorandum), January 20, 1967, Iron Mountain Box 2; Ben Gibson to Ben Cameron (memorandum), March 16, 1967, Iron Mountain Box 2.

68. Ben Gibson to Ben Cameron (memorandum), March 16, 1967.

69. Cameron interview, 48–49.

EPILOGUE

1. Hanford, *Minority Programs and Activities*, 1–4, 41–42.

2. Garrison W. Hedrick to Mr. Bretnall, Mr. Manning (memorandum), December 4, 1970, ETS Archives.

3. Hanford, *Minority Programs and Activities*, 1–4, 41–42.

4. John R. Hills to Ben Gibson, December 12, 1963, Iron Mountain, N.Y., College Board Archives, Box 1645, "Southern Regional Office."

5. Hanford, *Minority Programs and Activities*, 1–4, 41–42.

6. Stephen J. Wright Vita, New York, College Board Archives, 1, 2; obituary of Stephen Wright, *The New York Times*, April 19, 1996, Late Edition, Final.

7. Marie Taylor to Ben Cameron, April 12, 1967, College Board Archives; obituary of James C. Evans, *The New York Times*, April 23, 1988.

8. *The George-Anne* 54, no. 15 (January 10, 1974);; Georgia Southern faculty listings: www.georgiasouthern.edu.

9. Obituary of Ben W. Gibson, *The Herald Chronicle*, January 10, 1980; Jean Pennington Gibson, conversation with author, 2011; letter from Ben Gibson to Jean Gibson, July 1, 1979.

10. Ben Cameron Vita, College Board Archives; George Hanford to Trustees (memorandum), February 28, 1967; "Oral History Interview with Ben Cameron," College Board Archives, 47; obituary of Benjamin Cameron Jr., *Sewanee Messenger*, February 25, 1999.

Bibliography

PRIMARY SOURCES

Cameron, Doug. Conversation with author, 2008.

College Entrance Examination Library and Archives. College Entrance Examination Board, New York.

Davis, Jerry S. Conversations with author, 2005, 2007.

Educational Testing Service Archives, Princeton.

Gibson, Jean Pennington. Conversations with author, 2011.

Johns, Kingston. Conversation with author, 2005.

Moss, Donald T. Conversation with author, 2005.

SECONDARY SOURCES

Agnihorti, Bhishma Kumar. "Negro Legal Education and 'Black' Law Schools." *Loyola Law Review* 17, no. 2 (1971): 245–59.

Air Force Times. "Services to Offer Facilities For College Tests in South," April 10, 1963.

The American College Testing Program, "Student Information Bulletin." Iowa City, Iowa: American College Testing Program, Inc., 1963.

Atlanta Constitution. "Suit Asks Integration in Dougherty," April 8, 1962.

Bartley, Numan V. *The New South, 1945–1980: The Story of the South's Modernization.* Baton Rouge: Louisiana State University Press, 1995.

———. *The Rise of Massive Resistance: Race and Politics in the South During the 1950's.* Baton Rouge: Louisiana State University Press, 1969.

Bass, Jack. *Unlikely Heroes: The Dramatic Story of the Southern Judges of the Fifth Circuit Who Translated the Supreme Court's Brown Decision into a Revolution for Equality.* New York: Simon and Schuster, 1981.

California Voice. "Jim Crow Aptitude Test Draws Protest," August 19, 1960.

Couch, Harvey C. *A History of the Fifth Circuit, 1891–1981.* Published under the auspices of the Bicentennial Committee of the Judicial Conference of the United States.

Crespino, Joseph. *In Search of Another Country: Mississippi and the Conservative Counterrevolution.* Princeton: Princeton University Press, 2007.

Dalfiume, Richard M. *Desegregation of the U.S. Armed Forces: Fighting on Two Fronts, 1939–1953.* Columbia: University of Missouri Press, 1969.

Dunbar, Leslie W. "Oral History with Leslie W. Dunbar," Civil Rights Digital Library, the University of Georgia, December 18, 1978.

———. "The Changing Mind of the South: The Exposed Nerve." *Journal of Politics* 26, no. 1 (February 1964).

———. "The Southern Regional Council." *Annals of the American Academy of Political and Social Science* 357, no. 1 (January 1965): 108–12.

Egerton, John. *Speak Now Against the Day: The Generation Before the Civil Rights Movement in the South.* New York: Alfred A. Knopf, 1994.

Eskew, Glenn T. *But for Birmingham: The Local and National Movements in the Civil Rights Struggle.* Chapel Hill: University of North Carolina Press, 1997.

Fairclough, Adam. *Race & Democracy: The Civil Rights Struggle in Louisiana, 1915–1972.* Athens: University of Georgia Press, 1995.

The George-Anne. Georgia Southern College Newspaper, 54, no. 15, January 10, 1974.

Gilbert, Jonas. *Freedom's Sword: The NAACP and the Struggle Against Racism in America.* New York: Routledge, 2005.

Gilpin, Patrick J. "Charles S. Johnson and the Southern Educational Reporting Service." *Journal of Negro History* 63, no. 3 (July 1978): 197–208.

Georgia Southern University, faculty listings, www.georgiasouthern.edu.

Georgia Southern Online Magazine, Spring 2012, www.georgiasouthern.edu.

Greenberg, Jack. *Crusaders in the Courts: How a Dedicated Band of Lawyers Fought for the Civil Rights Revolution.* New York: Basic Books, 1992.

Gropman, Alan L. "The Air Force Integrates: Blacks in the Air Force from 1945 to 1964." Doctoral dissertation, Tufts University, 1975.

Hanford, George H. *Life with the SAT: Assessing Our Young People and Our Times.* New York: College Entrance Examination Board, 1991.

———. *Minority Programs and Activities of the College Entrance Examination Board.* New York: College Entrance Examination Board, 1975.

The Herald Chronicle. Obituary of Ben W. Gibson, January 10, 1980 (Sewanee, Tennessee).

Jefferson, Jevallier, "The Southern University 16: A Tribute to 16 African-American College Students Whose Sacrifices Improved the Lives of All of Us." The Black Collegian Online, First Semester 2004, www.black-collegian.com.

Karabel, Jerome. *The Chosen: The Hidden History of Admission and Exclusion at Harvard, Yale, and Princeton.* Boston: Houghton Mifflin, 2005.

Kruse, Kevin M. *White Flight: Atlanta and the Making of Modern Conservatism.* Princeton: Princeton University Press, 2005.

Leflar, Robert A. "Legal Education: Desegregation in Law Schools." *American Bar Association Journal* 43 (February 1957): 145–49.

Lehmann, Nicholas. *The Big Test: The Secret History of the American Meritocracy.* New York: Farrar, Straus and Giroux, 1999.

Lewis, John L., with Michael D'Orso. *Walking in the Wind: A Memoir of the Movement.* New York: Simon and Schuster, 1998.

Littlejohn, Edward J., and Leonard S. Rubinowitz, "Black Enrollment in Law Schools: Forward to the Past." *Thurgood Marshall Law Review* (1986): 415–55.

Lowe, Maria R., and J. Clint Morris. "Civil Rights Advocates in the Academy: White Pro-integrationist Faculty at Millsaps College." *Journal of Mississippi History* 69, no. 2 (2007): 121–45.

Mays, Benjamin E. *Born to Rebel: An Autobiography.* New York: Scribner, 1971.

Musgrove, George Derek. *Rumor, Repression, and Racial Politics: How the Harassment of Black Elected Officials Shaped Post-Civil Rights America.* Athens: University of Georgia Press, 2012.

The New York Times. "9 Students Arrested," March 30, 1960.

———. Obituary of Stephen Wright, April 19, 1996.

Nichols, Lee. *Breakthrough on the Color Front.* New York: Random House, 1954.

Orr, Marion, and Hanes Walton Jr. "Life on the Leading Edge of Democratic Reform: Student Perspectives on School Desegregation." *PS: Political Science and Politics* (April 2004).

Patterson, James T. *Brown v. Board of Education: A Civil Rights Milestone and Its Troubled Legacy.* New York: Oxford University Press, 2001.

Pratt, Robert A. *We Shall Not Be Moved: The Desegregation of the University of Georgia.* Athens: University of Georgia Press, 2002.

Pressly, William L. *The Formative Years at Atlanta's Westminster Schools.* Atlanta: McGuire Publications, 1991.

Roberts, Gene, and Hank Klibanoff. *The Race Beat: The Press, the Civil Rights Struggle, and the Awakening of a Nation*. New York: Vintage Books, 2007.

Sarratt, Reed. *The Ordeal of Desegregation: The First Decade*. New York: Harper & Row, 1966.

Sewanee Messenger. Obituary of Benjamin Cameron Jr., February 25, 1999.

Sosna, Marton. *In Search of the Silent South: Southern Liberals and the Race Issue*. New York: Columbia University Press, 1977.

Southern School News. September 1960, September 1963, September 1964, June 1965.

Tuck, Stephen G. N. *Beyond Atlanta: The Struggle for Racial Equality in Georgia, 1940–1980*. Athens: University of Georgia Press, 2001.

Tushnet, Mark V. *Making Civil Rights Law: Thurgood Marshall and the Supreme Court, 1936–1961*. New York: Oxford University Press, 1994.

Wallenstein, Peter. "Black Southerners and Non-Black Universities: Desegregating Higher Education, 1935–1967." *History of Higher Education Annual* (1999).

Wilkins, Roy. *Standing Fast: The Autobiography of Roy Wilkins*. New York: Viking Press, 1982.

Wright, Stephen J. "The Southern Negro." In *The New Negro*, edited by Mathew H. Ahman. New York: Bilbo and Tannen, 1969.

Index